Fantasy Football

by Edward Couzens-Lake

Fantasy Football

Published by
Legends Publishing
18 Darby Crescent
Sunbury-on-Thames
Middlesex
TW16 5LA

E-mail david@legendspublishing.net
Web www.legendspublishing.net

Dedicated to Mike Walker

Front cover photo:
Chris Sutton roars in triumph as Jerry Goss (right) wheels away in celebration fol-lowing his equalising goal against Bayern Munich at Carrow Road on November 3rd 1993 – the decisive strike that ensured a famous Norwich victory in this UEFA Cup Second Round tie. Darren Eadie (left) also celebrates while Bayern's Lothar Matthäus turns away from the scene, his face a picture of defeat. The match and the photograph reflect the pinnacle moment in an astonishing 18-month period for Norwich City FC, an era that started when Mike Walker was appointed Manager the previous summer.

contents

prologue

Fantasy Football primarily deals with the very first season of Premier League football in England, specifically the campaign enjoyed by Norwich City and its supporters. A season that was, perhaps, anticipated with some trepidation amongst many Norwich fans. The 1992/93 campaign would, after all, follow a somewhat disappointing season for the Canaries, one that had seen them not only lose nine of their last 11 League games, but also witnessed the departure of popular manager Dave Stringer.

Stringer's successor, Mike Walker, was relatively unknown, infact, to quote one contemporary writer, he was "...not even a household name in his own household." To add insult to injury, a few days before the season had even started, Walker saw one of his best players, talismatic striker Robert Fleck, sold to Chelsea. Fleck's departure, plus the poor finish to the previous campaign, made the Canaries odds-on favourites for relegation.

Those short odds became even shorter during half-time of Norwich's opening league game, with Arsenal 2-0 ahead at Highbury, and seemingly cruising to an easy victory, one Norwich player admitted that his thoughts in the dressing room ahead of the second half had been only of "damage limitation". However, by 4:50pm on Saturday August 15th 1992, the future seemed far brighter for Norwich City. Thankfully, "unknown" as he may have been outside of Norfolk, the appointment of Walker, known and respected by the players, turned out to be an inspired one.

The dearly departed Robert Fleck, meanwhile, had been replaced by Mark Robins, a proverbial £900,000 'snip' from Manchester United... and it was Walker's introduction of Robins in the second half of that Highbury clash helped turn the match and, in doing so, Norwich's season. What followed over the following nine months saw the same bookies that had been tipping City for immediate relegation, having to swallow their pride and offer new

Mike Walker deserved all the recognition and praise that he received

odds – only this time on the possibility of Norwich winning the very league they had been deemed certainties to depart.

It was never intended for this book to be a detailed, match by match account of that season, but what we hope it does achieve is to offer supporters a reflective view of the game, and of Norwich City Football Club, during that exciting, eventful era, using revealing, honest insights and opinions from some of the Norwich players at that time. And the title? Well, that's thanks to John Motson.

Those of us who were not lucky enough to have been in Munich that glorious Autumn evening, Norwich's very own Oktoberfest, will never forget Motson's excited, almost disbelieving commentary as Norwich went 2-0 up against the great Bayern Munich – and on their own patch.

"Crook takes it... oh, was it a bit of climbing there? And a chance on the far post... and it's in! It's Mark Bowen! And Norwich are two up... this is almost fantasy football..."

But for Norwich fans, the fantasy had started on a hot August afternoon some 14 months earlier – better late than never Motty! It was a wonderful ride. Thank you Norwich City.

FOREWORD

I was ten years old in 1992. I'd got used to getting the League Ladders given free with *Shoot!* magazine, showing the Barclays League Divisions One, Two, Three and Four, and displaying them on my bedroom wall – well, when I say 'displaying', I mean that the cardboard tabs bearing each of the 92 League club names were arranged in a painstakingly accurate order... until about mid-September in any case.

Because, by then, the novelty would have worn off and my attention span would have well and truly expired. Consequently, Norwich City would always be top of Division One, with Ipswich Town right at the bottom of Division Four, with the other 90 teams in-between ranked in some sort of irrational order of preference. That's how the League tables looked in my little corner of Norfolk and that is, by and large, how they would stay until *Shoot!* delivered the goods again the next Summer and rekindled my annual month of divisional OCD by giving away a nice, new wall chart and some more cardboard tabs, many of which would replace those that had been ripped up in a fit of pique as I lashed out at any team which dared humiliate my beloved Canaries. There were also those that would be lost 'up the Hoover' every season too!

The implications of the advent of the Premier League probably didn't resonate with me beyond the fact that the tables on my wall chart would now have different names – until I realised that you had to have a satellite dish to actually watch the games on TV. What kind of witchcraft brought viewers more than four channels? I didn't know anyone who had satellite TV, which was devastating for a football-mad schoolboy who preferred *Saint & Greavsie* to Phillip Schofield on *Going Live*, and who saw the visit of relatives on a Sunday afternoon as a massive blow to my hopes of spending more time with Elton Welsby, Brian Moore and the rest of the ITV Sport crew as they covered that week's only live game. Yes that's correct, just the one per week!

The start of the Premier League coincided further with another new beginning in my life – Fantasy Football. No, not the game that started to appear in the newspapers, but Norwich City actually challenging for a top flight title win – to become Premier League champions! I liked this new-fangled division from day one, following the Canaries' stunning comeback from 2-0 down at the favourites, Arsenal, to win 4-2, all *live* on Ceefax. What a thrill it was as the pixelated names of Robins (2), Phillips and Fox gradually appeared underneath my favourite team's name that afternoon. Des Lynam and his vidiprinter on *Grandstand* confirmed the result with barely a twitch of his trademark 'tash, and I busily set about the first League Ladders update of 1992/93.

I had my first visit to Anfield in October 1992 and celebrated with my dad, the man who had enriched my life with yellow and green almost before I could crawl, as Ian Butterworth fired us into an early lead with a rare strike. We were winning at Anfield! Sure, Liverpool were going through a transitional period and struggling to recapture the form that had seen them win the title three seasons earlier, a feat they are still attempting to recapture in fact, but they were still *the* club when I was discovering the joys of football, and many of my classmates had spurned their Norfolk roots for some faraway, Scouse land of milk and honey represented by Ian Rush, John Barnes and Mark Walters. Liverpool 0 Norwich City 1. It was going to be deliciously sweet when I got to school on Monday.

But four Liverpool goals later – and a missed penalty by Mark Bowen in front of the Kop – we set off back on the seemingly never-ending trip to Norfolk, and when I eventually sat in Mr Ringwood's mobile classroom at Woodland View Middle School in Spixworth, I remained stoically quiet about what I'd done at the weekend.

Still, in November 1992, Norwich City sat proudly on top of the table. This time, though, the stars had aligned and my bedroom wall was, for once, telling the truth. It couldn't last, and it didn't, but what a ride the lads gave us. John Polston's late winner against title rivals Aston Villa still ranks amongst my favourite football memories, a moment when the impossible started to look like it *just might* happen. Supporting a team like City teaches you some valuable life lessons though, and the fact that Norwich managed to finish third that year, with a goal difference of minus four, underlines how wonderfully hot and cold they could blow.

However, it was to be an all-too-brief flirtation with the high life. By 1995, I was watching the Canaries play Southend at Roots Hall in Division One, but, being in the First Division certainly didn't feel as special as it did when I'd first used my season ticket to sit in that blue plastic seat, my seat, in the rickety old South Stand at Carrow Road. Having rolled the boulder up to the top of the hill and peeped over the precipice at Bayern Munich and the San Siro, we hurtled back down, jettisoning millions of pounds' worth of talent on the way, until finally hitting the brink of financial oblivion – and before it became fashionable for football clubs to do so.

The Premier *League* became the Premier*ship* as branding, big business and inflated wages skewed everything in favour of the haves, rather than the used to have but not any mores, much like City. And, bar a one season wonder under Nigel Worthington, we were left with our noses up against the glass ceiling as *Sky* sold more of their satellite dishes and allowed us to see what was going on in that millionaires' theme park, that we loved playing in when it was just fields.

So, 1992 has much to answer for. Not so much because the year marked the start of rocketing ticket prices, obscene pay packets and the footballer as the tabloid star and fashion icon, but, for us Norwich City fans it cruelly teased us – we really could have been contenders. For two decades now, people like me have been staring off into the middle-distance at regular intervals, seeing beyond all the obscenity that is modern day Premier League football and looking, once again, at those League Ladders on our bedroom walls. That really was us. We have done it once, we must be able to do it again one day.

Chris Goreham
BBC Radio Norfolk

INTRODUCTION

We are routinely told that significant moments of world history are always qualified as such because people can, with instant recall, remember where they were and what they were doing at the time that the said historical event occurred.

My father, for example, clearly remembers that, at the time of the assassination of President Kennedy, he was busily cooking some chips in the kitchen at home, and sharing them with our family doctor who had called in to see my mother. No wonder at that, if he was in the kitchen!

I remember watching the first Moon landing at my village school, vaguely aware that something rather wonderful was happening, but more intent on going outside and doing what six-year-olds everywhere are expert at doing, that is, running around in circles, screaming at the top of their voices. It's the same with football.

Shortly after the 1971 FA Cup Final, I recall spending much of that Saturday evening throwing myself onto my back with my arms in the air, mimicking Charlie George's winning goal celebration earlier that day. Equally prominent in my mind are the cries from my mother, "get off that damp grass". Of course, the grass wasn't damp. But parents always claimed that it was, maybe it was some shared parental law they all had to follow?

Just before Tommy Smith scored Liverpool's second goal in the 1977 European Cup Final, it wasn't Steve Heighway's corner that made me sit up and take notice, but the fact that one of the advertising hoardings was for *Spar*, the convenience store chain whose influence, I realised, as Barry Davies squealed in delight at Smith's goal, reached far beyond the shores of Norfolk.

Likewise Gazza's tears and England's dramatic exit at the 1990 World Cup. I'd sat and watched the match with half a dozen or so friends at the time. At the final whistle they were distraught, as if a family member had died; else some other terrible personal tragedy had been announced. Forever a club

Norwich City players celebrate a season never to forget

before country man, I reminded them that it was "only a game", and fondly remember the cascade of peanuts and crisps that came flying through the air towards me (directed more accurately than Waddle's penalty I should add) in retribution at my blasphemous thoughts. And so on and so forth.

So seismic, of course, were those footballing events of February 20th 1992 that we can all, right now, sit back and remember the day, the announcement, and the ramifications of it all. What were you doing? I have to admit, at this point that, despite having this ability of recall to the extent that my friends find it a little creepy at times; I have absolutely no idea of where I was, what I was doing, or even where I was working. However, despite being as fanatical about football then, as I am now, I had to rely on Google in order to pin down the day and date that is argued by some as the day 'proper' football began; English football's Year Zero moment.

It was the day that saw all 22 clubs in English football's First Division resign from the Football League en-masse, declaring their intention to form their own league, a limited company, a new "elite". One that would have commercial independence from both the FA and Football League and be free to negotiate its own, lucrative, sponsorship and broadcasting agreements and contracts. The FA Premier League was coming.

Edward Couzens-Lake

THE [KICK-OFF] TIMES, THEY ARE A-CHANGIN'

Along with the announcement of the competition, which was initially to be known as the *FA* Premier League, there was an unfortunate consequence – the instant revision of the standing of the ('bloody but unbowed') Football League and it's 104-year-old history in England. Formed in 1888, it was to be swiftly relegated to a place on the bench – tradition and pedigree, if not forgotten, swiftly becoming the B.C to the Premier League's A.D.

Three clubs had particular reason to regret their relegation from the Football League in its last ever season as the pre-eminent competition in England; Luton Town, Notts County (how sadly ironic – the oldest professional football club in the world, the one whose black and white stripes were imitated, in admiration, by Juventus) and West Ham. They all missed out on the party and the greater glories to come. Indeed, for both Luton and Notts County, it was a pivotal moment in their histories – neither have climbed back into the top league since, with Luton exiting the Football League completely in 2009. Contrast this with the fortunes of Blackburn Rovers, promoted via the play-offs in 1992, and Premier League Champions just three years later – their success coming at the same time that County finished rock bottom of Divison One.

Football, by its very nature, is cyclical, with even the biggest, most wealthy and prosperous clubs having periods when success is all but a dusty memory locked away in the trophy cupboard (hello, Leeds United), so it is probable that Town and County's respective demises would have happened, Premier League or not. However, there is a stronger argument that, had they managed to survive relegation in 1992, their histories and footballing fates just might have been a little better than those which eventually befell them and that, in the entire history of League football in England, they had been unfortunate enough to be relegated at just about the worse time possible.

The financial riches they missed out on were in no small part down to the dizzying sums of money that were to come from television. Despite the long standing, established and expected tradition of the BBC and ITV sharing, and occasionally squabbling over, televised rights to the old First Division, the suits that ran the Premier League felt that their product had long been under-valued as a commercial opportunity, they now wanted the Premier League to be the goose that laid the golden football. ITV, rather than the BBC, had been the original pioneers of televised League football in Great Britain, their coverage of the First Division match between Blackpool and Bolton Wanderers in 1960 was the first-ever Football League game to be televised. *Match of the Day*, by contrast, did not begin regular broadcasting (and then on BBC2) until 1964. However, even then, the prime remit of the game was not to simply offer viewers a game every week, but to provide training and experience for those technicians and producers who would be taking on the arduous role of providing full and detailed coverage of the World Cup finals, to be held in England two years later.

An estimated 20,000 viewers watched that first ever *Match of the Day* programme – the game between (predictably, this was the BBC after all) Liverpool and Arsenal could only be seen in the London area, and then only by viewers lucky enough to be able to tune into BBC2. Multi-million pound and multi-million audiences and advertising revenue from the game was still nearly three decades away, but the seeds had been sown.

The eventual harvest was reaped by an Australian. The Premier League had set out to be radical and radical it was – awarding its first contract to televised matches to Rupert Murdoch's Sky television. Interestingly, even on their official website, the Premier League says that these rights were 'assigned', as if they were a precious jewel or priceless antique whose full value and worth could only be appreciated by someone who knew his subject as well as they thought they knew their own. Murdoch certainly knew his subject, having been involved with all aspects of the mass media for nearly 40 years before his company invested in English football. Sky paid the Premier League the then staggering sum of £191 million for five years' exclusive live coverage – confident that their own single-minded and aggressive marketing strategy would secure them the subscribers needed to help finance

City players being interviewed for Sky at the Trowse training ground

the deal. But not only that, Sky would be able to give the Premier League, its competition and its clubs, the sort of blanket coverage and attention that neither the BBC nor ITV would ever have been able to offer. For the Premier League, the offer from Sky was manna from Heaven. This, over time, proved to be the case for its member clubs as well.

Sky Television had incurred massive losses in its formative years. The initial four channel Sky TV package was launched in 1989 and was swiftly taken up by dozens of people. Hence the losses. At that time, both the BBC and ITV boasted massive audiences for their programmes and, quite simply, with Channel Four still seen as a novelty within British television, it wasn't so much that people didn't want, or were asking for, alternatives, but rather that the prospect of pay-per-view TV had never even entered the popular imagination, except, perhaps, as a short slot at the end of *Tomorrows World*. In effect, you can't desire something that you are not even aware of.

If Sky was to succeed, it needed a hook. Murdoch and his executives swiftly looked into football as being both hook and bait to a British public who were fast falling in love with the game again. The sport's new, commercial possibilities had first crept to prominence during the 1990 World Cup. Images of that year's competition were burned into the conscience of the nation – the cathedral-like stadiums, all peaks and pinnacles searing into dark Italian skies, *Nessun Dorma* and Pavarotti, the aria swiftly becoming the soundtrack of the Summer, and used by the BBC as the theme to their coverage of the tournament. Culture and football became richly entwined. The Italians may have had Pavarotti, but *we* had Nigel Kennedy – violin virtuoso and Villa fanatic, he was duly flown out to entertain the England squad.

Earlier in the year, respected post-punk band, New Order, had brought credibility to the England squads official song of the tournament, and footballing icon John Barnes became a rap star in the process. And, right on cue, and after an indifferent start, England found themselves in the semi-finals of the tournament. Countless millions sat and watched that semi-final on TV, many of whom had been attracted to the sport for the first time by the drama and colour (if not, ironically, for the quality of the football!) during that Summer's tournament. Football, as an event, had arrived, and Murdoch seized on those possibilities just two years later.

The suits and ponytails at Sky had, unquestionably, noted how the value of football as a televised sport was increasing. The Football League signed a two-year agreement in 1986 for £6.3 million, however, when the deal was renewed, just two years later, the price had rocketed up to £44 million, albeit over a four year period. Those negotiations in 1988 had included the first widely visible signs of the 'elite' clubs standing their ground, aware now of what their wider commercial value was becoming. Ten First Division clubs threatened to break away from the Football League in order to set up their own 'Super League', and, rather than risk calling their bluff, the League acquiesced to their demands and the status quo was maintained, albeit on somewhat weaker foundations than ever before. It is interesting to note that, this threat of a split in the ranks came a century after the original plans for the Football League were announced at the Anderton's Hotel in March 1888. Of the 12 founder members of the League, it is perhaps safe to say that only two of them (Aston Villa and Everton) would have been party to the potential new division all those years later.

If the Football League had thought it had come through potential revolution unscathed however, then those who governed the game at the time would certainly have been resting with some unease in their leather armchairs, having weathered this particular storm. One of a more perfect nature was looming on the horizon – one with more and more money being injected into the game, together with the massive surge of interest generated by the 1990 World Cup. Change was inevitable.

Clubs were investing money in new stadiums, or planning to relocate completely, while an increasing amount of well known companies were becoming involved in both the British and World game. *Littlewoods* had sponsored the League Cup from 1987 until 1990 (before becoming the first ever sponsors of the FA Cup in 1994) and Barclays Bank had first opened their account in football sponsorship back in 1987, sponsoring the Football League for six years. Football clubs and their sponsors became interchangeable – think Arsenal, think JVC. Similarly, another electrical giant, *Sharp*, became synonymous with

Manchester United. Even Liverpool, a club forever associated with the qualities of fair play and tradition had succumbed to the corporate siren – their relationship with Hitachi was the very first example of an English professional football club having a shirt sponsor, with that particular agreement being announced as far back as 1979.

For smaller clubs, the possibilities of sponsorship were still there, but they could rarely expect one of the multinational giants to be interested in teaming up with them – Norwich City are a fine example of this. In October 1983 City secured a sponsorship agreement with a company based in the small Norfolk town of Watton. *Poll & Withey* had previously secured a little niche in the history of glazing by making and installing a dozen double-glazed windows for the Kensington Palace home of Princess Margaret. The arrangement lasted for three seasons, including the 1984/85 campaign, which saw Norwich win the League Cup at Wembley. Millions of viewers across the world therefore became aware of the *Poll & Withey* brand (the actual shirt logo read *Poll & Withey* Windows) and, even though most of them would never require the company's services, the directors of the company must have been as delighted with the exposure their brand had secured through football as the marketing men at *Sharp* and *Hafnia* must have been – *their* clubs, Manchester United and Everton being FA Cup winners and League Champions respectively that season. It could, of course, be argued that Everton's relationship with *Hafnia* benefited the football club far more than it did the company in question, as few people at the time knew who *Hafnia** were, and, I suspect, are none the wiser today!

It seems clear, therefore, that the seeds for the corporate expansion of football had long been sown, the important failing of the Football League being their failure to recognise its pending arrival, while the clubs diversified as much as they could to increase their income and make themselves as much a brand as the logos on their shirts. The Football League had lain within its chrysalis for over a century, and, although time had rendered the outside of it dull and predictable, massive changes were taking place, quietly, effectively, and decisively on the inside. The clubs had long realised it, and, as the last decade of the twentieth century began, Rupert Murdoch was beginning to realise it as well – Norwich City had already benefitted from it in a modest way. But the Football League, oblivious, slept on.

As a prelude, British Satellite Broadcasting (later to be taken over by Sky) had acquired the rights for German and Italian football in 1990. The channel was very much a minority one, and it was strictly pay-per-view. But, never-the-less, there was interest, and there was an audience. The thinking at the time was logical and simple – if people happily paid a monthly fee to watch football played in Germany and Italy, what might they be prepared to do in order to watch live football played in England? Things had happened very swiftly, and, unlike the scare in 1988, this time there was no chance of the top clubs in England backing down and remaining part of the establishment, the Football League.

Crucially, remember, the soon to be formed new top division would have *total* commercial independence from both the Football Association and the Football League, leaving the FA (note how the prestigious abbreviation was kept in place at the beginning, like a divorced couple living together) Premier League freedom to negotiate those spectacular broadcasting agreements which were lurking on the horizon. One argument given at the time was that the influx of additional money would enhance English clubs' chances of success in Europe, which seems a spurious one today.

For example, English clubs had triumphed in the European Cup, later to become the Champions League, on seven occasions between 1975 and 1985 (after which, they were banned from Europe until 1990), as well as being runners-up on a further two occasions – in short, nine of the 11 finals of European football's flagship contest had involved English teams. Cynically therefore, maybe the clubs saw the income from the new league as being essential for their chances to compete for the top players, and pay the highest wages in Europe, rather than aid them in actual football success?

With the new league structure in place, it was now or never for Murdoch. The launch of the Premier League had coincided, as had been the clubs' intentions, with the end of the current TV deal and, with the BBC and ITV clearly eager to secure the rights, he needed to act quickly. His fledgling stations needed the income, and, popular as the coverage of the German and Italian football was, the income from that coverage was never going to help make Sky a growing (or profitable) concern. The smart money was on Des Lynam and the BBC securing some sort of live package, however, with the BBC at the mercy of licence payers, it was unlikely that the corporation would have the funds, or justification to commit to the large outlay required.

There would also have been scheduling problems, with the BBC unlikely to commit large amounts of airtime that any new deal might require – with talk of two, three, and maybe even four games being transmitted live per week under the terms of the new arrangement. For ITV, though, there were definite possibilities. The independent broadcaster had received widespread acclaim for their coverage of the Rugby Union World Cup in 1991, and, with the BBC, at that time, having many of the nation's top sporting events including Wimbledon tennis, Formula 1, and the British Open golf championship under its umbrella, ITV executives saw live Premier League football, along with the equally premier advertising rates they could charge for a 30-second slot during a high profile match, as a very promising opportunity. There can be little doubt that they would have bid against Sky, and that the bid would have been substantial. And certainly out of the reach of the BBC.

The possibility of ITV securing the rights to live Premier League football was one that Sky simply could not permit however – they had to win those rights. The future of the broadcaster may even have depended on it, therefore their offer had to be *so* big they couldn't possibly lose. And they didn't. Sky tabled a colossal £304 million bid to secure "live and exclusive" coverage of Premier League football broadcasting rights for the 1992/93 season, the payments covering an initial five year period – simply put, not far short of £62 million per season, which dwarfed the £11 million per season terms of the previous agreement. Sky had not only succeeded in blowing the previously dominant forces of the BBC and ITV out of the water, they had reduced them to picking at the feet of the table for any scraps of domestic football coverage that might be laying there – a situation that remains pretty much the same today.

Murdoch had taken a massive gamble. He was mortgaging his company on the fact that complete and blanket coverage of Premier League football would secure him the paying customers that his company needed to survive. The fact that, two decades later, Sky Sports retains its stranglehold on televised football in England and the Premier League indicates that the decision to go for broke and to put 'everything on football' paid off handsomely. Indeed, the two brands have become totally entwined – Sky Sports and live coverage of the Premier League – one could not exist without the other. Their relationship is now symbiotic and looks set to remain in place for the foreseeable future.

Amongst the broadcasters therefore, the change in football that prefaced the 1992/93 season saw its winners and losers. Sky Sports secured both its financial future, as well as its broadcasting credibility, while the BBC and ITV retreated to their London HQs, wounded and no longer complacent of the new kids on the block. The BBC had secured some sort of consolation prize however, with *Match of the Day* set to continue, offering a more extended highlights package of the Premier League games as part of the corporation's eventual deal with the Premier League. There were also, of course, winners and losers amongst the football clubs that were (or were not) affected by the launch of the Premier League and the influx of new Sky money.

One of the biggest beneficiaries of the creation of the Premier League were Blackburn Rovers. Prior to their promotion to the Premier League in 1992, most of the club's successes and significant history had occurred before 1930, with League and FA Cup success regularly on the Ewood Park menu. However, their relegation in 1966 was followed by 26 successive seasons of football played outside of the top echelons of English football – their rise to prominence was a further example of the commercial upheaval that was endemic in the game in the years leading up to the formation of the Premier League. Jack Walker was a million miles away from the car merchant or scrap metal dealer owner stereotype – Walker had helped turn the family business, Walkersteel, into a company that, as part of the family portfolio, was sold to British Steel for a quoted £360 million in 1988. Walker was therefore the Roman Abramovich of his day, and, with his generous financial input helping to attract some of English football's top names to the club, Rovers duly won the FA Premier League in 1995, just three years after their elevation from the play-offs.

Transformations of that magnitude within English football had previously been few and far between – there had always been the opportunity for smaller clubs to become successful, but it had been based on their ability *on* the field, which usually took time. Club chairmen usually gave their managers the freedom to do just that, and, because the staff at clubs knew they would be given time to put a winning side together, they made the most of it. A 'crisis' at some of the country's leading clubs back then was measured less in terms of Champions League qualification, or whether or not they could lure the biggest names to play for them, but often in far more mundane and sometimes comical terms.

For example, Ipswich Town joint-chairman, John Cobbold, described a typical 'crisis' at Portman Road would be that supplies of red wine in the boardroom had run out. So, whilst Mr Cobbold worried about his fine wines, manager Bobby Robson was left to get on with things on the pitch. Consequently, Robson had the time to put a fine side together, one that had not only gone close to winning the First Division Championship on a number of occasions, but also clinched victory in both the FA and UEFA Cups.

Once Jack Walker had invested those millions at Ewood Park, the definition of a 'crisis' at a football club had changed forever – it was now all about winning games and finishing as high up the table as possible. And, unlike Ipswich Town and their gentle, philanthropic and patient chairman, Blackburn had not gone about things in what might have been considered the *right* manner. They were portrayed as having *bought* the title – as a small club that had been lofted to previously unimaginable heights by a generous owner. This did not make Blackburn popular Champions. Indeed, there was a lot of antipathy aimed at them and their owner for going about things that way, and in a manner which some people almost regarded as cheating.

On the contrary, Ipswich had long been admired, a favourite club of many neutrals and the yardstick to which even their fierce Norfolk rivals would want to measure up to. Football had irrevocably changed and, whilst it was Blackburn's success that had made people finally sit up and take notice, the processes that had been put into place to facilitate that change had occurred some years previously. 1992 may well have seen the Premier League come into existence, but the seeds had, as we shall see, been sown a lot earlier than that.

THE
JOURNALIST

One very interested media observer at this time was journalist, broadcaster and diehard Canary, Mick Dennis. Mick had been following and reporting on football since the 1970s – his fledgling career in journalism commencing on Norwich-based publication the *Eastern Daily Press*, before moving onto work at national newspapers including *The Sun*, *The Daily Mirror*, *The Sunday Times* and *The Daily Telegraph*. He has consequently had first-hand experience of the changes, the movers and shakers in English football, and was there at the beginning. Not, as you might imagine, in 1992, but over ten years earlier. I met up with Mick on a hot Spring day in central London, and, after we had mutually rejoiced in Norwich's more recent Premier League success thus far, we started to talk about the formation of the Premier League and the circumstances that had led up to that pivotal date.

What did Mick recall about the period leading up to the formation of the Premier League?

"You really need to go back to the early 1980s to see how football was, inevitably, going to have to change. This was down to two forces gathering momentum in the game at the time. The first concerned gate receipts. These were always shared equally between the two clubs, so, for example, you have Manchester United at home to Norwich City, 50,000 people pay to watch, two clubs are performing – so the money is split two ways, 50-50. Simple. However, by the early 80s, some of the then leading clubs were beginning to realise their own importance, their own worth in the game. And they were asking questions. They were the bigger clubs – they were drawing in the big crowds, playing the big matches, parading the big players. Why, therefore, should they be expected to share the gate money with their, often 'lesser', opponents? The leading clubs were beginning to speak out a bit, and, by that,

I mean the clubs that were doing well at the time. Remember, at this time, there was still a chance you could still do well, based on your ability on the field, rather than your earning potential. Look at Ipswich as an example. In 1983, Watford finished second in the old First Division, and I remember Elton John getting in touch with me and saying he'd been involved with talks about the redistribution of gate money in the game. In other words, if you were doing well, you were one of the big clubs. And Watford were successful that season, so they were involved."

"Those clubs at the top, those clubs doing well, wanted to keep the gate money from their home games for themselves. And that's what happened. So, now, when Manchester United played Norwich in front of 50,000 at Old Trafford, they kept the gate money. And for the return fixture, Norwich against Manchester United, with maybe less than half that number watching – Norwich got to keep the gate money. You can see that, with the bigger crowds, the bigger clubs are going start making more money, and, all of a sudden, a little financial gap began to appear. It was a significant moment, a watershed one. The bigger clubs have the biggest crowds and therefore make the most money. It's hugely significant. This is all happening long before the Premier League began-but the interest in TV football is growing and that's what clubs and broadcasters noticed. This all came to a head in 1988 when ITV won exclusive rights to show live English League football. The amount of money they paid then, in comparison to what had been paid before, was enormous. The TV deal in 1983 had been £5.2 million over two years (BBC and ITV shared coverage) whereas in 1988, ITV paid £44 million over four years – a massive increase. They called it 'Snatch Of The Day' at the time."

"But, even so, even considering that huge amount of money for ITV to pay out, it was, for them, a cheap way of filling airtime. Look at it this way. It's a finite cost – they know what they have to pay, it isn't going to go up for any reason, so it's cheaper than putting on a couple of hours of drama. And they were guaranteed high quality drama, for two hours, at peak times. ITV did very well out of it. Big money, massive audiences. It was that combination – the fact that the home clubs were now keeping the gate receipts making the bigger clubs wealthier, plus the massive increase in football's commercial value. The bigger clubs were also shown more often, so they got more money. So the gap increases a little bit more. The Premier League was still four years away, but, really, it was just a matter of time then. For anything else to happen, there was a need for movers and shakers. These included people like Irving Scholar at Tottenham; David Dein** at Arsenal and Martin Edwards at Manchester United."

"They could all see just how much more money their clubs could make from the game. Firstly it had been 100% of the home gate receipts. Then the increased money from television. And, there were other possibilities, they could see what could be achieved through playing in Europe, they noted the massive revenue that clubs like Real Madrid were receiving. UEFA were quite happy for those clubs to look at any way they could of making more money, worried that the leading clubs in Europe would break away – but as long as there was harmony in the domestic leagues, it was okay by them. UEFA didn't want a breakaway European 'super league'. The idea had been mooted several times, with various clubs having made noises about forming one. UEFA could see that, as long as the bigger clubs in Europe were happy, then nothing would change, the status quo would be maintained. And if the likes of Arsenal, Manchester United, Tottenham and Liverpool all got wealthier and started to leave the smaller clubs behind, both on and off the pitch, then they weren't particularly bothered."

I wondered if the Premier League had also come about as a compromise, this time from the FA and Football League, and a result of the posturing of some of the larger clubs?

"It was. And it just needed someone to put it all together. That person was Graham Kelly. He'd been CEO of the Football League (1979-89) before taking on the same position at the FA. The Football League and the FA had never really got on. For a start, they were based at opposite ends of the country – the Football League were based at Lytham St Ann's, with the FA based in London. The Football League looked after the players, while the FA had the 'gentlemen' – the public schools, the universities, the Armed Forces. Kelly sought to bring them both together under an FA umbrella, and that the new league would be called the FA Premier League, which was how it started. The FA would basically run the game – it had everything, including the England side. The Football League would turn out to be the poor relation, its 22 leading sides had resigned en-masse to join the FA Premier League and, quite honestly, it would have been left to survive as a 'rump' organisation. Everything and everyone was focused on the FA Premier League and how it had been set up to help the game, the clubs, and, especially (and this is ironic, given the lack of co-operation shown by many leading managers today) England. Yes, it would especially "help England". They had a little catchphrase, 'for the good of the game'. They knew the value of their 'new' product straight away in a commercial sense and started working on the TV deals. ITV wanted to continue with their live coverage of football in this country, and exclusively, just as they had done since 1988. But Sky needed to drive up the sales of their satellite dishes, and Murdoch had realised that live football coverage would do just that. They simply had to win the first TV deal with the FA Premier League, and, of course, they did. The first TV deal that Sky signed with the FA Premier League was for £304 million over five seasons. In 1997, it had gone up to £670 million over four seasons. From 2001 to 2004, the figure was £1.024 billion over four seasons – so as much as ITV wanted live football, they couldn't compete. The BBC would probably not even have bothered to make a bid! It's easy to see how people started to fall out of love with the game.

The big clubs becoming wealthier, while others slip by the wayside. But it's important to realise that the Premier League has not been all bad. For a start, and, in conjunction with the Taylor Report, it's meant that going to a football match in England is now a much more manageable, pleasurable experience. Compare it to going to a big club match in Europe."

"The San Siro in Milan for example – everyone raves about what a magnificent stadium it is, well, it has terrible press facilities. It doesn't even have internet access, which is completely unacceptable, ridiculous. And, even on the top level, in the so-called 'good' seats, the loos are awful – they are just a hole in the ground. So the ladies, understandably, won't use them. And, because the ladies won't use them, well, the men do. Compare the overall football experience to Carrow Road, where the facilities are far superior. Plus far more families go to football matches in this country now – there are lots of women and children, not just young men. This is a legacy of the Premier League, it's made going to the football in this country a much more 'whole' experience than it is at places like the San Siro. In many ways, it's just a shell. Don't get me wrong, they're great places to watch a match, however, as an all round, satisfying customer experience, they leave a lot to be desired."

"The Camp Nou (Barcelona) is no better. Bare breezeblocks everywhere, unfinished work, open tread ladders up to the press boxes. The Bernabeu? (Real Madrid) Well, again, it's an amphitheatre designed for playing and watching football in, but the standard of facilities are not what you would now expect in England. The facilities at Carrow Road are, genuinely, better. I think one of the reasons that attendances are so regularly high at Carrow Road is because it is a pleasure to come to the football club. When the club decided to redevelop the old South Stand, they made sure the area behind the seating was exceptional – and it is. Plenty of space, clean, bright, good facilities, lots of loos, including plenty for the ladies. As I have already said, it's about the overall experience of going to football, not just the match itself. That's what really makes a difference here. You look back to the state of the ground in the 70s – I was at that game when the Manchester United fans started taking the place apart – one even got up onto the roof and fell off! Good job he was drunk, as he bounced..."

"The difference now when you walk to the ground, compared to what it was back in the mid-80s even, is staggering. The entrance to the old Barclay stand, the steps, the iron supports, the grassy bank. Norwich, of course, also needed an innovator, someone to drive change at the club. Early on, well, I'm thinking of Sir Arthur South (a club Director and then Chairman from 1966 to 1985), he was a lovely man and he wanted a successful, entertaining team out on the pitch. And we had a good team, a good Manager in Bondy (John Bond) and some great times under him. So yes, the facilities were in need of smartening up by then, but so did the football, in many ways Norwich had been left behind. Norwich's kids used to play games against some of the local teams – Great Yarmouth, Gorleston, clubs like that. Well, of course, their players loved the idea of getting an opportunity to kick a young Norwich player up in the air! Bondy wasn't having that; he said 'we've got to join the South East Counties League'. The club applied, but were told they couldn't, that Norfolk was too far away!"

"Bondy had an answer to that – he told them we'd play all of our games away. And, for two seasons, all of the youth games were played away from home. Bondy also wanted to know why we weren't signing all the best kids, how they were being missed by us and signing for other clubs. Well, that was because the club didn't have any relationship with the local schools. So Bondy appointed a Schools Relationship Manager. Change is happening at Norwich and its happening quickly. And you see where this is going? We're some way away from the formation of the Premier League, but the clubs were already beginning to think differently, to see the bigger picture, to expand and play a bigger part in the game. All of the clubs in England were thinking about how they could progress by that time, obviously, as the TV money and exposure of the game increased, the bigger clubs did so in a more obvious way, but the smaller clubs, like Norwich, were doing so as well. When the Premier League started, you then needed someone to hold it all together; currently that's Richard Scudamore, the Premier Leagues Chief Executive. He is as able a football administrator as I have ever met."

"It's a very tough job. When you think about it, he has a lot to deal with, even in that one league of 20 clubs. There are the top four or five, all with their own agendas, then there are another eight to ten clubs, which are all pretty much guaranteed to survive playing in the Premier League every year. Then there are those clubs that come and go, the 'yo-yo' clubs, there for a season or two, then gone again – maybe they'll return, maybe they won't. So yes, it's a tough job, three leagues within one, with 20 clubs all with their own way of doing things, with different targets and ambitions. With all of the issues that we have discussed – the gate money, the steady increase in both TV interest and income, the way the clubs were expanding and growing as businesses – it seems almost inevitable that the Premier League would have come about, one way or the other?"

"Even if Graham Kelly had said no to that initial proposal, something would have happened – it was inevitable and the seeds had been sown some ten years earlier. The clubs drove the change, not anyone else, and certainly not Sky. Although Sky were very happy to make the most of it and become, in effect, a business partner. The game has changed. On the positive side, it's great that facilities have improved, that more people are able to go to games and enjoy the whole experience. However, you will not see another club like Norwich go out and buy three reserves from Tottenham (Mark Bowen, Ian Culverhouse and Ian Crook) and see them become the core of a side that finishes fourth in the old First Division and reaches the FA Cup semi final.

Nowadays, for every promising player Norwich pick up like that, Chelsea will go out and buy a Gary Cahill, or Manchester United will sign another Javier Hernandez. That's the gulf now and it shows in league positions and possibilities. The Premier League will never be as competitive as the old Division One was. Never. The best a club like Norwich can ever hope for is to get up, then seek the consistency to stay there. But to win it, or finish in the top three....?" (Mick tails off, a distant look in his eyes, which speaks volumes!)

How about when we did finish third then? That side and the time leading up to that best ever finish?

"A lot of credit needs to go to Ken Brown and Mel Machin. Players came in and performed so well under Kenny in that 92/93 side – Bowen, Butterworth, Crook, and Culverhouse. They played and coached the right way, and Dave Stringer continued when he took over. Remember, we had a decent side and played some lovely football under both Kenny and Dave. It was all falling into place. I remember when John Bond left to go to Manchester City, and he regrets that now. Meanwhile the club were looking for a new manager and everyone assumed Bondy would take Ken with him. He didn't. Kenny may have been disappointed, but he moved quickly, and met with Sir Arthur South, asking if he could offer any good reason why he shouldn't replace Bondy as Manager? Sir Arthur couldn't think of one, so that was that – Kenny became Norwich manager!"

"Everybody said what a lovely man he was, and that's because he was! Kenny loved dealing with people, he was a people person – I think he enjoyed that side of management over the more rigid side of things like tactics, formations and so on. Mel Machin was the tactician, he was the one to talk and work through the intricacies of things with the players. Funny really – Ken was the cultural, ball-playing centre-half from West Ham, where Mel was a no-nonsense full-back who played much of his career at Bournemouth. He once scored a hat-trick for Norwich mind! So yes, it was a while before the Premier League came into existence, but the seeds were being sown at that time, locally and nationally, and you could see the changes coming at Norwich – firstly with Bondy and then with Ken and Mel. The clubs were driving the need for change and Norwich were no different."

"But clubs like Norwich could only keep up for so long. Eighties football couldn't have lasted for much longer as it was. The clubs were adapting and changing, but they were doing it for their own good and to their own ends. So something collective had to happen sooner or later. Another good thing that came about from all of that change was that the football pyramid truly became a football pyramid. A club that won their league, perhaps 17 divisions down could, theoretically, keep going and get to the top. For a long, long time it had been almost impossible to get into the Football League because of the old system of re-election. When the bottom club in the League were up against the top non-League side, it was the Football League themselves who decided who stayed or went, but now a club gets promoted by right, rather than by appeal. Equally, a club can slide all the way out and be gone forever, or they can fight their back in again. Everyone has a chance and anything is possible for a non-League outfit." I asked Mick if he agreed with my claim that the Premier League had 'saved' Sky as a viable business?

"Probably. The thing with Rupert Murdoch is that he invests in the product. Other companies, other company owners, they think of cutting costs to survive. Murdoch thinks of investing even more money to survive and, ultimately, prospers. Which they have done. One way or another though, he would have saved Sky. The way he did it; selling subscriptions based on football was brilliant, and, looking back, you can't see any other way in which he could have done it. He saw the future. People knock Sky, of course they do. After all, they were used to the product being free, not having to have to pay for football. But look at TV sport before Sky. It was ridiculous. A cricket test match would have been interrupted or transmission ended for the most ridiculous of reasons. Live sport, as opposed to highlights, wasn't taken seriously. The standard of coverage was very poor. There were very few cameras, little or no action replays or analysis. Viewers were taken for granted. Sky redefined TV coverage, and they need to, in order to stay ahead."

"They also know that, despite all the gimmicks, all the technological wizardry, what is absolutely key is the narrative. If a big football match is being played, viewers, first and foremost, want to see that football match, watch it unfold. The technology is impressive and important – but secondary to the narrative. Maybe the next step will be for the clubs to want to go their own way, and Sky will come under pressure that way. There currently is pressure from some clubs to fracture the collectiveness. The current cartel does help the smaller clubs with money filtering down and so on. Also, the big clubs have softened the blow to a certain extent by setting up their own TV channels – Chelsea TV etc. They control that and they control much of their media output. And, again, it's working its way downward. Norwich will release news of new signings, even team line-ups on their website first, before releasing it to the papers. The deal with Jonny Howson was confirmed on the website before it went anywhere else. That's no bad thing; it's their business and their choice. But it's another, huge change."

"Richard Scudamore has done exceptionally well to hold it all together. Part of that, part of keeping everyone onboard is this idea of the '39th game'. It'll aid the clubs with foreign owners – they can see their investment playing in their own back yard. Then we'll see these same foreign owners having the rights to sell their own games in their own countries. Look at Blackburn – they are huge in India now because of their owners. What we are seeing of course, taking all of this into consideration, is that the actual paying fan, you and me, are now a very small part of the picture indeed, whereas it used to be that 'we pay your wages'."

"Now of course, you have the celebrity fans, chairman and even the chief executive! Another huge change. Who would have known who their club's chief executive was even ten years ago? It's the same with administrators. Clubs would once have had an ancient clerk rattling around an office who knew which file went where, and how to register a player. And that was that. Now you see club premises full of telesales teams and young, very skilled administrators. Everywhere you look, massive, massive change. It's all part of this overall transformation of the game, which we keep on coming back to. The changes at Norwich have been, and continue to be, an ongoing project? Right through to the current owners. Except, of course, Delia and Michael don't get anything like the credit they deserve for transforming Carrow Road. Some things didn't change."

"Certain club chairmen didn't let their managers buy as many players as they'd like, one said to me that, 'the lowly managers don't know what to do with a lot of money'. Harsh, but true, to a certain extent I guess. Mike Walker certainly didn't have much money to spend. But he had something about him – he took us to third, into Europe, then saved a very poor Everton side from relegation".

Looking away from the Boardroom and Offices, what was Mick's highlight on the field during the 92/93 season?

"The away win at Aston Villa. I was right in the line of the ball when Daryl Sutch curled that great winner in for us and made it 3-2. We'd gone to one of the leading clubs, away from home, and won. We drove home singing along and I thought that anything was possible! And, for a while, anything did seem possible. But that's football – it was then – maybe not so much now."

How would Mick sum it all up?

"Massive change, which affected everyone. Clubs, players, supporters, TV viewers, the lot. It didn't all start with the Premier League, but that certainly moved things along and it'll never be the same again. But I think it has been good for the game. I remember some years ago, I'd been covering a boardroom-based story at Carrow Road, and, as part of my story, I door stepped one of the then club directors. As he went to leave his home I asked him the big searching, open-ended question. He just looked up at me and, in a broad Norfolk accent, simply said, "...thass a' rum ol' job, int'it?" before driving off. It summed up both football and the Canaries for the last quarter of a century or so very well!"

The Premier League, therefore, was not an overnight sensation, nor was it an impulsive act on the part of the FA to suddenly encourage the dramatic split that saw those 22 clubs wave a red card at the venerable old Football League. However, it did appear that, once their new league was up and running, the suits at the Premier League couldn't wait to sit around a big table and come up with lots of other new ideas to complement their baby and make it, well, look different! Whether or not some of their eventual implementations were an improvement or not is, even today, debatable, as is the question of whether or not some of them were really necessary.

One of their promises had been, as Mick Dennis has outlined, that the new league would benefit the England team, that it would be 'good for the game' – presumably it would also be 'good for the pocket'. The international game, of course, was where commercial opportunities already existed and were growing. England had already been granted the rights to host the 1996 European Championships, the FA's successful application coming, without a doubt, as a consequence of the Taylor Report, which had advocated all-seater stadia to be a legal requirement for all football stadiums in England's top two divisions. Would England's application to host the tournament (beating rival applications from Austria, Portugal and The Netherlands) been successful had it not been for the consequences of the Taylor Report?

However, with England's hosting of the tournament came changes implemented by UEFA. That year's contest (which England, as hosts, qualified for automatically) would be the first to include 16 teams (the 1992 tournament, in Sweden, featured only eight) as well as being the first to be given a "Euro" prefix, making it snappier, sexier and more attractive to sponsors. The FA could clearly see how commercially advantageous it would be for the England team to qualify for major tournaments – especially given that the 1994 World Cup, a mere two years away, was destined for enormous commercial success. FIFA and the United States were laying a mighty golden egg between them and the FA clearly wanted a piece of the commercial action.

With this in mind, the FA Premier League announced at the beginning of July 1992 that four clear weekends would be 'granted' (how big of them!) before midweek World Cup qualifying games – a hither-to unparalleled gesture to the national team and one that curried them a lot of favour with fans, if not club managers who, to this day see the national team and international matches as an irritating side show. England, under the management of Graham Taylor and Phil 'yes boss' Neal duly spoilt the FA's grand plan for riches by failing to qualify for the tournament, but the seeds had been sown. More changes followed. It was announced that referees in the Premier League would wear green, rather than the 'old fashioned' black, there would be a choice of three substitutes, one of which would be a goalkeeper, and that the half-time interval would increase from ten to 15 minutes – no doubt a decision that would please the clubs, as it would give their all-seated fans enough time to purchase food and drink from outlets during the extended break. Indeed, the only rule change that didn't seem to go down well was FIFA's banning of the backpass (yes, it really happened that long ago) to goalkeepers, or, rather, backpasses that the keeper could pick up.

So confused over the new ruling were the Premier League and its member clubs, that a special meeting was called on July 17th to discuss this new rule change, its meaning and possible interpretations. Clearly, too much time and effort had been devoted to changing the colour of the referees tops, rather than trying to keep pace with the changes in the game itself. However, the new rule had also caused confusion in Germany where a player ended up being sent off for kneeling down to knee the ball back to his goalkeeper!

The renowned Barcelona and Spain goalkeeper, Andoni Zubizarreta, said, "...if you stop the keeper from using his hands, you make it easier for the team that wants to defend – they don't even have to push a striker up to pressure the keeper. It seems ridiculous to me". Its effect was certainly felt in the Premier League, with the Leeds United skipper, Gordon Strachan, saying that the new rule "killed" the team, adding, "...we had been used to taking the sting out of games, giving the ball back to the goalie, re-organising and going again. You rest, you regroup. But that changed and we didn't adapt." But English football was going to have to adapt, and quickly.

The FA finally, at the end of July, introduced a ruling of its own that was connected with the game, that of compulsory random drug-testing for players. However, just as it seemed that the game and its improvement and development was once again becoming the priority, there were fanfares a-plenty just 24 hours later as *Coca Cola* twisted their sugary tentacles in the English game by becoming the new sponsors of the League Cup – the two-year deal costing £2.25 million. But how ironic that a competition outside the jurisdiction of the FA and their Premier League had stolen the thunder on this occasion. Stolen thunder or not, the opening day of the Premier League drew ever closer, and, as it neared, clubs tried to out-do each other with ever more outrageous recruitment programmes – all, of course, involving the money that had been awarded to them courtesy of the Sky deal with the Premier League. Champions Leeds signed David Rocastle from Arsenal for £2 million; Liverpool paid Tottenham £2.3 million for Paul Stewart; while Alan Shearer left Southampton to join newly minted Blackburn Rovers for a British record fee of £3.6 million.

And, in perhaps one of the first signs of the tail wagging the dog in English football, the Premier League clubs blocked proposed sponsorship deals from *Bass* and *Ford* as it would be seen as conflicting with existing club sponsorships. All-seater stadiums, record transfer fees, massive commercial deals live League football, and referees in green! The FA Premier League had arrived!***

---

*Hafnia were, and remain, a Danish meatpacking company.

**David Dein bought a 16.6% share in Arsenal in 1983 for £292,000, a move that was described by then Arsenal Chairman, Peter Hill-Wood, as "crazy", adding that, for Dein, it was "dead money". Dein eventually built up his shareholding in Arsenal to 42% by 1991. When he sold his stake in the club in 2007, he received £75 million... "Dead money" indeed!

***During all of the excitement surrounding the new Premier League and its accordant glitz, glamour and dancing girls, few people mourned the closure of the FA School of Excellence that same Summer. Closed, apparently, through 'lack of success'. You couldn't make it up!

A SUMMER
OF DISCONTENT

Norwich City, although regarded as one of the smaller clubs in the newly formed Premier League, could certainly regard themselves as one of its founder clubs through right. The Canaries had reached the top flight of English football for the first time in their history with Division Two Championship success in the 1971/72 season, and then, two decades after they had made their first appearance in what was then League Division One, Norwich prepared for the first ever season of Premier League football as an established top division side.

Since their promotion, City had spent 17 of the consequent 20 League campaigns in Division One, suffering just three relegations, all of which resulted in an immediate return to the top flight during the subsequent season. That period of time, by far the most successful one in the club's history, had also seen them achieve League finishes of tenth in 1975/76; fifth (immediately following promotion) in 1986/87; and fourth in the 1988/89 season. The latter two finishes, together with a League Cup (or Milk Cup, as it was at the time) success in 1985 saw Norwich qualify for European football on three occasions, their rightful and hard earned place amongst Europe's elite being unfairly denied to them by the blanket ban on English club's, following the atrocities at the Heysel Stadium in 1985.

In addition to all of this, the club had also reached three League Cup finals (with one victory), as well as a one defeated appearance in the quarter-final and semi-final stages. The FA Cup, long synonymous with the club as part of its giant killing heyday had been less productive since the famous run to the semi-finals of 1959. Even so, City had appeared in a further two semi-finals, as well as one quarter-final. All in all, a more than respectable record over two decades for a club which, prior to that time, had achieved little in the previous 70 years of its history other than a few eyebrow raising efforts in the FA Cup. Despite this, neither the City residents, or the footballing nation as a whole, had much faith in Norwich achieving anything at all in the first season of Premier League football – other than the ignominy of relegation.

The basis for this pessimism had been the club's poor performances during the previous campaign. The 1991/92 season, in Barclays Division One, had started with three draws and a victory – the opening run of four games without defeat was only ended by a Lineker-inspired Tottenham in late August. Even so, the Canaries recovered from that set-back with some impressive results, including victories over West Ham and Chelsea (Robert Fleck's brace in the 3-0 away stroll on November 23rd obviously making quite an impact on those who mattered at Stamford Bridge) then, following another victory, this time over Aston Villa on New Year's Day (2-1), Dave Stringer's side were in a respectable 12th place in the table. And things remained optimistic.

A Darren Beckford hat-trick on March 21st secured a 4-3 win over Everton, a thrilling game that had seen City fall behind – Beckford's final goal coming in the 86th minute to seal the win before what was, quite frankly, a lamentable crowd of just under 12,000. Norwich remained in 13th place, with seven games to go. All seemed well, and even a 3-1 Carrow Road defeat against Manchester United at the end of March (an extra 5,589 fans deciding that was a far more attractive proposition than the Everton game ten days earlier) did little to dampen spirits at the club – it had been another good season, with an FA Cup semi-final date against Second Division Sunderland to look forward to.

By the time FA Cup semi weekend dawned, the City, indeed, the entire County was full of optimism, that the game at Hillsborough against their lower division opponents, was as a good a chance as any for the club to reach an FA Cup Final. Even the injury to iconic striker Robert Fleck, one that had seen him miss the previous three games, seemed to be clearing up in time for the match. Fleck was spending a couple of hours a day in an oxygen tent in an effort to speed up the healing process for his cracked ribs, and, although the treatment method (then seen as bizarre and drawing inevitable comparisons with Michael Jackson) drew predictable guffaws from the national media, Fleck looked a certain starter in the match.

FA Cup semi-final and Premier League membership seemed assured (supposedly superior contemporaries West Ham were staring at relegation) under the popular Stringer, who looked destined to crown his four and a half years in charge at the club by leading the Canaries out at Wembley. Things were looking good at Carrow Road. Stringer was able to field a strong team, if not his strongest (Gunn, Crook and Phillips were all absent) for that semi and Fleck was available, if not 100% fit, and in the starting 11.

It was the same team that had seen off Southampton in the quarter-final replay, the game in which a certain Chris Sutton first came to national prominence. Bryan Gunn had been out since January, but had ably been replaced by his understudy, Mark Walton, in goal – Walton had played in Norwich's four previous matches in the competition and had only conceded two goals, he was only to concede one more in the semi-final, though, a goal that saw Sunderland win 1-0 and stun the 17,000 Norwich fans who had travelled to the game fully expecting victory.

That shock defeat had a very negative effect on the club for the rest of that season. Following defeat at Hillsborough, Norwich had just six games left, and lost five of them – the lone respite coming in a tense 1-1 draw at home to Wimbledon in the penultimate game. Even bottom club West Ham had a rare success against the Canaries during that run, the Hammers' 4-0 win at Upton Park on April 11th was their best result of the season. Further defeat followed at Notts County (1-0) and Sheffield Wednesday (2-0, another Hillsborough no-show) followed. Nerves were certainly stretched to breaking point at that time, and only that draw against Wimbledon secured safety. It was to be Fleck's last appearance and goal for the club during that first spell he had at Carrow Road.

Norwich ended the season with a home fixture against newly-crowned Champions, Leeds United. Rod Wallace ensured the Canaries seventh defeat in eight games with a memorable solo effort midway through the first-half, however, the game and result became of secondary importance to Norwich fans because of the shock news that had been announced the previous day. Dave Stringer, a popular player in his time at the club, who had stepped up into the manager's seat after the sacking of Ken Brown, announced his resignation from the post, stating that, in his opinion (certainly not the board's) it was time for a new man to take over.

Typical Stringer, modest and understated, quietly vacating the role which had made him Norwich City's most successful ever manager – a dignified reign which saw League finishes of fifth and fourth, as well as two FA Cup semi-finals. By choosing to leave right at the end of the season, Stringer had given the club ample time to find his successor, and, with Premier League status assured, albeit narrowly, the suits at Carrow Road would need that time to guarantee the right man for the job was found.

Speaking to members of the side who had played at the club under Stringer, their admiration and respect for the man is very apparent. This willingness to speak, nearly two decades later, and as one, in such a positive manner about Stringer, a man whose time at Norwich was perhaps overshadowed by the events that were to come, speaks volumes for him both as a person and as a football manager. He was certainly not going to be an easy man to replace, something which I, and many other fans would certainly have thought at the time.

The Dave Stringer-less Norwich ended that 1991/92 season in 18th position, three points above relegated Luton Town. There had been high points – lengthy runs in both cup competitions (5th round of League Cup) and some impressive league wins prior to the FA Cup disappointment, including a 3-0 thrashing of Liverpool at Carrow Road, a game that saw Fleck score twice in the final 20 minutes.

However, these positive moments stood, small and alone, in the seasons darker moments, which accounted for a 10% drop in the average crowds at Carrow Road (just 10,541 attended the home win over Luton on October 26th); the demolition of the old Barclay Stand, for so long a symbol of the club and a home from home, indeed, a spectating 'rite of passage' for many of the club's younger fans (during the visit of Arsenal in April, a wreath was placed on the side of the pitch in protest at the stand's demise, with a sit-down protest following); and, above all, the miserable League run at the end of that season. Nine losses in the last 12 games, including the heavy defeat at West Ham, and, with it, the sudden and rather unexpected threat of relegation.

Norwich used a total of 24 players during that final Division One season, with Rob Newman (41 league appearances); Mark Bowen and Robert Fleck (35 each) and David Phillips (34) leading the way. Of that notable quartet, three went onto become vital members of the following season's squad. The other, a popular and pivotal player in the side was to leave, although the timing of his departure was so critical, it really should be counted as one of the initial happenings of the following season, rather than a postscript to the last one.

You needn't have been a Norwich City supporter to question the wisdom of the decision to sell their star player and leading goal scorer with just three days to go before the new campaign started. Robert Fleck, signed from Rangers by Stringer as an early Christmas present for Canaries fans in December 1987, made an instant impact at Carrow Road, scoring in just his second game, a 2-1 win at Derby County, ending the season with seven goals from 18 League appearances, and finishing second in the club's highest goalscorers table for that season. He had been part of some of the club's most memorable matches and incidents in the years that followed, including, most famously of all perhaps, his last minute winner at Millwall in January 1989 ("people always ask me about that one"), a spectacular turn and volley that sent the Canaries home from that clash second in the table.

His energy, commitment to the cause, and effortless ability to wind up both players and fans from opposing sides, swiftly made him a hero among the Carrow Road regulars as well as his fellow players – Darren Eadie, still a schoolboy when he joined the club, and at a time when Fleck was the 'main man' around Carrow Road, may have found the experienced and much older senior player a daunting figure, but instead, he recalls Fleck as a "talisman" who was "...a great lad, who gave the younger lads a great welcome, and who looked after them". Fleck clearly had his admirers outside of the club too, and, although there had always been rumours of his pending departure to a 'bigger' club, he was always there at the start of a new season, ready to run himself into the ground for Norwich City once again. The Summer of 1992 was, however, going to be different.

Chelsea had long been cited as a club whose interest in Fleck was more than a fleeting one. They had previously raided Carrow Road two Summers earlier, signing Fleck's then team mate Andy Townsend, and it is likely that Townsend arrived from Carrow Road with a few words to say about Fleck that would have further piqued Chelsea's interest. They bided their time and, when it became clear that Fleck was looking for a move away from Norfolk, duly made their own move, signing him for £2.1 million on August 12th 1992. Chelsea were certainly making their intentions and ambitions for the new campaign clear – Fleck was joining two other new arrivals at Stamford Bridge in Mick Harford and John Spencer – signed from Luton Town and Rangers respectively, while Norwich had, at that stage, signed Gary Megson – on a free transfer.

And, while Fleck's departure from Norwich was hardly the biggest of surprises (Norwich had long secured a reputation as a 'selling club', although, to be fair, which club in football isn't?), the timing certainly was, especially with regard to finding a replacement. Fleck had ended the 1991/92 season as Norwich's top scorer with 19 in the League and Cup, Darren Beckford was second in the table with ten – the only other player who had reached double figures, goals wise, that season. With Fleck gone, Norwich looked as if they were going to commencing the 1992/93 season with a team that couldn't be relied upon to score any goals.

I met Robert to ask him about that move and eager to find out more about the iconic striker and his time at Norwich City.

THE DEPARTING HERO

R obert very much looked like the player I remembered when we met – an annoying trait I was to discover amongst the ex-Norwich players who have contributed to this book, who all appear to be immune to the ravages of time! Arriving at our meeting place in a very trendy VW Beetle ("it's my wife's car!"), we settled down and talked football, Robert's response to my claim that Norwich fans would be interested to hear what he had to say, being a softly spoken; "I don't know about that!" A typical response from a man whose modesty and gentle manner throughout the interview was completely in contrast to the fiery figure I remember so well. And, with fire in mind and fiery situations in particular, I opened by asking Robert what it was like coping with the pressures of playing for such a massive club as Rangers, where he started his career, in particular, an 'Old Firm' Derby.

"It's frightening! Frightening but terrific to play in, I played in three or four and they were amazing matches to be involved in. It's every boys dream in Glasgow to play in one of them, you're either Rangers or Celtic up there, so, to play in one...let's just say, if you don't win, you can't go outside for a few weeks, not until you've won another five or six matches on the trot, or played them (Celtic) again and won! But you mustn't think that playing for Norwich against Ipswich doesn't compare. Every derby match has its own moments, its own uniqueness, the rivalry and the hatred amongst some of the spectators. But Rangers v Celtic, that's huge in comparison"

I commented that the list of people who had come from Glasgow, at a young age, to settle in Norwich, and to stay put, was, well, let's put it like this: it wasn't going to be very long. Did Robert find his situation, then and now, an unusual one?

"I think it is, yes. I blame Chris Woods for that! When I was looking at a move, I first came down to Watford and met up with Dave Bassett, chatted with him and had a look around the club and ground. I didn't fancy going there at all. I'd been playing alongside Chris at Rangers, and he put in a good word about Norwich, good reviews – I'm glad he did, and I'm glad I came. It's a lovely place, I'm settled, met and married a lovely Norfolk girl. That makes it sound like it was perfect of course, and that I settle quickly, but that wasn't the case. It took time and it was difficult at first, my last game for Rangers was against Dunfermline, there was, I think, about 34,000 people at Ibrox. I went to Norwich, first game against Wimbledon at Plough Lane, there could have been no more than 4,000 there (Robert is spot on, the attendance was 4,026!), my debut, I brought six mates along...after the game, it was straight back to Glasgow and I was thinking, 'what have I done?' Perhaps it wasn't the best place for me to make my Norwich debut! But it was all part of the move, the changes. And people helped me to settle. I knew Bryan Gunn very well. He was a good mate, and, after I joined Norwich, I moved in with him for a while. It helped me to settle! We used to toss a coin to see who'd cook our meal that evening, I nearly always lost, 99 times out of 100, it'd be me doing the cooking..."

At this point I interrupted Robert and advised him that he had settled well and could, in this most guarded of counties, now be regarded as a local.

"I'll never be a yokel!"

A sign of Glaswegian passion, the sort that lit up many a football pitch during Robert's career. Fearing that he might feel insulted, I hastily repeated myself, insisting that I had said he was now a local, not a yokel!

"Oh, a local (smiles). Well, no. I'll never be a local and I'll never be a yokel. I love it here, but I'm a Scot, I'm Scottish, there's no doubt about that! Glasgow Rangers are still the first result I look for and my family are all still up there, but my life is down here now. I've got the best of both worlds. I like it here very much, but I also have Glasgow as well, and Scotland. Like I said, I'm a Scot first".

How did Robert's move to Norwich come about?

"Well, Dave Stringer took the job as Manager, he wanted to sign me not long afterwards. So he flew up to Glasgow with Robert Chase, I met with them both. I ended up taking the 7am plane back to Norwich, another meeting, this time in a portakabin – things were different then! And I signed. Bryan (Gunn) soon came over to welcome me, he brought some of the other lads, so I was looked after straight away."

Robert had been treated to what was, and remains, a real Norwich City tradition, helping new players settle in and feel part of the club as soon as possible. It would have been important for him to have felt 'at home' straight away, not all high profile Scottish players who headed south at that time settled so well, the prime example of the time being Ally McCoist, who had departed for Sunderland from St Johnstone in 1981 in the proverbial blaze of glory. Charlie Nicholas was another, and, more recently, there was Kris Boyd, a freely scoring striker at Rangers who struggled following another big money move, this time to Middlesbrough.

"No, Ally didn't settle at all (at Sunderland) which turned out to be a good thing for Rangers! But I was made to feel very welcome, and, what with knowing Bryan really well, it wasn't too bad at all. It was just as well; Norwich paid a lot of money for me! I actually think Norwich had tried to sign me before, when Ken Brown was Manager. There was talk and I knew about it. I think Dave (Stringer) was just following up on Ken's interest. But it was a fair bit of money for them. I have to admit, I don't remember too many of the first few games I played, unless I'm prompted, if I see a game or a goal on TV for example, else someone mentions one to me. The goal at Millwall? Yes, that's one that everyone does keep going on about! It's one of my more memorable ones, but I'm sure I have scored better ones and scored more important ones than that particular goal. I just enjoyed playing the game, the goals were part of it of course, but I loved to play football"

I mentioned that, in many ways, the way that Robert played and so obviously enjoyed himself whilst out on the pitch reminded me of Gazza.

"I've always looked at it like this. I always wanted to be a footballer – coming from Glasgow, if I hadn't have been a footballer, what would I have been? I don't know, working on the shipyards or something. Playing, to me, was a pleasure, a privilege; it was a hobby you were paid well for. Even then, it was expensive for people to come to games, and I wanted the fans who made the effort to feel part of it all and part of the team. They'd paid for their tickets and I think that, if you pay for your ticket, you can say what you want, call me what you want if you're playing badly, but, after the game has finished, that's it, over."

"A footballer is, essentially, an entertainer with the pitch as his stage. I'm sure that the people here had never seen anything like me down here, the way I played and got the fans involved. But I loved it! I loved the banter, the way it took my mind off things, helped me forget the pressures and worries. Yes, you go out to entertain. But as for Gazza? Well, I don't think I could lace his boots up, he was fantastic. A character and a great player, there was nobody to touch him. But I liked to try to entertain as well".

With Robert seeing himself as an entertainer, I wondered if he had played a big part in the inner sanctum of the dressing room, where banter was, and remains, king – and did he miss it as much as he missed playing?

"Well, I have played in some of the charity games. You turn up, get in the changing room, old faces come along, you might not have seen them for two or three years but, once they're there, it's like you've never been away, you're straight back into it. The banter, dressing room banter, it's one of the very best things about football. Yes, you do miss that. It's a tough place the dressing room at a football club. For new or young players, when they first come to a club, it's a case of 'sink or swim' when they come in there. It must be very hard for all the foreign players in the game today; they must find that part of the game very difficult to understand. It wasn't like that when I joined Norwich, the foreigners then came from Scotland!"

"We had a couple of Spanish lads at Norwich when I was there – Victor Segura was one. Another came over on trial but never signed – Bakero? Yes, Jose Bakero. But it didn't matter who you were at Norwich, everyone was always made to feel very welcome. They must have found it very strange. But, regardless of who you were, or where you came from, there were no cliques at Norwich. Falling out, yes... fights, yes. But you sort that out in-house, in the dressing room. Done. By Monday, back at training, everything is OK again, back to work as normal, friends again. But it's like that at all workplaces, in football, however, it just gets reported and blown up all over the place. But why on earth is it thought of as newsworthy in the first place – look at what you have got, a big group of young, healthy, competitive men, that's what is going to happen! And like I said, we all stuck together, we may not have all got on well, all have been friends with everyone, but we all stuck together, especially when we were all out on that pitch! I got on well with everyone at Norwich mind. Everyone! (I didn't find that surprising!). Bryan, Mark Bowen, Ian Crook, Ian Culverhouse, Ian Butterworth, Robert Rosario. I played a few games in attack with Robert, taking the knocks whilst he scored the goals. He was an underrated player. When he left Norwich and went onto play for Coventry and Nottingham Forest, people began to realise what a good player he was. He was a pretty boy!! But he'd put his head in where it hurts. Great player, great character to have in the dressing room. But we had lots of characters, lots of funny guys in that dressing room. And a good manager in Dave Stringer. He was one of the gentlest men I have ever met. Gentle, that is, until you got him into the changing room. He then became a changed man! If you then crossed the line with him, you knew all about it, and he'd let you know in no uncertain terms if he wasn't happy with you, and in front of everyone else if necessary. David Williams did much of the training and the tactical plays, whilst Dave did the man management side of things. You did not cross him! But, otherwise, he was so very quiet! I just missed out on playing with Dave Williams, he was coming to the end of his playing career when I joined and had teamed up with Dave. But I played alongside him for the reserves, and what a great player he was. A great passer, good technique, strike of the ball and a good communicator. He'd have a bit of a sulk now and again, but he was a great tactician."

You were obviously coached and brought up to play the 'right' way at a huge club in Rangers, one that offered as good an apprenticeship for young footballers as any in Europe could offer – did you think yourself pretty much the finished article, or did you improve even more as a player whilst you were at Norwich?

"Well, you can agree or disagree on that one. I'd come from a big club, and had already played in a team containing some greats – Ally McCoist, Chris Woods, Terry Butcher, Trevor Francis, and Ray Wilkins. All exceptionally good players, so I was, remember, already playing at a very high standard when I joined Norwich. Mind you, when I came down here, I was playing alongside and against some very good players. Alan Hansen – I remembered playing against him when he was at Partick Thistle! So yes, I had to improve – but did Norwich improve me? Playing with and against great players. Maybe they did. Of course, I eventually moved on from Norwich, but it's what I wanted at the time. I would have left the previous year and there was talk of me going to one of four or five different clubs. But I ended up promising Dave Stringer and Robert Chase that I wouldn't leave, and that I'd stay for one more (1991/92) year. But it was always known, to them, that I'd be leaving at the end of that season. It wasn't the best of seasons for the club, especially given what they'd achieved before in terms of league finishes. And I didn't have a particularly good season either. People forgot all of the good years I'd previously had with Norwich! But I was always going to leave. I went down to London to talk to Tottenham and Chelsea. I met with Terry Venables at Tottenham first, but I was never going to join them, I only went there and met with him out of courtesy. In my mind, I was always going to join Chelsea. They'd asked Norwich about me the previous year – I was on holiday and got a call, Chelsea are after you! I then spoke to Robert Chase and he said 'no', so I agreed to that one final year. But Chelsea became the club I wanted to join. I went to speak with them that following Summer, the day after I'd seen Venables, sat and met with Ken Bates. I knew I wanted to sign for them; it was a case of 'where do I sign?' I don't regret it."

"It seemed to me to be absolutely the best move I could have made at the time. I guess people have since thought it was a bad move for me as I didn't work out quite as well as had been expected, but it was the right choice to make and I have never regretted making it. Given the choice again, I'd still sign for Chelsea. I don't regret anything. I was lucky to play alongside some great players there – big Mick (Harford), Tony Cascarino, Spenny (John Spencer). They'd all come along just before me, I arrived shortly before the start of the season, so it was a bit of a rush at the beginning. Ian Porterfield was the

Manager who signed me, Don Howe was his Assistant. Perhaps Don was the problem for me? His philosophy was that you defend from the front, maybe not the game I'd been used to. I mean, I was doing OK, and, by Christmas, I'd scored a few goals – and I was never a prolific goal scorer – but I was up there with the assists, indeed, I had more assists than Dennis Wise, and that's a hell of achievement, because what a great player he was! So, maybe my game was improving now – a different way of playing, new team-mates. I thought I would progress and become a better player. But Ian and Don got the sack, and after that it was always a struggle, for me and for my game. Dave Webb came in, decent, honest guy; I went to see him and he was straight with me, he said, 'Robert, I want to play with the big men up top, Mick Harford and Tony Cascarino – but I will need you, you'll get used. I said I'd do my best, and I wanted to, like I said, he was a good, honest man. In one game though (Robert laughs at the memory!) I think it was against Blackburn, he played me right midfield! He'd asked me to do a job and I did it to the best of my ability, it wasn't my best ever game, but.... anyway, he didn't stay in the job for long, and I was gutted about that, but then Glenn (Hoddle) came in. I thought this would be a good thing. He'd been at Tottenham, played and talked the game the right way, good football, a good Manager. Anyway, he sat down with me, it all sounded good; '...this is what we'll do, you're part of my plans Robert, you'll be playing, I liked the way you played at Norwich, bla bla bla...' – but it didn't work out that way. I believed that I was better than what Glenn had in the team, but...and I've still no regrets. However, even at that time, I didn't regret the move and didn't see myself going back to Norwich, or wanting to. I went out on loan to some other clubs instead, initially to Bolton, under Bruce Rioch and Colin Todd. I remember that, one week we were playing Southend, then Millwall on the Saturday, so the team stayed in a hotel in London, even though I still lived there! I went to Bristol City on loan later on, under Joe Jordan and John Gorman – he's Glenn's best mate. I loved it, loved it there, and Joe wanted me to sign, I know I wanted to stay (in 13 league appearances for the Robins during 1995, Robert scored three goals), but, for one reason and another, that didn't work out. There was even a chance to go to Celtic when Lou Macari was Manager..."

Much as I didn't want to, I had to interrupt Robert at this point, I couldn't believe what I was saying – he would have joined Celtic? It was like saying he'd have considered a move to Ipswich – maybe even worse than that!

"Yes I would – but that's how desperate I was to play again! I needed to get out of Chelsea, Glenn wasn't even talking to me by now. And yes, it was Celtic, but I saw it as an opportunity to get playing, score a few goals and get a permanent move back down in England. However, Chelsea moved the goalposts and it didn't come off – and, looking back now, that was probably a good thing! And then Norwich wanted me again. I went and spoke to Martin O'Neill, he said, 'listen, this isn't going to be just a loan, we want you back full time'. Martin was like Dave Webb, very straight, very honest. I like that in a Manager, if he talks to you straight, gives it to you straight, then you'll work your bollocks off for them over ninety minutes, and that's what I wanted to do for Martin. It's a respect thing with managers – especially with ones like Martin O'Neill. Whatever else you might think about them, it's vital you respect them? And I had a lot of respect for Martin."

Much has been said, and doubtless still has to be said, about Martin O'Neill's six month stint as Norwich City Manager. Infact, there is probably a book in there somewhere! The story goes that O'Neill was frustrated at the reluctance of the club to release funds that would help him continue to rebuild a squad that, although full of talented young players, could have done with a little experience and professional nous. O'Neill identified one player in particular as being ideal for his needs, one who would, had he joined the club, been a striking partner in arms for Robert, the player in question being Dean Windass.

"That would have been nice, yes, to play alongside Dean. But things don't always work out. We had a good side at the start of his time here, we thought it was good enough to get back into the Premier League – players like Darren Eadie, Andy Johnson, Jon Newsome, John Polston, Bryan of course, Spencer Prior...Spencer, yeah, bloody hell (Robert's words and expressions indicate good memories of that team and time!), plus in time, we had some good players come in on loan. Jan Molby was one of them. He was a fantastic player. So down to earth, a great big Dane with this amazing Scouse accent! He gave us all a big lift when he came here (Molby joined Norwich on loan from Liverpool in December 1995, making five appearances and scoring one goal); he just knocked the ball about, a great striker of the ball, great passer. You could get players like that to come in for a spell at that time. You probably couldn't now, the changes in the game, the wages they'd be on. We showed that everyone had a chance of doing well, given a good squad of players and Managers, which Norwich had. But will a club the size of Norwich ever finish in the top three of the Premier League again? No, definitely not. Not a hope in hell. We had our time right at the last moment, before the gap became too big. A fourth place finish and two FA Cup semi final appearances. And we'd have qualified for Europe as well, had it not been for the Heysel disaster. People forget that. People say that Mike Walker is the most successful manager Norwich has ever had. They're wrong. The most successful Manager Norwich have ever had is Dave Stringer. Two FA Cup semi-finals and a fourth place finish."

I wondered, not for the first time, if Robert, with that thought in mind, would you have fancied his team from 1988/89 in a game against Mike Walker's side from a few years later? I did allow for the slight difficulty in that some players could have represented both teams, so am assuming that they would have done just that, played for both! Theoretically, in that case, which side did Robert think would have come out on top?

"Yeah. I think we'd have beaten them...(Robert pauses, then speaks, quietly but great conviction and a little bit of that fire he showed as a player briefly shows in his words and conviction)...we could have pushed Arsenal and Liverpool all the way for the title that season. The worse thing that happened was getting to the semi-final of the Cup in 1989. Dave was starting to rest players and think about the Cup more, rather than going all out for the league. We spoke about it, it was decided, this is what we were going to do, and some players it was, 'yes, the FA Cup semi-final, how often do you get that close to Wembley?' But we could, we should, have gone for it in every game. You should have been playing in every game, play, play well, if you don't, then you're out, then someone takes your place. I've spoken to Bryan and Dale Gordon about it, we agree, we should have pushed it in the league that season. We were doing well (holding second place in the table into mid-March) then we played Newcastle at home (the Magpies were nineteenth!), well... Mirandinha scored and we lost, 2-1. After that it was 'never mind, we're still in the Cup' and we seemed to give up on the league – plus I missed out on that first semi-final, indeed, I nearly missed the second one (in 1992). Back then though, with a good side and a chance of winning the league, attention turned more to the Cup from about March onwards. So we just focused on that, not the league. A nightmare! Of course, the FA Cup meant more then, certainly to fans. I'd like to think it still does today. I never won the Scottish Cup – won the Skol Cup a couple of times though, the medals are at home in a cupboard somewhere!"

I wanted to further question Robert on the point he had made about Dave Stringer's 1989 side maybe not going all out to try and win the league that season, and to rest players, rather than selecting the best side available and giving their all in every match. Would he have wanted to play in every game, do footballers really want to play in as many games as possible?

"Very much so, yes. I wanted to play in every single one. If the Reserves were a few players short in midweek, I'd put my hand up, I'd volunteer to play. But it wasn't just me; there were loads of players like that there at the time. Like I said, I just wanted to play and I wanted to win. People ask me, do I wish I was still playing the game today? My answer is 'no'. They then say, 'well, what about the money?' That's not playing for the love of it. Listen. I won a league, a couple of cups. I've played for my country in the World Cup finals. When is my country going to play in a World Cup finals again?"

There is a great clip from the 1990 World Cup finals, which features Robert wildly celebrating in the background after a Scotland goal – just as any member of the travelling Tartan Army would have done. Did he remember the game?

"Sweden! (big smile!) I've got the photograph. But I shouldn't even have been there, it should have been Davie Cooper. I was in Dubrovnik, on holiday with my wife, daughter and mother and father-in-law. Davie was injured, so Norwich were trying to get hold of me to let me know I was needed. They managed to do so, I had to leave and go off to Malta to acclimatise, then off to Italy. For the first game (Scotland lost 1-0 to Costa Rica) I wasn't even on the bench – but you're there, you're at the World Cup finals, it's every boy's dream. We lost that game, second up is Sweden. All of a sudden, I'm starting, and from nowhere. Fantastic! Third game, Brazil. I've done well against Sweden, so I'm thinking, I'll be starting again – but I wasn't playing, Ally McCoist did. I wasn't happy, especially as McCoist hadn't started in either of the last two games."

"During the Brazil game, me and Andy Goram were warming up, up and down the touchline. We weren't watching the game though, we were watching the Brazil fans! They're great to watch, but the Scottish fans are the best in the world, colourful, good humoured – fantastic, the whole experience. You'd pay to play for your country in the World Cup finals. They're just there to support their team. And we felt well we could have done well – we were full of confidence. Great squad and players. But you go into the first match, Costa Rica, and, with no disrespect to them, we should have won. But we lost, and we're on the back foot straight away."

"But we beat Sweden, and we should have at least got a draw against Brazil. The keeper made one of the best saves I've ever seen – the ball came in, wet pitch, it just bounced over my foot– if I'd got a connection, I'd have scored. It falls to Mo Johnston, he's about four yards out. He smashes it, but the keeper, Taffarel, he made a fantastic save. If only it had fallen to me! If I had put that away, well, I'd probably still be running around Turin celebrating today. The team spirit was cracking, a real eye opener."

"I'd made my debut against Argentina in a friendly, they were then the holders. That was a big to-do. But then to actually go to the World Cup. A bonus, wonderful team spirit. You can't buy memories like that. My memories are very special to me, and personal. And they're for me alone, I wouldn't do an autobiography like so many players have done. I've been asked, someone asked me about it only a couple of weeks ago, but I said no, I won't do it."

One of Robert's memories might have been an early game he had for Chelsea at Stamford Bridge, with the Premier League pacesetters Norwich City in town. Chelsea had gone ahead and Robert had set up their opening goal for Mick Harford. Did he remember much of that day, and, dare I say it, the final result?

"Yes, and I'll be honest here, and I don't care who knows it – Bryan knows anyway! He and his wife had stayed with me that weekend, so I told him! Anyway, the Norwich team were late arriving for the game, which was good, as we got into them from the kick-off. I had a chance early on, went through, only the keeper to beat! There I was, heading towards Bryan Gunn and all the Norwich fans – and it just hit me, I thought, 'I can't score, I can't score!'. It was Bryan – who was staying with me, the Norwich fans and team, I just couldn't do it, Norwich had been such a big part of my life! So I laid it back to

Mick who went onto score, he turned and celebrated, I just turned the other way to him and slowly walked back towards the centre circle."

"I couldn't do it. Not against Norwich or Bryan, especially as he was staying! Infact, if I had ever scored against Norwich, in any game, I wouldn't have celebrated. I had, have, too much affection for the club and their fans. The fans were amazing to me, I've a lot of respect for them, they never criticised me. They knew I would never hide, would always give everything, even if I was having issues with the club or the management. Dave Beasant was unfortunate in that game, making the errors that let Norwich back into it. The fans and the management let him know all about it, but, you know what they say, if a striker misses a couple of good chances, he can make up for it and those misses are forgotten. With a keeper, well, with Dave that day, he made a couple of mistakes that won the game for Norwich, but he was criticised afterwards too much. You know, Dave was the definitive gentle giant, he'd do anything for you, anything to help out. He was devastated after that game, I don't think he even changed afterwards, he was in his car and gone. But nobody in the changing room said anything against him afterwards – and that's football, you stick together. The fans had their say, and Ian Porterfield, well, he did have a lot to say, and pretty much immediately after the game as well. That should be kept in-house, in the changing room. Norwich had a great start to the season, including doing the double over us and I was pleased, of course. Really chuffed for them, I knew most of them – I even knew Gary Megson because he came in whilst I was still there, so I got to know him – it was only Mark Robins I didn't know. So yes, of course I was pleased for them. But I was jealous as well, jealous that I'd left and they ended up doing so well, they ended up third whilst we finished in eleventh. I'd gone to Chelsea thinking we had the better team and squad, but it wasn't to be. I came back to Norwich, and ended up finishing my career at Reading. That came at a time when Norwich were getting rid of all of their players, or so it seemed! I went to play there under Tommy Burns, bless him. I tried to help them stay up, but it wasn't to be, and that was sad. It was my only relegation as a footballer. But they were, like Norwich, a lovely club, a community club. I enjoyed my spell there, and. Like I've said, have so many good memories".

How would Robert sum himself up today as a footballer I asked?

"Well, I wouldn't have called myself a prolific goalscorer. I was more of a creator; I liked to play in and around the 18-yard box, just behind the main striker. I did my bit, tried my best for all the teams I played for, and the fans. I guess I was just an honest footballer. Yes, if you're going to say anything about me at all, just say that he was an honest footballer."

Robert was now creating more memories in his current role, working as a Classroom Assistant at a local school for children with special needs. I asked Robert if it was a case of the children not really knowing who he was, or what he used to do – but exactly the opposite with their parents, Fathers especially!

"Well, the kids see me on a pitch and at games. They like that! And they see me doing interviews. But I don't ever feel I was a footballer now. I mean yes, I am when people like yourself want to interview me for your work, I'm happy to do that. But I'm not a footballer now. This is what I do now, and it's fantastic to put a smile on the kid's faces doing this. I get enormous job satisfaction. It's lovely! It was difficult and new at first. But I got used to it, I'd been around kids when I was a player, doing hospital visits and such like. I became involved with the school, the job came up, and I was lucky enough to be offered it. It's fantastic. It makes the sort of things that wind you up in football seem very trivial! Now I just want to help make the school the very best place it can be for them. I'm a Glasgow boy. I've seen a lot there. I've seen a lot in football. Came down to Norfolk, found it to be a lovely place. Moved and played some football in London – the football didn't go so well, but I don't regret it. Then I came back to Norwich again. It's all been very rewarding – and yes, I feel very rounded, I've seen some things, done some things. But I'm settled now."

Chatting to Robert had been an absolute joy! It's said that you should never meet your heroes, lest you be disappointed. When Robert was playing for Norwich, it was that passion, the commitment, the smile on his face – and the unquestionable skill he had, that endeared him to me and so many Norwich fans, and to this day. A good footballer, an honest man and a good man. I was not disappointed.

Prior to leaving Norwich to join Chelsea in August 1992, Robert had made 130 league starts for the Canaries, plus a further 13 as substitute. He started a further 29 FA and League Cup games, coming on as a substitute in a further two games. A total of 174 appearances for Norwich during that first spell, during which he scored 62 goals, a ratio of one in just under every three games – not too shabby at all for someone who doesn't consider himself a natural goalscorer!

Following his spell at Chelsea, as well as loan appearances at Bolton Wanderers and Bristol City, Fleck returned to Norwich City for a second spell in August 1995, three years after his initial departure; one of the two signings Martin O'Neill made during his short spell at the club, the other being Martin Rush. He made a further 104 league appearances for the club during that time (including eleven from the bench), plus fourteen FA and League Cup appearances, including coming on as a substitute in a further two games, scoring 18 goals in total. He left the Canaries for the second and final time in March 1998, joining Reading, playing (but not scoring) against Norwich on the last day of that 1997/98 season.

A whole new Ball Game

The Premier League, with its softly-softly introduction had slowly gathered momentum and, by the beginning of August 1992, the hype and expectation had gone into overdrive (maybe even overkill?) with the main benefactors of the new game, Sky Television (how ironic that, with the ban on tobacco advertising, Sky Sports have taken over as Rothmans as sponsors of the very book that was so wary of the changes that might come in the game) produced and networked across their whole output the fact that football had changed, had changed for the better – and, what's more, it was all going to be shown on Sky! The time had come, football was, officially, a circus, prime time entertainment, live entertainment, and by God, how they were going to milk their sacred calf.

Naturally enough, Norwich City had not been selected to be one of the teams 'privileged' enough to be featured in the opening television games. Indeed, it is likely that, even if the Canaries were due to play against a team of Martians, such was their standing in the game at the time, it would barely have got a mention. Mike Walker and his team travelled to Highbury for their opening match, football writers and associated experts gave the fixture a cursory glance, awarded George Graham's team the three points and moved on to wax lyrical about Liverpool. Insult seemed to be added to injury for those Canary fans who attended the game when they had their first look through the Arsenal programme (at £1.50, the same price as the Norwich one) and read the programme notes by George Graham. It was, and remains, the tradition for the opposing teams Manager to say a few words about their opponents on the day, to pick out a few players, as well as say a few things about his opposite number – although it is doubtful that Graham even knew who Mike Walker was, much less knew him. But no, not a word. Graham (or maybe his ghost-writer?) spoke about a pre-season signing (John Jensen); a signing who didn't come off (Geoff Thomas), as well as looking forward to the season ahead and Arsenal's chances of success ("I disregard all the bookmakers who make us favourites. That's a dangerous game in such a gruelling contest"), indeed, the length of the league programme then became the focal point of Graham's piece as he added; "My concern is over the number of matches. Our players play too many games. We need to reduce the size of our top division. I'm disappointed there won't be any reduction from 22 clubs until 1994. I'd prefer an 18 club Premier League – the sooner the better." Nearly 20 years on, George still does not have his wish – but he betrays his thoughts slightly by adding, in the same article, "I wish we were in Europe this season." Clearly, therefore, too many League games was a bad thing – but perhaps you could never get enough in Europe.

Interestingly, on the page immediately following Graham's there was a piece from the Premier League Chief Executive, Rick Parry, which included a colour photograph of him, one that is larger than that of Graham on his page. No doubt this piece was included in all of the home team programmes on that opening day. Parry spoke of "...the dawn of a new era in English football..." and "...the pursuit of skills and a spread of inventive football across the grass swards of the country...". Compelling stuff, inspiring maybe (or not), but, as with Graham's wider pontifications, there was no reference to what really counted to the fans, that is, the day's game, the players and the matches to come. Something seemed to have been forgotten already – Norwich fans could perhaps be excused for thinking it might have been their team!

Certainly most of that build up to the new season seemed to focus more on the Premier League as a single entity, rather than a collective of the 22 'elite' clubs of English football. The game was, and is, of course, more important than any one club or player, but, even so, on this opening day, the "new age" that Rick Parry spoke of, the excitement and speculation that always surrounded the opening of a league season seemed strangely muted, as if people were waiting for something to happen. Ignoring the fact that it was the games that were about "to happen". Sky seemed to have little doubt that this happening was their coverage, and their Premier League launch features reflected this. Played out to the middle class, middle of the road soft rock offerings (was this the audience demographic of Parry's brave new football world?) of the Simple Minds' *Alive and Kicking* (were Sky suggesting that football had died, and that they had resuscitated it?), the one and a half minute long feature used to promote the league and their coverage of same didn't so much break the mould of marketing the game in England, as strap it to a nuclear warhead and disintegrate it. Things truly never were going to be the same again, and the feature became an immediate talking point the day after it was first broadcast.

It opened, music suggestively playing in the background, to a montage of casually dressed footballers, all of whom were clearly going somewhere together. Convention shattered already! These players were not at their respective grounds and clubs, were not on a pitch, indeed, there wasn't a ball or blade of grass in sight! Clad in t-shirts, jeans and casual jackets, those one-time working class heroes were seen boarding a coach; tantalising glimpses of the likes of Strachan, Beardsley and Wark (and, ever so briefly, Ian Butterworth, the one sighting of a Norwich player in the whole advert!) chatting, teasing, a bit of banter, then a dressing room, a team line up – with them all wearing football shirts with a 'Sky' logo on – and, as the lyrics of the song commenced ("You turn me on..." – no really, I know it sounds preposterous, but this is really how they were marketing the game!) the viewer observed the glamorous Anders Limpar, then of Norwich's opening day opponents, stirring in his glamorous bed within his glamorous house, dutifully being offered early morning refreshments by his glamorous wife.

Indeed, as the advert treacles its way to a conclusion, the viewer could be confused as to quite who the football coverage is being aimed at, such is the proliferation of scenes in the gym, the changing room, and the shower – quite clearly not the average football fan. Football had clearly been 'sexed up' with players portrayed as laughing, loving family men – characters with lives of their own, far away from the sweat and mud of the pitch. Likewise the supporters have been equally sanitised, happy family groups, mixed and laughing their way to the game as a jolly policeman hitches a small girl up onto his horse – its football Jim (or should that be Rick?)... but not as we know it!

All of this, of course, was a million miles away from the reality of that opening Highbury afternoon for Norwich. Arsenal's ground resembled a building site, with the infamous mural of fans replacing the real ones (though it is argued that the mural offered more atmosphere) with the travelling Norwich fans shoe-horned into one of the stands. If football was being perceived as 'sexy' this season, then the reality of travel to away games and the facilities on offer were pretty much the same – small seats with minimal leg-room, expensive, largely inedible food and toilets that might have featured on a list of UN chemical weapon factories. The reality of 'going to the football' was nothing like the Disney-like fantasy that Sky were promoting, but, of course, they were promoting a game to people who had absolutely no intention of ever attending one for themselves.

Speaking before the game, Mike Walker looked back on the previous season's efforts from his new charges, hinting at where he thought improvement and change was needed; "...we have a reputation as a good passing team and we will build on that. However, John (Deehan) and I have emphasised our play in the last third of the field. We were lacking there last season. We need to deliver more crosses and improve our finishing. There has been a tendency to make one pass too many... we also need to be more effective when we lose possession. Norwich sides have never closed opponents down enough, so we're also working hard in that area."

Walker was clearly concerned about his team's inability to score goals the previous season. Norwich had ended the 1991/92 with just 47 goals from 42 league games – an average total of just 1.199 goals per game. Their pending opponents, Arsenal, in contrast, had scored 81 goals in the same number of games, an average of 1.928 per game. It doesn't sound as if there is a great deal of difference between the two figures – but, in football terms, and, over the course of a season, that gap is positively seismic and had to be addressed. Indeed, Arsenal had scored one more goal (30) in all of their away fixtures, than Norwich had managed in all of their home ones. And, with leading goalscorer Fleck now at Chelsea, the logic, if not, urgency of Robins' purchase from Manchester United made a lot of sense.

Walker did not select Robins in his team for that opening game. He opted instead to play Rob Newman in attack alongside Chris Sutton, no doubt hoping that the duo's physical presence (Newman was 6' 0", Sutton 6' 3") would upset the Arsenal defence, the expectation being that the two of them would be able to make the very best of the crosses that Ruel Fox and David Phillips would be sending their way.

Walker had bemoaned his sides brevity in the crossing department during the previous season, but in Fox and Phillips, he had two men with more than enough ability to send a series of threatening deliveries into the Arsenal penalty area. Whether or not Arsenal would actually be bullied into submission by Walker's most English of tactics remained to be seen – however, it was a positive objective and one that showed that he was coming to Highbury with the intention of getting a result. His pre-match quote of wanting to make the most of an early visit to Arsenal, before they had been able to settle into a rhythm, now waiting to be proven.

Both Norwich fans and ex-players have since admitted to me that, at half time in that opening match, they had thoughts of nothing more than damage limitation. The Gunners had looked comfortable from the off, and, after half an hour, had begun to realise that their opponents seemed to have little to offer as an attacking threat. So, when a free-kick was awarded, which Nigel Winterburn delivered towards the far post, it was perhaps no surprise to see Steve Bould make a quick run into the penalty area, heading home the opening goal, despite the very personal attention given to him by Ian Butterworth.

Barely ten minutes later, Arsenal were two up, this time Lee Dixon had made a run into the City half, and, with little or no attempt to close him down made, played the ball into an almost identical area to where Bould had been successful earlier on. This time his low pass found Kevin Campbell who turned and beat the unfortunate Butterworth before calmly slotting the ball past Gunn. In *Norfolk 'n' Good*, Kevin Baldwin gloomily summed up his feelings, that "...suddenly, Norwich had discovered their form from the end of last season. A free kick, a free header. Arsenal 1 Norwich 0. A low cross, a low shot. Arsenal 2 Norwich 0..." Arsenal fans and players duly celebrated, those celebrations oddly mute, as if this is what they had expected, 'job done', rather than actually being borne out of excitement.

For Norwich, it was a different story. A new season, a new league and all the opportunities and hope that went with it. But 2-0 down, at Highbury, on a hot sunny afternoon, with a third of the first-half yet to play – and Ian Wright on the bench for Arsenal. It probably didn't look as if it could get any worse. Fifteen minutes into the second-half, all was as it should be in English football. Arsenal were winning whilst 'plucky' Norwich were losing. Rick Parry's brave new world seemed, to Norwich fans, as looking like nothing more than the preservation of the status quo, albeit in shiny new wrapping paper. Wrapping paper that was red and white.

And then, at about 4:15pm, Mike Walker gave Robins his debut. Perhaps he sent Robins on with the instructions to loosen up and to get some match time, prior to the Canaries' next league game, at home to Chelsea (for whom Fleck was now making his debut)? Alternatively, he might really have said to the diminutive striker, who replaced Sutton, was that phrase of football legend, '...two goals down son, half an hour to go, make a name for yourself, go and win it for us...' – whatever he did say however, Robins' arrival on the Highbury turf did lead to the game turning in such a significant and unexpected manner, for all parties concerned, that the final third of the game turned out to be, in my opinion, one of the most significant in the history of the club – a fact that is as relevant today as it was two decades ago.

Think about it. Had Robins not had the impact on the game that he did, had Norwich proceeded to their expected defeat, no-one would have said anything. Nothing was expected of the fixture or the players, they had turned up, done (undoubtedly) their very best, but succumbed to a better side. Thus there was no momentum to take into the next game, one which could have easily ended in defeat as this one had done, thus precipitating another mediocre season that saw the club finish, at best, between mid-table and the drop zone. No heroics, no European run the following season, no time in the sun for players like Jerry Goss and Bryan Gunn; no near canonisation of Mike Walker; no resultant high expectations from the fans in just about every season since. Yes, promotion back to the Championship in 2010 had seen a touch of realism attach itself to many Norwich fans who had admitted, as had their Manager, that survival, consolidation at best, was the best they could hope for in the 2010/11 season. Was that the first season since the spectacular 1992/93 campaign that had seen a lessening of the expectations and pressure that had so often weighed down the club in the 17 seasons that had since elapsed, and was Mark Gordon Robins the spark that led to all the disappointment and frustration that was to come?

It's an unlikely hypothesis, but, such is the way that the smallest things, the seemingly most insignificant moments of all, can shape history, including sporting history. For example, what tiny shoot formed, silent and initially insignificant in Sir Stephen Redgrave's mind that, just four years after famously saying "...if I go anywhere near a boat again, you have my permission to shoot me...", led him to do just that, and, against all the odds, win a fifth consecutive Olympic Gold Medal – when it would have been so easy for him not to do so? The theory that Robins' scoring exploits for Norwich in that game were the catalyst for all the heartbreak that followed is an interesting one – but I digress. Half an hour to go, Sutton off, Robins on. The transformation is immediate and startling.

69 minutes Phillips takes a free-kick for Norwich, close to where Winterburn had taken his in the first-half. The lofted ball into the Arsenal penalty area is similar, as is the end result; Robins swiftly making his move between Smith and Dixon to place a diving header beyond Seaman. 2-1.

72 minutes Goss plays a speculative high-ball across the Arsenal penalty area, towards Seaman's far post. The keeper should really collect, but he hesitates, leaving David Phillips to steal in and lift the ball past him and into the goal. 2-2.

82 minutes Its Goss, again on the Arsenal right, this time he plays a through-ball along the ground that Denis Bergkamp would have been proud to call his own, allowing Fox to dart in ahead of the lumbering Bould, beating Seaman at his near post. 2-3, and all five goals so far have originated in the same area of the pitch, with two of Norwich's three down to goalkeeper errors – but who cares?

84 minutes Awarded a free-kick on the edge of their penalty area, Seaman plays a long, high-ball up to the edge of the Norwich area. Phillips and Smith challenge for the header, the ball is cleared and falls to Newman who lifts a high up and under back in the opposite direction. As the ball descends, it is Tony Adams' responsibility to clear and he really ought to deal with it, but, inexplicably (or perhaps not?) he fails to control the ball and it bounces off his chest and away, free of him and the watching Bould. Robins duly strikes, pouncing on the loose ball and lobs the ball over Seaman from nearly 30 yards for his second and Norwich's fourth. 2-4 and, at this point, the Arsenal fans, clearly confused, are simultaneously booing their own team whilst applauding Robins for the skill and anticipation shown.

Arsenal 2 Norwich 4 Norwich City sit atop the very first ever Premier League table, an honour and distinction that can never be taken away from them. A league table, of course, after just one game is an irrelevance, a curiousity and certainly nothing to be taken seriously. Most football "people" say that no league table has any significance until Easter, so those fledgling Premier League stats for the first day are disregarded by most, never-the-less, TV and newspapers alike produce that first league table and it duly does the rounds

Ruel Fox and Jeremy Goss congratulate Mark Robins after his second goal against Arsenal at Highbury

with Norwich City on top. And if it was such an irrelevance, then why bother printing it in the first place?

Needless to say, events at Highbury are the days talking point within the game. On Radio Five, the BBC's Charlotte Nicholl brings shame to her profession by describing Robins second and the game's final goal as a 'hoof'. The pass towards Robins may have been one, but the finish was not, it was sublime. Was she even watching the game? As for *Match of the Day*, well, admittedly, they broke their unwritten code about ignoring Norwich, however, with highlights of all the day's games to feature, that choice was no longer theirs to make.

The game's goals were described by a bored sounding Ray Stubbs who, when recounting Norwich's third goal, said that Mark Robins had been sent on by Norwich Manager "*Ian* Walker" to score a couple of goals. Yes, Ian Walker, the City Manager's son and Tottenham goalkeeper. The corporation had featured the Norwich game (Stubbs called it the "shock result of the day by far" in the sort of tones you would normally expect at a funeral) but had, at least, swiftly resorted to type by demonstrating the sort of lazy research and journalism that Norwich fans have come to expect from the national media. At least they'd know who Mike Walker was by the middle of the season.

Meanwhile, after the game, and wearing a rather fetching terracotta blazer that might have come straight from the wardrobe of Sky presenter Richard Keys, Robins, in a brief interview admitted that "...the pressure is on me now isn't it? Hopefully the lads will keep on winning". The quiet smirk that could clearly be heard coming from the interviewer as Robins spoke was telling, as far as that presenter and, quite possibly, everyone else was concerned, Norwich had enjoyed their 15 minutes of fame and would now settle down to being anonymous again, their act of footballing blasphemy at Highbury tolerated, if not quite forgiven. The following Wednesday evening saw Norwich commence their home league fixtures with the visit of Chelsea.

Fleck was unable to play in the game, part of deal that had taken him to Stamford Bridge barely a week earlier meant he missed out, so, suitably suited and booted, he sat in the director's box as a spectator. Despite his enforced absence however, Chelsea still had a formidable side. They'd kicked off their Premier League campaign with a 1-1 draw at Oldham Athletic, and had a starting XI that featured Canaries past and future in Andy Townsend and Graham Stuart, the current Liverpool Assistant Manager Steve Clark, and the undoubted class of central defender Paul Elliott.

They also boasted two of football's 'hard men' in midfielder Vinnie Jones and forward Mick Harford. Chelsea's nut, clearly, would not be an easy one to crack – indeed, the likes of Jones and Harford were probably relishing the opportunity to crack a few Norfolk ones. The Canaries had lost their embryonic place at the top of the Premier League table to Blackburn and, horror of horrors, Ipswich Town. However, both of those sides only had four points from their opening two games, another Norwich win could see them retain their unlikely position at the top. Early days, of course, but what an opportunity for Mike Walker's side to make a further point to the doubters?

Norwich found themselves under pressure early on and nearly went a goal behind from a set piece, a free-kick taken in a similar position to the two that had led to yellow feathers being plucked at Highbury, the architect, one Andy Townsend, causing confusion by feigning the kick, leaving it for right-back Gareth Hall to float a high-ball into the Norwich area, allowing Elliott to majestically rise and power a header goal-bound – but Gunn made the save. Chelsea, encouraged, pressed on, and, when Ian Culverhouse uncharacteristically lost possession on the edge of the Chelsea penalty area, Graham Stuart knocked a long, cross-field ball to Townsend who swiftly sent another cross into the Norwich area. This one eluded the Norwich defence, but not the afore mentioned Stuart who, after starting the move, proceeded to finish it, galloping almost the full length of the pitch to make the most of the space afforded him and score with a free header. Norwich would have to come from behind again to get anything from the match, and, with the score still 1-0 at half-time and the Blues seemingly happy with that, Walker needed to weave his 15 (rather than ten minutes, which had been the case up to the beginning of this season) minute magic again during the interval.

Which he clearly did. Norwich had lost John Polston to a hefty kick in the face before half-time, an injury that Polston looks back on later in the book, and one serious enough to keep him out of the Norwich side for the next five matches. Walker's pep talk, plus the sight of their bleeding and dazed centre-half lying semi-conscious in the dressing room seemed to put some fire into Canary bellies, and they hit Chelsea hard right from the off. Pace and energy levels stepped up a gear or two, and, for a while, the Chelsea side, backtracking as one, lost control. Almost an hour had passed, Norwich pressure had been building, and, with it, confidence. One player who typified that confidence was Welsh international David Phillips. A goalscorer at Highbury, his previous 110 league appearances for Norwich had resulted in just nine goals, a modest return for the talented ball-playing midfielder with an eye for a pass similar to that of Ian Crook's, and a ferocious shot to match.

He duly proved the latter cutting in from the left, sending home a fierce shot from 25 yards, leaving Beasant helpless – the second of nine league goals he would score that season, a career best for Phillips and proof not only of his quality, but the largesse of Walker in allowing him the freedom to attack the opposition defence. Phillips' shot was so hard that Chelsea defender Clark very obviously got out of the way of the strike, not that it made any difference, as the ball was still accelerating when it hit the back of the yellow Carrow Road goal net. The scores were now level and, from then on in, there would be only one winner of the game.

The Norwich winner was scored by Robins and its similarity to his second Highbury goal is testimony to the speed of his mind – a long ball from

Megson was pounced on by Robins, who, in one deft movement, calmly lifted the ball over the head of the formidable Beasant (Beasant, a full six inches taller than Robins and some 42 lbs heavier is *not* someone he would want to collide with) and into the net for one of the more memorable goals of the season and his third in two matches – game over!

City were back on top of the table. Six points from six, the same number of goals scored and two respectable scalps to boot. Needless to say, the aberration gives the tabloid writers ample opportunity to conjure up some "imaginative" headlines, and references to the Canaries 'flying high' and being 'top of the perch' are legion. Whatever Mike Walker has brought to the mix, it is working – Kevin Baldwin observed after this game that he (Walker) seemed to have "...come up with a new type of game-plan, apparently based on the old Muhammad Ali rope-a-dope technique. Do nothing for an hour, let the opposition score a goal or two – then surprise them late on."

City were surprising everyone already. It was, of course, not completely unknown for the side to win their opening couple of top flight fixtures. Back in the 1988/89 season, under Dave Stringer, Norwich had won their opening four league fixtures – this was different though. With glamour clubs Arsenal and Chelsea seen off, things were stirring at Carrow Road, if not amongst the fans, then certainly the players, who all now speak of the confidence and momentum the results, and the performances that went with them, as being key for what was to happen over the following 18 months or so. The die had, most certainly, been cast.

Mike Walker refused to get carried away with Norwich's excellent start. Writing in the programme for the Chelsea game, he said that, whilst the win was an excellent one, "...there was plenty of room for improvement. We didn't start well and came under plenty of pressure from the home side in the opening period... we must learn to concentrate from the beginning of each match and not rely on a comeback."

Which is exactly what the team needed to do in that consequent game against Chelsea! Not surprisingly, he made a reference to the team's poor start in that match as well after the game, admitting that, again, "...we gave away a goal. But at half-time I said, come on, we're only 1-0 down, it was 2-0 at Arsenal..." He praised his team for their confidence and self belief, reserving special praise for Robins, "...the little fella stepped up again, good awareness for the second goal". Robins himself remained modest, reminding people that it was all "...still a new experience for me, playing on the biggest platform in the game – I'm just delighted to be here". There would be no arguing that point from any Norwich fans.

The Premier League rumbled its way through August. Sky's first live TV game, Nottingham Forest's home clash with Liverpool, played on the Sunday after the opening fixtures, was a five-hour extravaganza, the hyperbole that surrounded it seemed to be attempting to make the point that this was the biggest television event since the Moon landings – and one that, quite probably, cost as much to put on. It seemed that, had it not been for Sky, there would be no football at all. "Sky Sports proudly presents... FA Premier League football... A whole new ball game! Ford *Super Sunday*, exclusively live from the City Ground, Nottingham Forest versus Liverpool... in association with Fosters."

A plug for the two sponsors, and who better than Ford and Fosters? After all, who was going to be watching the games and paying the subscription? The men, of course. And what do men like? Cars and booze! Simplistic marketing, but deadly efficient at the same time. Sky had put the hook in the water, taken the chance, as had the sponsors – the bite they got was good enough to net them a 20-year near monopoly of live Premier League football in England. As Richard Keys said when opening that very first programme, "Weekends will never be the same again!" He was right.

The honour of scoring the very first 'live' goal on Sky that season went to Teddy Sheringham as Forest prevailed, 1-0. They were a team of few stars, the glitter was provided by Brian Clough, whose presence overshadowed his team, a squad of honest and capable professionals, men such as Brian Laws, Steve Chettle, Gary Crosby and Ian Woan, all of whom featured in the televised victory over Liverpool. Sadly, the first-ever season of Premier League football was to be the last as a Manager for Clough; his side lost their next six matches (including another Sky-fest, this time at Norwich) and ended the season relegated.

Liverpool, like Forest, were also a pale shade of the side they had been. Bristling Manager Graeme Souness had selected striker Dean Saunders for the opening game, but the two of them were rumoured to not see eye to eye, and by early September, Saunders had moved to Aston Villa, where he proceeded to score six goals in his first four league appearances. Souness had led Liverpool to an FA Cup victory the previous season, but his time at Anfield had been fractious and lacked the harmony that marked the reigns of previous bosses – Paisley, Fagan and Dalglish.

Both Liverpool and Nottingham Forest had won the European Cup in the previous decade, however, the fires at both clubs now burnt low and it is interesting to now observe how Sky, the new kid on the block, the brash footballing upstart, had chosen to show a game that featured two tired clubs who were not expected to challenge for titles and glory that season, a responsibility that laid with current Champions Leeds United and their nemesis, Manchester United. The fact that one of those clubs played no part at all in the title race, together with the rise to prominence Aston Villa and Norwich City, helped make the 1992/93 Premier League season as open, unexpected, and interesting as any that have followed since. Indeed, by the time that all of the Premier League clubs had played their opening two fixtures, only two of them – Norwich City and Coventry City – had maximum points. In their next game, at home to Everton, the Canaries had gone behind for the third consecutive game, with Peter Beardsley scoring for the Toffees, Ruel Fox rescuing a point for Norwich a little over 20 minutes before the end. Robins played and came close to scoring again – however, his late shot curled narrowly wide.

Norwich were now second in the table, and, with two difficult looking away fixtures coming up, football fans outside of Norfolk, and the national media in general, looked forward to not having to bother about the Canaries in the future. They'd been 'knocked off their lofty perch' and that was that. Following a 3-1 defeat at Manchester City, a game that saw, for the fourth consecutive match, Norwich go a goal behind, this belief that their time had been and gone seemed a justifiable one. It was perhaps now, therefore, with the season under way and the euphoria of those opening games well and truly worn away by events at Maine Road, that Walker and his team needed to prove their mettle and show that they weren't going to be a novelty act. Five consecutive league wins saw to that.

Whilst the new league and season gathered momentum, the FA did its bit to remind supporters that the new set up had the international team in mind just as much as it did the new 'elite' that served it. A rule was introduced that decreed that any player who withdrew from an England squad must, at the time of his withdrawal, either provide a medical certificate or have his fitness assessed by the England team doctor. For many observers of the game, this seemed akin to regarding errant players as naughty schoolboys who had to produce a 'sickie' for not turning up for classes.

It didn't go down particularly well with some of the players, and most certainly not the clubs, who felt that the skills and capabilities of their own medical departments were being questioned, as well as the honesty and professionalism of their players. It is an issue that remains very relevant in the international game today, although, with the ultimate 'split' of the FA from the Premier League, it is no longer perceived by the Premier League clubs as their 'problem', and the constant and often predictable withdrawal of players from England squads, especially before friendly games, is a good indicator of the gulf between the FA and the Premier League, formed and intended as partners, but, in today's modern game, very much of the sparring variety.

Much of the attention on the international game in England, naturally, centred around England's qualification for the 1994 World Cup, being held in the USA. For Norwich fans, the tournament had little 'local' interest, the club's involvement with the national team leading up to the commencement of the qualifying games in 1992 had always been minimal, with a total of five players having been selected for the national side – Phil Boyer, Kevin Reeves, Mark Barham, Dave Watson and Chris Woods. Of that quintet, Woods, now at Rangers, remained an England regular, which provided Canary fans with some interest in the fortunes of the national side. However, of the squad that commenced the 1992/93 season, few looked likely of ever catching the eye of national Manager, Graham Taylor, who, clearly felt 'do I not like that' when it came to trips to Norfolk, despite the form of players like Ian Crook – whose skill and guile was repeatedly ignored by Taylor, the man who picked such footballing artistes as Carlton Palmer and David Batty for England instead. The nearest Norwich had Palmer and Batty, was midfield 'destroyer' Gary Megson, whose influence on the side was growing.

Megson had started all six games, forming a midfield quartet along with the afore-mentioned Crook, David Phillips and the reborn Jerry Goss. Maybe if he had been younger, Megson might have got a call from Taylor? However, his chances of playing for England remained at nine below zero, along with the other players in the side who might have been deemed worthy of at least some consideration, Mark Robins being another.

Robins might have been someone who *did* merit a chance; he had played six times for the England U-21 side in 1990, notably scoring five goals in England's 7-3 victory over France in the Toulon Tournament; he also scored against the USSR in the same tournament, as well as another two in a friendly win against the Hungary U-21 side. However, after that match, Robins U-21 career came to an end, simply because he had reached 21 years of age and no longer qualified to play for the side.

It is to his great misfortune perhaps, that one of his successors at that level was Alan Shearer (a player who Dave Stringer had looked into signing in 1989 as a possible partner for Robert Fleck – how the history of Norwich City might have changed if that had come to pass) who scored 13 goals in his first 11 games for the England U-21's, swiftly progressing to the full international side as a result and, in doing so, consigning the international chances and progress of Mark Robins to the pages of history.

Whether or not Robins' international chances would have been enhanced had he stayed at Manchester United, else moved onto to one of the bigger clubs, even, as had been the case with ex-Canary Woods, to Rangers, is debatable.

It is fair to say however, that he was unfortunate not to get his chance after a fine first season at Carrow Road. Robins ended the 1992/93 season with 15 league goals from 34 starts (plus three as a substitute), including strikes against teams such as Arsenal, Chelsea and Manchester United, as well as a televised hat-trick at Oldham Athletic, and, along with Graham Paddon, remains a player who, in my opinion, should have got an opportunity for England whilst he was at Carrow Road.

Following that defeat at Maine Road, one which saw Megson score his only goal for the club that season, Robins missed his first game of the season due to injury, his place being taken by Lee Power, as the Canaries headed for a tricky league meeting at Crystal Palace. The south-London side have long been regarded as a 'bogey' side for the Canaries, and, although the fixture history between the two clubs did not, as it does not now, reflect that, it was not an ideal time for club and supporters to be travelling to the salubrious surrounds of Selhurst Park.

Six points out of six in their opening two games, with the same amount of goals scored had lifted the spirits of the fans, the consequent one point from the next two, that one coming in the game against Everton which the Toffees were unlucky not to win, had immediately damped them again. With Robins missing, a hard game was expected, however, for the first time that season, Norwich went ahead, Power justifying his selection and the number 9 shirt he was wearing, by scoring with a close-range header after just 15 minutes, and, although Palace swiftly equalised after a defensive mix-up, Norwich sealed the victory with just over a quarter of an hour to go. Power the goal-scorer became Power the provider, his lofted pass into the Palace area being superbly volleyed in by an acrobatic Phillips. The win turned out to be a pivotal one in the club's season, setting up a televised home encounter with an already struggling Nottingham Forest side – victory would be enough to see Norwich back on top of the Premier League table.

THE
WRITER

Kevin Baldwin didn't wait 20 years to put his thoughts, memories and opinion of Norwich City's 1992/93 season into writing – he seized the moment and started putting his thoughts down on paper on the very first day of that first ever Premier League season. And, showing the sort of self-minded dedication and discipline that many footballers lack, kept going right until its end, reflecting on each and every one of the team's 47 League and Cup games that season, all of which, without exception, he attended. The end result of Kevin's efforts was the excellent book, *Norfolk 'N' Good*, a very personal and amusing account of the Canaries' season. Now, two decades on from the book's publication, I sought Kevin out to talk to him about that campaign and his thoughts then, and now, on the Premier League and the club's achievement in finishing third. I asked Kevin if he thought the 1992/93 season had been even more of a surprise (to him, me and every Norwich fan) because we had struggled towards the end of the previous one?

"Well, we did towards the end of it, yes. But to me, it was always going to be the season that we finally reached the FA Cup final. I think we were all convinced. I remember coming out of the quarter-final replay against Southampton – we had scraped a win somehow, and hearing the news that Sunderland had beaten Chelsea in their game. With us due to play the winners of that game, and with Sunderland being a league below us, I was thinking, 'great, it's not Chelsea', we're virtually in the final. But of course it didn't happen. The team just didn't turn up. Fleck got off his sick bed – he'd been in an oxygen chamber, but he wasn't fit. It was just a very dismal end to a season that looked very promising. I actually drove away from Hillsborough after the League game there shortly after the semi-final; we lost pretty poorly,

(Norwich lost 2-0, their eighth defeat in nine league matches) and I was thinking 'God, we're going down'."

It wasn't looking good, was it? We'd finished very badly, Dave Stringer had left, and then, barely a week before the season started, we sold Robert Fleck!

"Yeah. You got the feeling it was going to be a long season! But something happened during that first league game. It's one of those strange things, the sort of turning point that transforms a season. If we hadn't have recovered at half-time in that opening game at Arsenal. I don't think we would ever have had the season we had, it just transformed the next nine months. Suddenly, all things were possible. I'd say it was probably one of the most significant moments in the history of the club in terms of where one result, one half, took us over a period of some considerable time. After the game I was listening to some Arsenal fans on the train and they were going on, 'we didn't deserve to lose that 4-2', and maybe, certainly going on the first-half they didn't. At the time I was just thinking what an amazing turnaround that was, its only in hindsight that you realise the significance of that one game. Then the Chelsea game came along and you could see that they were all buzzing, that there was lots of confidence and self-belief there"

"I didn't let myself get too carried away though. I just thought, OK, we're having a good start to the season, let's get as many points as we can to give ourselves the best chance of securing our place in the Premier League for another season. Mike Walker said he wanted to get to 40 points as quickly as possible, and, of course, Paul Lambert had the same attitude. So often before, when we've have a good start, you worry about the collapse, as had happened at the end of the previous season. So yes, it was a case of let's accumulate as many points as we can before Christmas, then we can just hang on in there for the rest of the season. So I wasn't getting too excited, it was, like, yes, let's get the points now. I wasn't thinking we would achieve anything, no, the thought that we might finish in the top three was..." (Kevin tails off, a faraway look in his eyes!).

Feedback from the players at the time about the appointment of Mike Walker as Manager had been very positive – in the main because he was a familiar figure to them and that they had already grown to like and respect him. For the fans, it might have been different. Walker would have been a relative unknown and it may have appeared that the club were going for a safe, cheap option by appointing from within, a 'yes man' (which Walker turned out to be anything but!) even. What did Kevin, as a fan, make of the appointment?

"I remember reading a very good piece about him that season, and one that wasn't written by a Norwich fan. It said that he was a Manager who could make substitutions that made a difference, something which a lot of Managers couldn't do – they couldn't read the game like he could – make the change that changes the game. For example, bringing Mark Robins on at

Arsenal. We're well into the game, 2-0 down, yet Mike thinks OK, what can I do to try to win this game? I'll put Robbo on. After that, if ever we were struggling in the first-half of a game, I would just be thinking, let's get to half-time, he'll sort this out. That win is a very fond memory for me, but it wouldn't be my stand out memory for the season. That would have been when John Polston scored in the home game against Aston Villa, towards the end of the season. Of all the Norwich games that I have seen, I think that is the best quality football that I've witnessed. The Villa game was an extraordinary one, both teams were absolutely at the top of their games, we played well, so did Villa. You just had two good teams, really having a go at each other. I don't know how it only finished 1-0."

"And Garry Parker missed the most open goal that you will ever see, right in front of the Barclay! He hit the post, should have scored. That was just before Polston's goal as well. It was special for Polston as his first child had just been born, and I think he'd been up all night, so he hadn't had any sleep. But he still played and got the goal in front of us in the River End. It came at a crucial time, as we had Villa that week (24th March 1993) and Manchester United a short time afterwards (5th April). By that stage, to have any chance of winning the title, we had to win both games, so there was a lot of pressure on for the Villa game. For us to win that one and play the way we did... now, I came away from that game thinking, we are going to do this. Those were the heights, when he scored. That was definitely the highlight."

"Mind you, following that game, Manchester United took us apart – I don't think Mike could have ever done much about that. Mind you, everyone in the ground felt that their two first goals were offside. They undid us in the first half hour. But we still played well, we needed to win, we had to play to win. If we had scored early on – it might have been interesting. But 3-0 down? I guess a lot of people were rooting for them, they hadn't won it for ages. So it was a big thing for United then, their first one after so many years."

"There were some low points as well. I suppose there was the heavy defeat (7-1) at Blackburn. But that was just one of those strange games when every time the opposition attack, they score. Everything Shearer touched went into the net. We came out of the ground laughing, it was just such a freak result. If anything, it's better than losing by a 'normal' score, you just forget about it and move on. We lost to Ipswich twice of course. The one at home, just before Christmas I think, that shocked everyone, we'd been doing so well, so that was a bit of a set-back."

"The 5-1 in the rain at Spurs, I think that was pretty dismal! But you need to look at the Manchester United game again really, everything was resting on that, and for it to go wrong, and to go wrong so quickly in the end. So yes, that game, that was the low spot. Maybe the lowest point of all would have been if, after the season we'd had, we ended up not qualifying for Europe? It was freakish that Arsenal and Sheffield Wednesday were playing in both the

League and FA Cup finals. We were desperate for Arsenal to win in order for us to qualify for Europe. I remember the first game; I couldn't bear to watch it, I just went to the cinema. I don't know what I watched, I was just sitting there thinking, 'I wonder what's happening?' So, to come out after all that, and discover that it had gone to a replay! And of course, the fact that it was an ex-Norwich player (Andy Linighan) who scored the goal that put us into Europe – what are the odds?"

Kevin had chosen an excellent time to write his book – after all, when he started it, the club had endured a forgettable season with a last minute scrap against relegation and a lost FA Cup semi-final, so he was hardly going to be aware of the drama that was going to unfold as he commenced putting pen to paper. Did he think his book would have done so well had the season not been such a memorable one?

"No, I don't think so. Indeed, I got the proof of that with the follow-up, 'The Second Coming' which didn't sell anywhere near the same numbers. But I was talked into that! People were very kind about Norfolk 'N' Good, saying you've got to do a sequel, you've got to do a sequel. I was all for leaving things as they were, I even started quoting successful film sequels, saying how rubbish they were, but then someone said 'yeah, but Godfather II was better than The Godfather'. Everyone was going on about it, saying I had to write it, so, eventually, I thought I'd give it a go, so I did, and when it came out, everyone said 'Mmmmm, no, it's not so good', and I'm thinking 'great, thanks a lot!'. It's a shame, because I think the second book covered a far more typical season, a much more typical supporter's experience of following Norwich City."

Kevin's follow up to *Norfolk 'N' Good*, the aptly titled *The Second Coming* was his diary of the 1996/97 season and followed the sides (then) Nationwide Division One season, following the return to the club of Mike Walker, who had been at the helm during that first Premier League season. After the usual promising start, Norwich had their traditional pre-Christmas slump (including consecutive 5-1 and 6-1 defeats) and eventually finished a lowly 13th in the table. Mike Walker had been, therefore, a common link between the two books.

"Yes. In the first one, he had just become the Manager, nobody really knew who he was and everyone was wondering how he would get on. I was bloody lucky that I chose to write that first one then and we ended up doing so well! In the second one, well, everyone certainly knew who he was, and expectations were very high. But that first season was really his and the teams time. And the fans. Personally, I look back at that time with a lot of pride. I did 11 years without missing a game."

"My wife looks back at that time, before she knew me, as a time when I was a lost soul trekking an awful, barren desert! I was going from game to game, watching and playing at the weekends, as far as I was concerned, I would carry on doing it indefinitely. Was it a coincidence that it all changed when I met my wife? I don't know."

We're coming up to 20 years of Premier League football. How do you look back on that first season now – using that ever useful weapon, hindsight?

"We were doing well, but, very slowly from the start of that season, I got the feeling that this was turning into something special and that we should enjoy it, and that it could, quite well, be a one-off. We were eight points clear at the top of the Premier League table at the start of December, but still I thought we should enjoy it, make the best of it. Even during the following season, there was that sense of it being taken for granted, the first UEFA Cup match against Vitesse Arnhem, I sat there, looked around me and thought 'why isn't this place packed out'? (a little under 17,000 attended that first ever competitive European fixture). When we were playing Inter Milan, Barry Davies said 'this is all good experience for Norwich' and I was thinking, whoa, hang on, this is pre-supposing that we are going to be playing European football regularly! It was something special, something to enjoy, and something we all needed to make the most of as it may never happen again. You would hope that the club can get back into the Premier League and establish itself there. But the game is different now. When the Premier League was launched, it looked cosmetic, just a re-branding exercise. We now know different."

The Ballad of Sutton And Power

Lee Power had certainly done his footballing credentials no harm in the opening month of the 1992/93 season. Lewisham born but qualified to play for the Republic of Ireland (making 13 appearances for their U-21 side), he had joined Norwich as a trainee, making his debut for the Canaries on April 28th 1990, aged just 17, and yet to sign as a full time professional. The game in question was a six goal thriller, Norwich and Aston Villa earning a point apiece at Villa Park; Power replacing Fleck in the second-half. Whether or not Power (or, indeed Norwich) had aspirations for him to one day replace the popular Glaswegian in the Norwich attack is open to conjecture, however it might well have been the case that Power had cause to be disappointed when Norwich signed Mark Robins just before the start of the season. Robins was the 'chosen one', identified as the heir apparent to Fleck's place in the Norwich attack, a decision that would leave Power standing in the Norwich shadows.

Following his debut towards the end of the 1989/90 season, Power found first team opportunities a little more forthcoming during the following campaign, starting in 13 league games under Dave Stringer, with a further three appearances coming from the bench. He'd also played in the Canaries' 2-0 defeat at Middlesbrough in the League Cup Third Round, a game notable for one ex-Norwich man, Trevor Putney, who returned after a long spell out injured for Boro' against his former club.

If Power had been downhearted at Robins' arrival at Norwich, he certainly didn't let it show. He made his first appearance of the 1992/93 season at Manchester City, replacing Robins in the second-half. Norwich lost the game 3-1, but, with the knock that Robins had suffered in the game keeping him of Norwich's next fixture, Power found himself starting that one (at Crystal Palace) three days later, scoring in the 15th minute to put City ahead, the first time the club had opened the scoring that season. Mike Walker clearly had enough faith in Power to pick him for that televised game against Nottingham Forest where, as we have seen, he scored and won the 'Man of the Match' award. It seemed as if Robins was going to have to expect a serious fight for his place, something he might not have expected to be the case when he signed. Challenged or not, Robins responded in the best possible way towards the end of City's first match in September, a narrow 1-0 Carrow Road win over Southampton. He had been named as a substitute for the second consecutive game, finally replacing Ian Butterworth in a brave tactical move that saw Robins score the only goal three minutes from the end – Phillips and Goss the architects.

Despite his promising start to the season, Power's appearances for the club were then, for a while, few and far between. He came on as a substitute in consecutive league games against Blackburn (which Norwich lost 7-1) and QPR, a 2-1 home victory, failing to score in either game. More to the point however, another young striker was, by then, making the most of the opportunities that Mike Walker was giving him, his goal in that win over QPR was his first in the league that season, he had, however, also made his mark in the League Cup, scoring both in City's 2-0 win at home to Carlisle in a second round, second leg tie. His name? Chris Sutton.

It seemed, therefore, that not only did Power have to worry about Robins being brought in above him, he also had the problem of Sutton, just nine months older and also a former trainee, catching up and overtaking him. Robins' selection for the side, when fit, was a given. Which one of Norwich's two young tyros would be riding shotgun for him?

Chris Sutton was just 19 years old but he had already earnt his stripes as a Canaries player, having made his first team debut back in March 1991, replacing Fleck in a 1-0 win for Norwich over QPR at Carrow Road. He followed this up with another appearance as a substitute, coming on for Ian Crook in Norwich's following game, a 2-1 defeat at Aston Villa. For older Norwich fans, the name Sutton on the team sheet was not an unfamiliar one, for Chris's father, Mike, had played for the club from 1963-66, his position being the ubiquitous one of a 'utility player'.

Sutton junior could also have been described as a utility player, his preferred position upon joining the club as a trainee had been centre-half, however, it soon became clear that, with his sheer physical presence and height, he could prove more than a match for his fellow defenders as an attacking player; a centre forward in the traditional sense, and one who would be a willing and more than capable target man alongside the smaller, more mobile striker that was Fleck, and, in time, Robins.

Despite his cameo appearances from the bench at the end of the preceding season, Dave Stringer held Sutton back at the beginning of the 1991/92 campaign, giving him his first start for the club in a 3-3 draw against Crystal Palace at Carrow Road on December 7th. For that game and his next seven appearances, Sutton played in the centre of the Norwich defence, accompanying more seasoned players as he did so, those centre defence partners being Rob Newman, Paul Blades and John Polston – all three providing the experience and knowhow. However, following those initial eight first team starts, Stringer withdrew Sutton from his team for one game, before re-introducing him to the starting XI for the game at Highbury on February 11th, Norwich gaining a credible 1-1 draw, with Sutton starting in attack alongside Fleck. Two games later, Sutton scored his first league goal for the club in another goal fest against Crystal Palace, the Canaries prevailing this time by 4-3, with 'Sutty', as he became know, scoring the Norwich opener.

He had, by this time, already made his attacking mark on the club and within the game in the FA Cup. Selected to play against Notts County in a 5th round tie at Carrow Road on February 15th, Sutton scored twice in a convincing 3-0 victory over the Magpies, his first a typical poacher's goal, seized upon after Steve Cherry had parried a Rob Newman shot into his path; the second, and Norwich's third, from a diving header. He famously scored his third FA Cup goal of that campaign in the Quarter-Final replay against Southampton, although it is unclear as to how much intent he had in scoring the goal that sealed Norwich's progress into the Semi-Final, his looping header, four minutes from the end of extra-time looking as if it was fashioned more from accident than design. Regardless of that, he had been in the right place at the right time, and there was little Tim Flowers could do to keep the ball out of the net. Thanks to Sutton, therefore, Norwich had a second FA Cup Semi appearance in four seasons to look forward to, and, thanks to highlights of that replay being shown on the BBC's *Sportsnight* programme that same evening, John Motson having the pleasure of introducing the latest Canary prodigy to the football watching nation.

Sutton ended the 1991/92 season having made a total of 21 league appearances (five as a substitute), plus six in the FA Cup and two in the League Cup. He scored five goals in total, three of which were that contribution to the Canaries FA Cup run. Disappointment followed for both him and the club in the Semi-Final defeat against Sunderland, as he was substituted for Daryl Sutch in that game, leaving City with only the half-fit Fleck in attack. For Fleck, disappointed as he would have been at that defeat, there was the promise of bigger and better things to come with his pending move; for Sutton, the season had ended with him having made an impact, appearance and goal wise – and at an opportune time, with he and the Canaries set to commence Premier League football the following season. If there was a rivalry between

Sutton and Power for a place in the Norwich first team, then Sutton seemed to have stolen a march on his team mate with his form and goals towards the end of the 1991/92 season.

However, as we have seen, it was Power who took the initiative at the start of the following season, scoring against Crystal Palace and Nottingham Forest, that latter televised game bringing him to national prominence in the same way that Sutton's goal against Southampton had done in the FA Cup.

Mike Walker's appointment as Norwich Manager in the Summer of 1992 at least meant that the new Canaries boss would have been familiar with both Power and Sutton, having been their Manager in the clubs Reserve Team prior his elevation to the top job. Both would need to prove themselves to him as first team players now. And Walker gave them both a chance. In the clubs first ten Premier League games of that season, both featured strongly, with their appearances breaking down as follows;

	Games Started	Games Substituted	Games As Sub	Scored
Lee Power	3	0	2	2 (from 5)
Chris Sutton	9	1	1	0 (from 10)

Power's goals in the games against Crystal Palace and Nottingham Forest had raised his profile at both club and in the game, however, it was Sutton who had started nine of those ten games, his lack of a goal being down to the fact that Walker, like Stringer beforehand, had given him a run of games in the centre of the Norwich defence. Sutton duly found himself played in attack again in the game at home to QPR on October 17th and scored his first of the season in a 2-1 win for the Canaries. Power had started that game on the bench, coming on to replace Robins, resulting in this game being one of only three that season that saw the two of them start in attack – however, of those three games, both scored two goals apiece, so maybe Walker missed a trick by not giving them more playing time together?

Of course, the signing of Robins meant that the possibility of the two of them forming a permanent Norwich strike force was improbable, but, as the season wore on, it was clear that the versatility of Sutton meant that he was getting more games in the league – of the 32 league games he started, Sutton played in the Norwich defence for 20 of them, with just 12 played in his more favoured position in attack. Taking into consideration the fact that he came on as a substitute in a further five league games meant that, of Norwich's 42 league games that season, Sutton had been involved in 37 of them, the same as Mark Robins, and exceeded by only Mark Bowen, Bryan Gunn, David Phillips (who started in all 42 league games) and Ian Culverhouse, who missed just one start, a 1-1 draw at home to Middlesbrough on October 31st. Any guesses as to who had replaced Culverhouse at right-back that afternoon? Yes, for 'one game and one game only', it was none other than Chris Sutton. His combined abilities in both defence and attack were swiftly making him

Daryl Such high-fives Chris Sutton after Sutton scored against QPR

an automatic first team choice under Mike Walker. After a promising start, Power's season tailed off into one of disappointment and unfulfilled promise. He ended that first Premier League season with just 11 league starts, plus a further seven as substitute, his final goal tally of just six in the league a disappointing return on what had been an exciting, never mind promising, start to the season.

His Norwich career tailed off the following campaign which, of course, saw Norwich play in Europe for the first time. Sutton cemented his place in the team and, ultimately, a £5 million move to Blackburn Rovers by scoring 25 goals in 41 league starts whilst Power made just two starts, with a further three as substitute. The high spot of his season perhaps being another substitutes appearance, against Inter Milan in the UEFA Cup 3rd round tie at Carrow Road.

It was his only involvement in the club's European run, and, although he started City's next two league games; at Oldham on November 27th and at Old Trafford a week later, he was swiftly replaced by Efan Ekoku once the latter had recovered from injury. Things went from bad to worse for Power in the league match at Ipswich on December 18th, coming on as a replacement for Ekoku, he swiftly 'earned' two yellow cards and was dismissed by referee Mike Reed. It was the last time he would play for the club under Mike Walker, and, following the appointment of John Deehan as Manager a month later, he made only one more appearance for the club, again as a substitute, this time at home to Arsenal on February 13th. It was hardly a St Valentine's Day massacre for the Canaries who gained a respectable 1-1 draw against the Gunners, however, that same game also saw Ekoku score his ninth goal of the season. Power had therefore fallen behind in the pecking order of strikers at Carrow Road, with Sutton, Ekoku and even the injury ravaged Mark Robins all ahead of him in terms of selection.

The 'race' between Chris Sutton and Lee Power to establish themselves as a regular starter and goalscorer for the Canaries was, in reality, anything but that. Sutton had the advantage of versatility, a quality that was as vital in the game then, as it is now – especially for clubs like Norwich, for whom the benefits of having a player who could slot into more than one position were obvious. Power had burned brightly upon his elevation to the first team, but had been unable to maintain the early promise that he had displayed in the 1992/93 season. And, with Fleck's departure, the need for Norwich to have a dependable striker was paramount, hence the signing of Robins.

In his excellent website *Flown From The Nest* (www.ex-canaries.co.uk), Steve Whitlam argues that much of the cause for Power's decline could have been the intense media attention that his initial rise to prominence created, which, at one time, led to him being (ridiculously) christened the 'Norfolk Gazza'. We've seen this before at Norwich of course, other players have suffered exactly the same fate, arriving on the scene in a blaze of glory and potential that swiftly becomes hype. More recent examples of those that burnt brightly, but all too briefly, in the Carrow Road cast include Ryan Jarvis (Canaries first team debut at just 16, Premier League strike against Liverpool at 18, released by Leyton Orient, with spells at Walsall and Torquay (on loan) to follow, and Michael Spillane (Canaries debut at 16) – both young players that great things were expected, but which never materialised.

It could be said that the pressure was even more intense upon Ryan Jarvis who appeared to have it all – a Norfolk born striker who came into the team at a time when Norwich fans had almost forgotten what it was like to have a local boy in the first team ranks. He, like Power, unquestionably and absolutely had the ability to go all the way in the game, but, for whatever reasons, their Norwich careers went downhill almost as quickly as they had ascended the peak.

With regard to Power, Whitlam adds that he might have lacked the mental strength, that determination to succeed at all costs in the game, something which his team mates, especially Sutton clearly had in abundance. Maybe the fact that Sutton's father had enjoyed a successful stint at the club further helped him with the demands and expectations of a young footballer (although it can be equally well argued that being the off-spring of a footballer, especially one who has played for the same club can be a distinct disadvantage) coming through the ranks at Norwich? Whatever the reasons, the change in fortunes for both players was staggering in scale. Power and Sutton had lined up in the same Norwich side in January 1993 for that 4-2 win over Crystal Palace and both had scored goals in the game, the three points consolidating the Canaries place in the top three of the Premier League.

Just under two and a half years later, Sutton was celebrating the end of his first season at Blackburn Rovers with a Premier League winner's medal, having struck a potent striking understanding with Alan Shearer. For Power, the end of that same 1994/95 season saw him in somewhat different circumstances at Bradford City, who had just finished 14th in the 'old' English Division Two, equivalent to League One today. He scored five goals over two seasons and 30 league appearances for The Bantams before, in July 1995, moving to Peterborough United. Although it should be pointed out that his time at Bradford had been hampered by a viral condition which seriously affected his fitness and career.

The Ballad of Sutton and Power draws to a close in the current day. A successful, if not medal-strewn career for Sutton in the game at Norwich, Blackburn Rovers, Chelsea, Celtic, Birmingham City and Aston Villa saw his first move into football management at Lincoln City end in disappointment in 2010 – despite that however, it seems likely he will return to the professional ranks in some sort of managerial or coaching role. For Power however, his departure from professional football altogether has brought him the success that was denied to him within the game. Following his departure from Norwich in 1994, Power played for 12 (including some on loan) clubs in England and Scotland before commencing work as a football agent, Then, following his involvement in setting up the sports publishing company CRE8, he became involved, at board level at both Luton Town and Cambridge United, including having a spell as caretaker Manager before becoming Chairman – poacher turned gamekeeper if ever there was a case of it in professional football! He has also been a board member at Rushden and Diamonds and includes horse racing amongst his other professional interests – indeed, unlike most players, who enjoy a flutter on the horses, Power has gone one step better, having been an owner.

Power and Sutton were just two of a squad of 57 players who were registered at Norwich City at the end of the 1992/93 season – from senior players like Bryan Gunn, Jeremy Goss and David Phillips, through to the club Trainees and Associated Schoolboys. It would have been a onerous task to have been responsible for all of the matters associated with such a large number of people and dealing with all of the paraphernalia that comes with them.

The man in the hot seat at the time was Andrew Neville, and, determined to get an idea of life behind the scenes at the football club during that momentous era. I tracked Andrew down for a chat. Despite the fact that I arranged to do this just at the time that Andrew, who is now Football Director at Leicester City was snowed under by the work and demands of running the administrative side of a football club, he very generously gave me some of his time to look back at his days at Carrow Road.

THE CLUB SECRETARY

Andrew Neville would have been one of the busiest members of staff at Carrow Road over the Summer of 1992 and heading into those first few months of Premier League football. Andrew kindly agreed to let me know a little about his time at the club and the responsibilities and recollections of his role at Carrow Road at that time. I asked Andrew for recollections of the weeks leading up to the start of the 1992/93 season and the appointment of Mike Walker.

"Mike had been Reserve Team Manager and it was noticeable that he had built a rapport with players and fans. So yes, looking back, internally, it was a good appointment to make at that time and, I believe, the right one. The key to it all was appointing John Deehan as Assistant Manager, the two of them got on well and worked well together. Dixie (John) was the joker in the pack, whereas Mike was most definitely the boss. I've always believed in managerial partnerships and the strengths they bring, it seemed apparent that Mike and John would work well together. Yes, it was a good appointment and a good team, that was very obvious early on – although the appointment of John might not have been Mike's decision to make. Morale at the club had been low towards the end of the previous season, and, in addition to that, as we got into pre-season and started getting some games under our belt, we didn't do so well. I can't recall the games now, but I do remember that we lost quite a few of them! And Robert (Fleck) wanted to go. When you consider the difference between the clubs, between Norwich and Chelsea, even then, you can't blame him. So he was knocking on the door and wanting out – it didn't help that we hadn't been doing very well, hadn't had a very good season. So it wasn't just about 'needing the money'. There were times after he had gone when he was knocking on the doors again, wanting to come back! But that's how it is in football, people are moving on, in, and out all the time, it's a very fluid industry and, of course, not just with regard to the players. So we headed into that first Premier League season on a bit of a low, morale was low. Then we noted that we had Arsenal and Chelsea in our first two games!"

Mike Walker had been able to add Gary Megson and Mark Robins to his squad in time for the beginning of the season. As Club Secretary, Andrew would have had a lot of involvement in all outgoing and incoming moves, staff wise. What did he recall of those two signings in particular?

"Well, with regard to Megson, that was a bit of a battle. There were certain individuals at the club who didn't want Gary on board, and were against our signing him. As far as player recruitment was concerned, the Chairman saw the players' value as being someplace on a curve. It started with them in their mid to late teens, went up as they reached their mid-20s, before dipping back down again as they got into their thirties – the idea being that a player's value slowly appreciated, then, as he got older, it depreciated again. So Gary didn't occupy a good place on his curve, as he didn't have a sell on value. He was 31 when we signed him on a free from Manchester City. But Mike wanted him, Mike wanted Gary and he wanted Mark. And he got his way, despite the opposition from some individuals at the club.

Mark was a bit easier! Mike wanted him; we went out and got him. It was a relatively straight-forward deal. It was a big fee for Norwich at the time – but we had the Fleck money in the bank, and, looking back, it was a shrewd bit of business all round. Again, Mike knew what he wanted. Megson was to be his leader, his 'manager' providing all the experience on the pitch, Mark was to be the goalscorer. I thought they were two great acquisitions."

"There is a big difference, mind you, in going out and buying a player now, to what you did then. It's huge, there's so much difference! Back then, for example, there were no agents to pay. Indeed, right up to the time I left Norwich, in 1998, I don't think we ever paid any agent, any fee at all. We used them of course, and they were already part of the game by then. But we didn't pay them! With Mark Robins, we would have contacted his club directly – and as you should do! In the case of Manchester United then, it would have been their Chairman, Martin Edwards. You negotiated a fee, then you spoke to the player. It was a lot simpler all round – you would have arranged his basic wage, signing on fee and bonuses. We had a very good bonus structure at Norwich at the time, the bonuses were not far off the basic wage – you couldn't afford to do that now! Today, players' contracts are very complicated and run into many pages. It's a different world. One player who I had a lot to do with, transfer-wise, is Darren Eadie. Martin O'Neill had rung me about Darren while I was still at Norwich – and I blanked him! Martin wasn't happy about that – he wanted him, he'd identified Darren as the sort of player he wanted while he was at Norwich – small in stature, but big in heart, that's the sort of player Martin likes! Needless to say, when I did end up at Leicester, Martin was eager to pursue Darren's signing again, which I worked on, with Norwich. Darren was a great player and is a nice lad."

When the Premier League was launched, did Andrew feel it was the start of a 'new era' for football in England – or more cosmetic exercise?

"I felt it was just the 'old' Division One under a different name. People kept calling it that for quite a long time anyway. One major difference, of course, was Sky's arrival on the scene. Their involvement, certainly in the early years was, I feel, more about the brand and the razzamatazz. I don't even think clubs got the facility fee then that they do now. This is a payment that clubs get in the Premier League if their game is shown live. You get it regardless of whether you are at home or away. When Leicester were last in the Premier League it was something like £500,000 per game – especially handy if you are the away club and have fewer match day expenses to come out of that."

"For the 2011/12 Championship season the fee is about £10,000 per game, which shows how the disparity between the Premier League and the Championship has widened. The Premier League is massive and everyone wants to be part of it. But it is not what it was in that first, or those first few seasons. You look at players like Denis Bergkamp and their rise to prominence and the impact he had here. He and other players that came to play in England in the early 90s. That's when it started to grow, with them. Now we all want to be there, but for the money rather than the football which was the initial lure. We're all breaking the bank to try and get there. We are at Leicester. But it just wasn't like that when the Premier League was launched, there wasn't the disparity between the clubs, especially the financial one."

I told Andrew that, much as I would dream of having his type of role at the club, indeed, any role, I did wonder whether I could sufficiently do the job to the sort of standards expected, in the main because I was a fan and that, sometimes, my heart might rule my head. When he was working at Norwich, was he, did he, become a fan of the club – or did he approach the job with total professional detachment?

"I was a Chelsea fan when I was a kid during the late 60's and early 70's – the era they won the FA Cup and the European Cup Winners Cup. I started to go to Norwich with my father and sister when we first got promoted to the 'old' First Division, back in 1972 and started my Norwich supporting days in the Main Stand."

"Then, further into the 70s, I became a regular in the Barclay, pen two or three. When Justin Fashanu scored that great goal against Liverpool, the goal of the season, I was right in line with the ball – so I was a long-time City fan by the time I started working for them. Watching games in the Barclay as a kid was a rite of passage. They were called pens, but they were really just cages weren't they? You could hear coins and the like tinkling as they were thrown from one end to the other and hitting the fencing, it was crazy. I don't know how we all put up with it. And the surges – well, you could see that Hillsborough was an accident, a tragedy that was waiting to happen."

"I always stood with a barrier behind me, so any surge would stop before it got to me. But at games at the bigger grounds, like Wembley, you just had to go with it. So I grew up with the club. By the time the 1992/93 season came around, I was a fan – and had a few favourite players. I always found Mark Robins to be a nice lad, very level headed. But we had lots of good players. The three Ian's – Culverhouse, Butterworth, Crook – he was the playmaker. Gunny (Bryan Gunn) was very popular. It was a good blend."

"Mark though, it felt as if he was the key to our success. In that opening game at Arsenal, he scored twice and Norwich scored four in 15 minutes to turn that game around. He was an important player and that was a big win in an extraordinary game. There had been this mood of pessimism prior to the season starting and it was still there at half-time during that game! I was in the Arsenal Boardroom with Dave Stringer and his wife and we were chatting about it, the gist of the conversation was, '...this is Highbury, we shouldn't win this, aren't expected to, if we come away having lost 2-0, 2-1, 3-1... then that's expected, that's OK'. But Mark came on and, again, he was the key, he helped us turn the game around and we won 4-2!"

"We didn't look back after that, it gave us a massive boost. And that stayed around the club all season. Not long afterwards, we had the first sighting of the 'Sky effect' with the televised home game against Nottingham Forest. That was one of their Monday night games. They were, as I have already said, very big on the pre-match entertainment, what with the Sky Strikers – everyone wanted to see the Sky girls as well as the Sumo wrestler costumes and the fireworks. We won 3-1, went back to the top of the table. I remember that game very well."

"Forest at the time were still considered a big club – we played really well. It played a prominent part in what was a very good first half to the season. We were, something like eight points clear in the run-up to Christmas. Then we had Manchester United away (December 12th), I remember driving up to that game thinking, 'if we win today, we're 11 clear of United, that's a big gap!' They'd not long signed Cantona of course, he played, also Sharpe, Hughes, Giggs... they took us very seriously and won 1-0. That checked our progress. Of course, when we played them at home later on that season, they were 3-0 up after 20 minutes, which checked our progress even more!"

I said I had talked to Jeremy Goss about that game and how he recalled their tactic of playing four in attack in an away match and using the width and pace of the players involved to have a go at Norwich right from the start.

"They were excellent. We actually thought every one of their goals was offside, they were so quick on the break and left us exposed. But none of them were! Funnily enough, one of the linesmen that night was from Gorleston, a mere 22 miles away from Norwich. Mark Robins got one back for us, but we couldn't compete against United that night. We couldn't really do enough to catch them after that; they now had the momentum that we'd rode at the start of the season. So we finished third, exceeding all expectations. But there was a bit of disappointment. We'd gone close, we'd led the table for a long time and been well clear at the top. It was the first season of Premier League football and ended up having a massive opportunity to end it as the best team in England. Just before the Manchester United game, we played Aston Villa at home, they were, and had been, consistently in the top three themselves."

"But we won 1-0, so, going into that United game, we still felt we had a good chance. I remember the Villa game particularly well, Garry Parker, who I now know very well, missed an open goal, he rounded Gunny, did everything right – but put it wide. There was still a chance, even after we lost to United, but we also lost, heavily (5-1) at Tottenham and, of all clubs, Ipswich. So it all petered out in the end. It was disappointing – it shouldn't have been, looking at the relative size and aspirations of the club. But it was."

I had to ask Andrew about the Norwich Chairman at the time, Robert Chase. He became a very emotive subject of debate and argument amongst Norwich supporters, indeed, even today, the mention of his name and stewardship of the club draws a variety of reactions from fans. What were Andrew's thoughts and recollections of having to work for him?

"He and I had a grudging respect for each other, which was good, else I probably wouldn't have lasted as long at the club as I did! So yes, we were able to work together. He did some good things. Maybe he could have listened to other people a bit more – perhaps sometimes, with that in mind, it did look as if everything was more about Mr Chase, not about the football club. Mind you, in my role, I was always going to align myself to the Manager rather than the Chairman anyway. To be honest, I haven't spoken to him since the day he left the club. After he'd gone, Gordon Bennett (the then Chief Executive of Norwich City and, like Andrew, a popular figure at the club) carried on with our respective roles between us and kept things going. People should remember what a big part Gordon played in the running of the club back then. As Youth Development Manager, Gordon was responsible for bringing through players like Craig Bellamy, Darren Eadie and Andy Johnson.

We worked closely together when he became Chief Executive. He's a good bloke, I like him a lot, and we got on very well. Times were hard at the club in those years following our successful couple of seasons in the Premier League, but he worked hard and helped keep things together."

I have an abiding image of the afore-mentioned Mr Chase reveling in the post match atmosphere after the home game against Bayern Munich. Back then, I suspect, most of we supporters felt he could do little wrong. What did Andrew particularly remember from those games?

"I'll always remember when we were in Milan for the away fixture to Inter. Mike Walker had said his son, Ian (then Tottenham goalkeeper) was coming over to watch the match, so I found myself outside the San Siro shortly before kick-off, waiting for him to arrive – looking up at this huge stadium, hearing 'On the Ball City' drift over the sides and down towards me. 'On the Ball City' in the San Siro! It was quite a foggy day as well, that made it all a bit eerie! We were, side-wise, massively depleted for that second leg. The three Ian's were all missing; Efan Ekoku wasn't fit, we really were under strength – yet we still should have won it, what with the chances we had in that game. But good times, good memories. Even the stick we got for the playing strip at the time – looking back on it now though, it was pretty horrendous!"

"I also remember the away match we played against Chelsea. We'd booked ourselves into a hotel that was a long way from Chelsea's ground. The team coach set out to the ground as usual, but, for some reason, all the bridges over the Thames that day were closed, so the team were very delayed getting to Stamford Bridge. I was at the ground, and, at 2:15pm I got a call, "the Norwich team haven't arrived". I eventually met the coach as it arrived at the Directors entrance – the players were tumbling off the coach, one sock on and one sock off, they'd been forced to change while travelling!"

"Not surprisingly perhaps, we were 2-0 down at half-time, and, to add insult to injury (former Canary) Andy Townsend had scored for them. However, somehow, we came back strongly in the second-half and won the game 3-2. Chelsea keeper Dave Beasant had a terrible game, and, for our third and winner, the shot looked as if it was going past the post and wide, however, Beasant managed to get hold of it and push it into the goal. The reaction of the Chelsea crowd towards him at the end was very unpleasant and Ian Porterfield, the Chelsea manager (very publicly) said that Beasant would never play for the club again. The away game against Oldham was also special; it felt as if it marked another stage in our progress as a club. Both the team, and some of the fans, were flown to the game, it was another one of the Sky Monday night games. We won 3-2, Mark Robins scored a hat-trick. That felt a big result and a big moment for us. Then (Andrew laughs, in full reflective mode now!) later on that season, we had the away fixture at Nottingham Forest. We won and quite easily, 3-0, which kept us at the top of the league, but also meant that they were one from the bottom and struggling badly.

I was walking back from the dressing room, and, as I did, I saw Brian Clough walking towards me. I moved over to one side of the corridor so he could easily walk past me, but no, he walked across and kicked me! He wouldn't have known who I was – just that I was someone to do with Norwich! I'll never forget that. I was chatting to the Forest Secretary after that game, he said to me 'now go on and win it' We were still doing well, but, in winning that game, making things a lot worse for them and they ended up being relegated. But we had a bit of a 'blip' after that. Our next match was at Wimbledon and we lost 3-0."

"As far as the not so good memories are concerned, one word. Blackburn. We got a right hammering there (7-1). In those days, we used to fly to a lot of games, even the ones we didn't really need to fly to, however, it wasn't the team that was flying, it was the Directors and some of the staff, myself included. After the game, we were told that Bryan Gunn would be flying back with us – we did wonder at the time why just the one player would be doing so, however, that's what happened. We found out later that night that (Bryan's daughter) Francesca, who was suffering from leukemia was seriously ill, hence him needing to get home to be with her and his family. That was a very sad time for us all, especially for Gunny and his family."

"John Deehan, was a very important figure in everything we achieved I think. We needed a brilliant team spirit and we had it, he was part and parcel of that and all the happy times. He and Mike were a brilliant team, yet, when they went their separate ways, neither of them had the success or recognition that they had during that time they worked together. And that was their strength, working together as that team. But Mike became too popular. Chairmen at football clubs do, as a rule, have big egos. Some of them are happy to bask in the reflected glory, others would prefer it to be direct. Mike was taking a lot of the glory and a lot of the attention. When, after the Milan games, he very publicly said that the club's purse strings needed to be loosened, well, I think Mike's leaving of us was inevitable once he had said that. He had, in some eyes, gone too far. Dave (Stringer) was different, he was happy to get on with the job, he didn't court the glory or the media, he was content for the Chairman to take all the glory. He and David Williams were another example of a great managerial team, we played some great football under them, and made an FA Cup semi-final. It's astonishing that Mike hasn't, as far as I know, been offered a job anywhere in English football since he left City for the second time in 1998. Look at what Mike did; he took a small club to third place in the Premier League, playing some great football, and into Europe with some great victories; he then went onto Everton, keeping them, and they had a poor side at that time, in the same division, saving their Premier League status. That shows what a good Manager he was."

Looking back, I mused, it seems all too clear (as if it wasn't obvious enough already) that supporting Norwich is a story of peaks and troughs, moments of utter joy, followed by those of despair and, as we all know, personal tragedy – putting the football into perspective.

"It is. There were a lot of ups and downs. We played Sunderland in the (1992) FA Cup semi-final and that was as disappointing as it gets with regard to the football. We just didn't play at all well, and nowhere near as well as we had been playing at that time. You think that this is the time, this is our moment, our opportunity to get to the FA Cup final. But it wasn't to be. But I have been lucky, I was at Norwich during one of the most successful periods in their history. I've seen and felt both ends of the football spectrum. But, when you are doing well, as we did at Norwich during that season, it gives you an awful lot of satisfaction. It was a wonderful, special time and I look back on the period I spent working at Carrow Road with a lot of happiness."

Norwich fan Andrew applied for a position as Accounts Administrator with Norwich City in April 1987, joining the club a month later. During his first few months in the role he was introduced to some of the secretarial work that needed to be undertaken at the club by the then Club Secretary, Nigel Pleasants. At around the time that Ken Brown left the club (November 1987). Andrew was appointed Club Secretary, which has always been considered as one for the "older man" – indeed, it is thought that Andrew was the youngest Club Secretary in the Football League at the time of his appointment. During the next few years he had various job titles in addition to his original one – Football Secretary, Head of Football Administration and Head of Football Operations, all of which, he admits were "...the same thing, but just under a different heading!"

He first met Martin O'Neill in 1995 when O'Neill arrived at Carrow Road as Manager and became a family friend. A year later, after O'Neill's departure to join Leicester City (despite Neville's publicised attempts to keep him at Norwich) Andrew, together with everyone else at Carrow Road became increasingly aware of the financial plight of the club which resulted in everyone "pulling together to keep the club afloat and operational" and which culminated in Delia Smith and Michael Wynn-Jones investing in the club.

In late 1998 Andrew was approached with an offer to become Club Secretary at Leicester City, ending up being reunited with Martin O'Neill. Andrew is a hugely likable person who has 'lived the dream' about as closely as it is possible for those of us who could never aspire to having a career in the game as a player. The mention of his name still elicits a positive response amongst those players who remember him from their time at Carrow Road, and I am sure that he is a highly valued and popular member of the team at Leicester City – he is definitely a football man. Football clubs could not function without people like Andrew.

Norwich played just four league games in September 1992, but were unbeaten in that run, earning three wins and a draw, including that return fixture against Chelsea at Stamford Bridge that Andrew Neville (as well as quite a few of the players) remembers the most due to the fact that the club arrived late and the players had to change on the coach! The first game of the month, a Carrow Road encounter with Southampton saw Mike Walker pick up the Manager of the Month award for August pre-match (try as they might, the judging panel just couldn't see a valid reason for awarding it to Alex Ferguson on this occasion), but, far from succumb to the Manager of the Month 'curse', Walker sent out a side buoyed by that televised win over Nottingham Forest, a side that proved its early durability by not playing particularly well on that occasion – but still winning, an 87 minute goal from Robins securing the three points late on and consolidating Norwich's place at the top of the table. Following the win at Chelsea, the Canaries entertained Sheffield Wednesday at Carrow Road on September 19th and earned another 1-0 win, Rob Newman duly earning the scoring plaudits on that occasion. The win against the Owls (who had ex-Canary favourite Chris Woods playing in goal) was a club record fifth successive top-flight victory.

One ex-Norwich player making the news – though not as he would like – that September was Dion Dublin. Released by the Canaries without making a first team appearance in 1988, Dublin had steadily rebuilt his career at Cambridge United (52 goals in 156 league appearances) before signing for the Red Devils for £1 million in August. In just his sixth appearance for the club against Crystal Palace, Dublin broke his leg, and, apart from a brief substitutes appearance against Oldham the following March, that was pretty much it for Dublin and his United career. He went onto join Coventry that same Summer where he rediscovered his goal touch with 61 goals in 145 league appearances, including time spent forming a formidable striking act with one Darren Huckerby, which the two, all too briefly, recreated at Carrow Road from 2006 to 2008.

With Norwich ending the month of September two points clear of second place Blackburn Rovers, national attention switched to European club football. Reigning Champions of England, Leeds United (nine points behind the Canaries) impressed in the second leg of their European Cup first round tie against Stuttgart by winning 4-1, Eric Cantona, later to join Manchester United, amongst their scorers. When it was revealed that the German side had broken the rules of the competition in that game by fielding four foreign players (the maximum permitted was three) a classic fudge by UEFA ensured that they were virtually unpunished, Leeds were awarded the game 3-0, handily making the aggregate score over the two legs 3-3. The clubs had to play another game, this time at the neutral Camp Nou in Barcelona, Leeds eventually prevailing 2-1 and earning a second-round tie against Rangers. The allure of playing in the competition, European football's blue ribbon trophy remained the ultimate reward for the Premier League Champions, both professionally and financially, for clubs and players alike. Most English pundits were still tipping Norwich for probable relegation however – "it can't last" was the general attitude, with the BBC's Alan Hansen the club's biggest doubter.

Away from the Premier League, Norwich began their League Cup campaign on September 22nd, the long trip to Carlisle ending in a 2-2 draw, Robins and Goss the scorers. On the same evening a greater shock was the near defeat of media darlings Liverpool in the same competition, a 4-4 Anfield draw against Chesterfield raising eyebrows; the four goals conceded were the most Liverpool had conceded in any home cup-tie since 1898. Liverpool slipped up again four days later, losing 3-2, again at Anfield, this time to Wimbledon. Liverpool ended the month in 19th place, with only goal difference keeping them out of the relegation places.

Norwich's major concern, however, was at the other end of the table. Their first fixture of October would take them to Ewood Park, where Blackburn Rovers, complete with Alan Shearer, ten league goals to the good for the season already. For early Premier League contenders, as both clubs were, it was a fitting test in which to commence the month – second versus first with only two defeats between the clubs in their 20 league games thus far.

Defensive Holes in Blackburn, Lancashire

When deciding which of the league games they would feature for the opening months of the 1992/93 season, the suits at Sky had neglected to select the meeting between Blackburn Rovers and Norwich City on October 3rd 1992. So the fixture stayed where it was, a 'traditional' 3pm kick-off on a Saturday afternoon. For Norwich fans however, it was the second consecutive Saturday that their team had been involved in a 'first versus second' clash in the Premier League, for it had been Coventry City that occupied that position in their meeting just a week earlier, the spoils shared in that 1-1 draw. The point had been good enough to keep Norwich at the top, but, by virtue of a 2-0 home victory over Oldham Athletic on the same day, Kenny Dalglish's newly-promoted side crept into second place themselves.

Much of Blackburn's ascendency was down to the benevolence of their Chairman, Jack Walker. His involvement with the club had started in 1986 when he donated funds to the club that enabled a new stand to be built at Ewood Park. It is also widely believed that it was Walker's money that made possible the arrival of Steve Archibald and Ossie Ardiles during the 1987/88 season. Despite their high profile presence at the club however, Rovers still ended that season in fifth place, albeit only one point off a promotion place. Momentum was building, and both the fans and Walker knew that it was inevitable he would take sole charge of the club, eventually doing so in early 1991.

Despite the continued backing of Walker cash rich Rovers did not, as many had suspected, storm to Division Two glory in the 1991/92 season. Indeed, Blackburn finished in sixth place, their position in the play-off's only guaranteed on the last day of the season. Rovers duly squeezed into the final by beating Derby County 5-4 on aggregate, where they met Leicester City in the final at Wembley. They prevailed and won their place as founder members of the Premier League by virtue of a Mike Newell goal. Walker celebrated by signing Shearer from Southampton for a then British record fee of £3.3 million.

One of Shearer's new team mates would be an ex-Canary, midfielder Tim Sherwood, who had been one of Dalglish's first signings the previous February, opting to leave a Norwich side that was sitting comfortably in First Division mid-table at the time for a stab at possible promotion glory at Rovers. Of course, the fact that Walker and Blackburn would have been able to substantially increase Sherwood's wages might have had something to do with his decision to leave Norwich, either that or the fact that Walker clearly rated Sherwood as a footballer of some considerable merit, he is reported to have once said to Dalglish, "...why do you want to sign (Zinedine) Zidane when we have Tim Sherwood?".

Despite their status as Premier League new boys, Blackburn started the season as they meant to continue. Following an opening day 3-3 thriller at Crystal Palace (Shearer scoring two on his debut), consecutive wins against Arsenal and Manchester City followed, and, on September 5th, Rovers went one step better than Norwich, beating Nottingham Forest 4-1, a result that consigned Clough's team to the bottom of the table. In Shearer and Newell, Rovers had a formidable front pairing – but quality shone throughout the side. David May, who would go onto win a Champions League winners medal with Manchester United, was a mainstay at right-back, together with Colin Hendry and Kevin Moran in the centre of that defence.

Sherwood provided the steel in midfield, playing alongside the experienced Gordon Cowans, while Stuart Ripley, whose form that season would earn him an England call-up, prowled the right flank, with another future England international, Jason Wilcox, working the left. A formidable squad, backed by a generous and hugely wealthy philanthropist, with a legendary Manager at the helm and goals in abundance guaranteed by Shearer – who had already plundered ten in the league prior to the Norwich match. It would be the surprise Premier League leaders biggest test of the season so far .

An even bigger surprise was the ease and magnitude of Rovers' victory. Norwich capitulated, losing 7-1, with Shearer magnificently leading the line, able support being provided by the enigmatic Roy Wegerle. Shearer scored twice (the mists of time have clearly affected the memories of many Rovers fans, so many retrospective accounts of the game have him scoring a hat-trick) as did Wegerle. Even Sherwood got in on the act, after scoring the fourth, he smiled and waved at the Norwich fans standing behind the goal

– not a popular move from a player who hadn't exactly left Norwich on good terms with those fans. In *Norfolk 'n Good*, Kevin Baldwin mentions Sherwood's goal and consequent wave, adding "...the Norwich supporters waved back, but not using all their fingers." With Gordon Cowans and Stuart Ripley also scoring, the defeat was, and remains, the biggest ever suffered by a team that entered the game leading the top division of English football.

That defeat immediately drew out the footballing soothsayers, attracted to the carnage of Norwich's defeat like moths to flame. It was credit to Mike Walker and his team that the Canaries resisted the clarion call for collapse and humiliation by winning five of their subsequent seven league games – with even this run punctuated by another mauling, this time at Liverpool, and to the tune of 4-1. The Canaries had even gone ahead in that game, Butterworth scoring after barely a minute – with his defensive partner, Bowen, going on to miss a penalty. Writer Rob Hadgraft summed up the defeat succinctly by suggesting it was "more comfort for those convinced City's leadership is a flash in the pan..."

Whether it was or not might come down to the club's next away game, one that was due for live broadcast by Sky – Norwich remained in second place, but the game that was to test their mettle was the long, cold and wet evening trip to Oldham. With the rapidly escalating conclusion that the softies from Norwich 'wouldn't fancy it'. That first fixture of November would soon tell whether or not the club's unlikely success up to this point could be maintained – or if the Canaries would be down and out again before the Christmas decorations even came down from the loft. In the meantime however, there were other matters for Mike Walker and his team to worry about. Twelve goals had been conceded in those three league matches so far played in October and, before the club had the chance to prove the doubters wrong in that Sky game at Oldham, there was the small matter of another home league game to come, this time against Middlesbrough on October 31st.

Under the wily stewardship of Lennie Lawrence, 'Boro had enjoyed a reasonable start to the Premier League season. Leading up to the game, they had not been out of the top ten and had enjoyed some good results, including a 4-1 home win over reigning champions, Leeds United. In Paul Wilkinson they had a striker who was reliable, consistent and on-form, indeed, prior to the Norwich game, Wilkinson had scored seven goals in his 13 league starts. Clearly maintaining their form and momentum from the previous season, which had seen them promoted, they were also no mugs when it came to scoring goals throughout the team – in addition to Wilkinson's seven, a further 15 goals had been scored, making a total of 22 in those opening 13 games. So there was no reason to think that the pending Carrow Road clash could be anything more than an automatic three points for Norwich; Lawrence and his side would have travelled to Norfolk with nothing less than victory in mind, one that would consolidate their place in the table and leave them just six points adrift of Norwich. Defeat for the Canaries would mean that the team would only have taken three points from the 12 available in October, a fact that might even have the club's own fans wondering if their sparkling early season form was about to fall as flat as it had been in the closing months of the previous season. Baldwin neatly summarises the growing doubts that might have been gathering as, "sneaking up on them like a storm front", on many Norwich fans.

As at Blackburn, City put together some neat moves and fancy approach work, but never actually got into the box. The crowd was very quiet, presumably concerned at seeing the return of last season's form. The speed and directness of the performances at the start of the season had disappeared and the nearest Norwich came to a goal was when the Boro keeper Pears had to head a back-pass over his own bar.

How quickly doth optimism and belief desert the thoughts of a Norwich fan – but Baldwin was not alone in his concerns. The game against Middlesbrough marked the first third of the season complete, and, at that point, and despite the heavy defeats at Blackburn and Liverpool, Norwich were still second in the table, five points ahead of title favourites Manchester United and a massive ten points clear of Liverpool.

If Norwich had needed a confidence boost going into the game, the crowd were not particularly forthcoming with intent to provide one. It almost seemed as if many of the fans merely sat on their hands, waiting for a goal, and a goal from Middlesbrough at that. Luckily for them, Wilkinson obliged just after the hour, finding a criminal amount of space in the penalty area to score from a header. The goal, as Baldwin points out, seemed to finally give those disaffected fans the opportunity to have a loud and very public dig at the players who they thought were particularly wanting. Rob Newman ("too slow"); Ian Crook* ("won't tackle"), and Jerry Goss ("ruddy useless") all came in for some stick and the atmosphere around Carrow Road slowly became rather desperate and tardy, the lack of support in places clearly affecting the players' confidence.

However, a goal did come, and, when it did, how ironic that the scorer should be another one of the players who had come in for some criticism from the stands? Ian Crook (*quite frankly any Norwich fan who thought an ability and tendency to rush into a heavy tackle and imperiously stride away with the ball, leaving his prostrate opponent behind him has no understanding of the game of football or what a unique talent Ian Crook was) crossed to Darren Beckford whose knock-down was thumped past Pears by a delighted Daryl Sutch. Honours shared and crowd noise generated by collective delight rather than criticisms.

The point meant that Norwich entered November level at the summit with Blackburn, their vastly inferior goal difference keeping them in second place. It had been a relatively disappointing month for the Canaries with only one win to show for it in the league and, if the momentum that they had created at the start of the season had not exactly been brought to a halt, it certainly needed a kick-start to get it going again. With over a week before the televised Oldham game, Norwich fans wondered who might provide it, with rumours beginning to develop that Walker would be forced to bring in some new personnel, either that, or, as the well worn footballing phrase in times of crisis (what crisis?) says, 'give the kids a game, they couldn't do any worse...."

As far as "the kids" were concerned, it had long been known at Norwich that the "kids" – or trainee professionals as they were known at the time – would have as good a chance at Norwich as they would anywhere at getting a game in the first team. Another old footballing cliché, "if they're good enough, they're young enough" coming into play here. This had already been shown to be the case with one time Carrow Road trainees Robert Ullathorne, Lee Power and Chris Sutton already being given a chance to impress in the first team – for example, at just 21 years of age, Wakefield born defender Ullathorne was already a 'relative' veteran of 28 league and cup games, having made his debut as a teenager.

With his gradual introduction into the first team picture under Dave Stringer, as well as the growing prominence of Sutton and Power therefore, many of the other trainees at the club could aspire to be selected for the first team themselves, three of whom, like the afore-mentioned, were strikers. Ade Akinbiyi, Jamie Cureton and Darren Eadie were the three who were perhaps closest to a first team debut that season, with Chippenham born Eadie the stand-out individual of the three, a player who was gaining rave reviews at youth and reserve team level. Eadie had been just 17 at the start of the Premier League season in 1992, but was already being spoken of as a first team player and potential star of the future. No pressure there then for someone barely out of school and over 200 miles from home.

THE PROMISING YOUNGSTER

Darren Eadie began the 1992/93 season as a 17-year-old trainee, a little over a week older than contemporary Lee Power who had already started to make an impact on the first team. He was part of an impressive group at the club at that time; in addition to himself and Lee Power, Chris Sutton, Andrew Johnson and Daryl Sutch had also joined the club as trainee's, Sutch, in particular set to have a good campaign that season, making 14 league starts and scoring two goals. All five turned out to have good careers in the game, testimony to the youth and scouting network that Norwich had at time.

I met with Darren during what was a particular busy week for him, one that saw him preparing for the launch of his business. As with all of the ex-Norwich players, he looked fit, healthy and ready to play a game with only minute's notice. He had been a real fans favourite at Norwich; the nearest you will get to an old fashioned, out and out winger, with pace to burn and skills and trickery in abundance. But not only that, a real enthusiasm for the team and for the game, a combination that made him a joy to watch –

and, like quite a few of his contemporaries (Craig Bellamy, Keith O'Neill, Andy Johnson, to name a few), he was a player who Norwich didn't exactly discovered on their doorstep?

"No, I'm from Chippenham. Born at the hospital there – though I think it's gone now. It's about four to five miles from Bath, about 20 miles from Bristol maybe? Norwich weren't the only club who came in for me at the time. I had trials with Swindon schoolboys. I also played for Southampton at that level. I was playing for them against Norwich – Jamie Cureton was playing for Norwich that day as I recall, when Norwich first approached me – I ended up signing as a schoolboy. So I had a lot of growing up to do here, having signed at such a young age. Initially I shared a house in Norwich with some others, it was a chaotic time. Gordon Bennett and Sammy Morgan ran the youth side, Gordon was brilliant, he was so committed to the club and his work, on occasion he'd drive down to Chippenham and pick me up, then take me all the way home again afterwards. After he left the club, I did a lot of work under Keith Webb. He was also good for me and my career. I didn't really want to stay though when it came to moving up here. But my mum and dad made me stay! I soon settled though, it was very like Chippenham – very quiet, very rural. So it felt like home after a while. And we ended up being a good group of lads; I think five or six of us made the first team, which is a good total. We were all coming through at about the same time that Manchester United were having so much success with their young players! But lots of decent young players would have chosen to come to Norwich at that time, that they would have a good chance of successfully coming through the system and making the first team. Norwich have always had that reputation and still do, there are some good young players at the club now as well".

You're one of a legion of young footballers who has been coached and helped along the way by Gordon Bennett?

"Yes, Gordon was brilliant. I think his title was Youth Development Officer. He helped me a great deal, and not just with regard to the football – he even helped me set up my first Bank account, and that's the one I still use today! He kept us all happy, kept us going and we all became friends. I got on well with Sutty (Chris Sutton). He was the year above me, so I watched him progress his way into the first team – he started out as a centre-half but moved up front and was very effective there. He was my room-mate for a while, so it was good to tap into his experience and knowledge about things, it also helped with the transition from youth team football to playing in the first team, what with him being around and having made that step himself. It can probably be quite daunting making that step up, from the youth team through to the first team. It wasn't too bad at Norwich however. The Youth Team worked very closely with the First Team anyway, so it wasn't such a big step as it could have been. The good team spirit was there throughout the club, from top to bottom, and the seniors would soon welcome you in

Darren Eadie at the start of his senior Norwich City career

and make you feel part of things. Mind you, I still had my errands to do! I cleaned Ian Culverhouse's boots, also Rob Newman and Ian Crook's. We also had other jobs at the club – cleaning the loos, keeping the changing rooms and showers clean and tidy, making sure the kit was all in one place, neat and tidy. One Summer I remember, we had to paint the dressing rooms! It's a rite of passage... or it was. All the time, you're being asked, 'this is what you need to do to become a professional footballer, how much do you want it?' And I think the game and young players suffer for it now as, of course, it isn't done that way now. Young players, you talk to them, ask them about their ambitions, they say 'I want to be rich'. It's all about the money with so many of them, not the joy of playing the game. Their motives are all wrong – they want to be rich first, then be a footballer. But they need that dedication and drive, they won't succeed in the game and they won't 'get rich' without that, and it doesn't matter how good they are. Norwich ended up getting someone in to clean the boots for the players. I didn't agree with that. It was a good experience for the younger players, me included. 'Your' players would mentor you, if you looked after them, then they looked after you – there'd be a good tip at Christmas. It was a good way, a gentle way of getting to know a first team player."

Darren proceeded to follow his contemporaries into the first team, ending up making his first team debut in a rather important game.

"Yes, Vitesse Arnhem at Carrow Road, UEFA Cup game. I was in training when Mike Walker called me over, he said David Phillips had been injured, so I was being called into the squad as cover, and would be on the bench. I was nervous, of course. But the team was playing well, we were 3-0 up when I came on, replacing Gary Megson – and how good is that, there's about 15, 20 minutes left, at home, 3-0 up, on I go, played out wide on the left. I soon got the ball, someone had found me in acres of space so I thought, 'OK, this is it, run with the ball as fast as you can' – so I did! I think my run led to us getting a corner, and I could hear the buzz in the crowd, 'who's he then?', that sort of thing. It was a perfect introduction for me. I wanted it then, I couldn't get enough of the ball. Mind you, I was knackered when the final whistle went – that's when it caught up with me, the mental pressure of it all, the expectation. But I was pleased, and remember thinking that, whatever else happens now, I've done this, first team appearance, UEFA Cup. I'm glad that it all happened when it did though, it might have been different just six months down the line. I'd had some involvement with the first team on match days by then. We went to watch the games. I was at the 3-3 draw at Middleborough on the last day of the (1992/93) season. My mate Andy Johnson played, and scored. It was good to be involved, it helped me get ready for when I would be getting into the team. Mike Walker had a lot of faith in us and in me, confident of our abilities. But he was super confident himself. He had belief in himself, the lads as a whole, all of the team. He trusted the older lads to look after the younger ones, it was a good mix, we all got on well and he was there for all of us. There was me, Ade Akinbiyi, Jamie Cureton and Deryn Brace, who played in Europe (with Wrexham), as has Ade. We had a good bunch and a great team spirit. And of course, there were a lot of experienced players who you could look up to and get advice from. Ian Culverhouse was one. And Ian Crook. I loved playing with Chippy (Crook), he'd always find me, he has such an innate ability with the ball. I'd reciprocate for him, make sure I found him whenever possible. I started to get a few games, even up front, played a few there alongside Sutty. And I scored on my league debut. That was a few days after the Vitesse game. Mike picked me to start against QPR at Loftus Road, we drew 2-2 but yes, I scored – Sutty set it up. That was such a good team to come into, I had Mark Bowen right behind me, he had so much talent and space. Then there was Gossy in midfield, putting in all the hard work. I look back at the team at the time and the players, and I do think what a great team it was and some great memories. I've still got all the shirts I swapped. I remember tackling Lothar Matthaus, how good can it get? You dream of those sort of moments when you're kicking a ball against the wall! Luckily, at that time, Gordon Bennett kept us in our place, helping us along the way."

Did you enjoy playing under Martin O'Neill – he would have managed you at Norwich and Leicester?

"You couldn't help but improve as a player under Martin O'Neill. Paul Lambert seemed a very similar sort of Manager, I would have enjoyed playing under him as well I think. But yes, I moved onto Leicester and Martin O'Neill again, from Norwich. I did not want to leave Norwich. I was happy here, on a good wage, playing good football, we were settled in the area – I had no intention of leaving. But, the club needed the money at the time and I was a commodity – I was told if I didn't move, the club would be in real trouble. But that's football. Players and Managers move on for different reasons, and it's always happened. "You can't blame people for moving on to improve themselves – though maybe it's different now. If you're doing well of course, nobody wants to leave. Success breeds loyalty."

I mentioned the former Secretary at Carrow Road, Andrew Neville, who has contributed to this book and who, when doing so, spoke about either having to resist offers for Darren or eventually arrange his transfer himself.

"Andrew has handled every contract I've ever signed. I knew him at Leicester as well as Martin – and Martin really wanted me there. I had a very strict medical before I signed for Leicester, the surgeon who examined me said, 'with that knee he could play for another ten years – or barely another ten games, I can't be certain either way'. Martin said, 'I don't care, I want him here'. It means something to you when your Manager says things like that. I never saw that much of him mind. The thing is though, when you've a Manager like that, you want to impress him when he is there, you want him to react. My first impressions of him at Norwich were interesting! I remember John Robertson coming along as part of his 'team', infact, he'd just be there as one of Martin's mates to start with. We were out training when we noted this old chap wander over, in his suit, asking if he could borrow a pair of boots and join in. We didn't know who it was – anyway, he puts the boots on, still wearing his suit and joins us on the pitch, this old chap, barrel-chested, whiskey in one hand, fag in the other. And he still had it! He could play, up and down that wing. Martin O'Neill is great at getting the best out of a player. Paul Lambert is the same, so is Sir Alex Ferguson. You don't want too much familiarity with your Manager. Yes, he's there for you, but there is no doubt who the boss is and what he says, goes. Players respect that."

I suggested that Martin O'Neill seemed to be a completely different character to Mike Walker?

"Mike was a completely different sort of character to Martin. He was far more 'pally' with you' he'd muck about with you on the way to away matches, play-fighting with the players at the back of the coach. But a lot of us had known him as Reserve Team Coach, so we'd sort of grown up with him. He gave the players some slack but we respected him, he had the balance between being your mate and having the authority exactly spot on. Respect is crucial; you have to respect the Manager. Watching the game now, you can tell which teams and which players are working for their Manager and which ones aren't."

Darren is a very easy going, friendly, and likable person, the sort you can imagine walking into a bar and immediately making friends with everyone in the room. Given that aspect of his character, did he ever find himself playing alongside someone who he didn't get along with or like?

"Yes I have. And he was a great player, he still is. But we didn't get on. But you don't have to get on with everyone, and that's going to be the case in any walk of life. There were about 25 of us, all together at the club, were we all going to get along with each other? Come on, Ed! We mostly bonded, of course, but you can't have it all. There were lots of characters at the club. Who were they? Butts (Ian Butterworth) and Cully (Ian Culverhouse) were the serious ones. The jokers? Foxy (Ruel Fox), Sutty, Lee Power. There was a lot of banter and football banter, at the top level. It is relentless. It's really 'sink or swim' if you're new to an established dressing room. It must be like coming into an army barracks, you can't hide or you'll get destroyed. It's a very male orientated environment, of course, and you've got to learn to take it and take it well. At Christmas, the young players – and I did my turn – had to come and sing a song to the senior pro's, some Christmas carols maybe. Now, making your debut in front of nearly 17,000 people and all the TV cameras? Not a problem. But singing a song in front of 25 older pros? That's horrendous, you'll get battered. One year, one of the young lads came in and sang a carol – well, he got it all, eggs, flour, shoe polish. Again, it's 'how much do you want this' it's about your desire to be a footballer, to achieve that goal. But, despite that banter, the older players would always keep an eye on the younger ones. Fleckie (Robert Fleck) was one of them, he looked after the young lads. He was a sort of talisman for us, he led by example. If he did a bad pass, he'd get down and do some press-ups. He was a great lad, he always had time for, and a big welcome for the younger ones. He was a character, like Gazza. On the pitch he made such a difference. We miss people like him, the characters in the game. He had his moments (huge smile breaks out on Darren's face), sometimes, at half-time, he'd pull his shorts and slip right down to his ankles, and sit there, with everything hanging out! Maybe it helped him relax or unwind at halftime, but, if the Manager was going to give him a bollocking, how could he do so, with, well, him sitting there like that? Great character."

Like so many ex-Norwich players who moved on, Darren had settled back in the area –he must like it?

"I love the City and the County. And I was, and am, very proud to have been a part of this club. Sometimes it feels like you're living in a goldfish bowl. Yes. But you expect it. If you're out and about and someone asks for your autograph, it usually means that you're doing well – you might be in the middle of meal of course, but, even so, I'd say 'just let me finish my food', I'd still go and sign for them. It strokes the ego. I rarely got abuse."

Had Darren ever thought about getting into coaching like some of his ex-team mates? Mark Bowen had been part of Mark Hughes team and was, at the time of writing, with him at Queens Park Rangers. Rob Newman had done coaching and management, and was presently at Manchester City. Ian Culverhouse was the Assistant Manager of Norwich. Did he feel he could, or would, join the coaching ranks one day?

"Well, I could still be playing. I had to quit when I was 28, I'm now 36. I don't like watching, I miss playing. When I watch a game, I get all analytical about it, I can't enjoy it. When you have to quit, it tear's the heart out, it really does. I have my memories of course, I will never lose those. I remember a game at Old Trafford against Manchester United. I was just taking it all in and happened to look across – and there, standing right by me was Eric Cantona. I just thought, 'bloody hell, it's Eric Cantona!'"

Darren, as he said, had to quit the game at an early age. A great loss to football and to Leicester City, his club at the time. But, here he was, back in the City, happily chatting about his career, and running his own business. He had moved on – but was he happy?

"Yes. But it took a while after I quit to settle down. I enjoy watching my son play – but I still find myself wanting to be out there. And there's a tinge of jealousy as regards the game at the moment and people having success. I guess it's different when you choose to retire, you may not miss it as much? I don't know. Maybe I'll fully come to terms with it when I'm about 70? I know that I do miss playing. And I think many players, maybe in a similar situation; they are reluctant to admit that. But it's difficult to explain and I think that, unless you've done it, unless you've played, you can never really understand how it feels. I'd love it if my son became a professional footballer, it'd be brilliant. It's the best life in the world. I'm enjoying life. I love my fishing still and I have lots of other interests. I'm also very proud to have been part of the history of Norwich City. I was there during some very good times for the club and I am remembered positively from the fans, which is nice! They were good times and I enjoy looking back at them. Those great moments, they're there and gone in a flash – what I will always remember more, and with greater pleasure, is the friendship and banter. There's nothing like it, it's a wonderful life."

Darren's love for the game came across so strongly in the interview. If I'd have produced a football and suggested we had a quick kick around on the nearby hallowed turf of Carrow Road, I think he'd have been out there and ready before I'd even got up from my place!

It was one of the worse days of my Norwich supporting life when he moved to Leicester, but, of much greater hurt, was his eventual early retirement through injury, hurt not just felt by me and thousands of other Norwich (and Leicester City fans) but deeply within the game of football itself. Many young players could do with sitting down and listening to Darren, they could learn a lot, not least to make the very best of the fantastic opportunity they have and how to make the very best of it...while it lasts.

As far as that first Premier League season is concerned, Darren just missed out on making his first appearance during that campaign – although he was involved with the squad, and, as he mentions in the interview, part of the first team squad that travelled to Middlesbrough for the clubs last game of the season. His time was surely near, Walker had marked him out as one for the very near future by taking with the team on that occasion, and he duly made his first Norwich appearance in the 2-2 draw at QPR on September 18th 1993, scoring on his debut via flick-on from his best mate and contemporary, Chris Sutton. In total, he made 153 league starts for Norwich, with 15 more as a substitute. He also made 32 FA and League Cup appearances for the club, scoring a total of 38 goals in all competitions. He joined Leicester City in 1999, making a total of 40 league appearances for the club, scoring two goals. He also played twice for England U21's in 1994, scoring one goal.

Darren is currently a Director of Sellebrity (www.sellebrity.org.uk) an online auction site that sells items that have been donated by celebrities. Items are sold on the site with the money raised going to charity.

Norwich saw further action in the League Cup during October 1992, the draw delivering them an away game at Ewood Park, home of Blackburn Rovers who had so emphatically plucked the Canaries at the start of the month.

For the tie on October 28th, Walker made three changes to his starting XI from the 7-1 defeat, including John Polston, Gary Megson and Darren Beckford in place of Daryl Sutch, Rob Newman and Mark Robins. City's improvement was much improved but the damage was, again, done by Shearer who scored first in Blackburn's 2-0 victory.

On the transfer front, Norwich sold Paul Blades to Wolves for £325,000. Blades had joined the club from Derby County in 1990 for a then club record outlay of £700,000, with the player originally forming a central defensive partnership with Ian Butterworth. However, with Norwich signing another central defender at around the same time, John Polston from Tottenham, it was clear that only one them would ultimately secure a first-team position along Butterworth. The day before Blades left Norwich, an ex-Norwich player was also on the move, Wayne Biggins, who left Stoke City in order to join Barnsley for £200,000.

Biggins was a true footballing nomad, when he joined Norwich in 1985 he had already played for five other clubs, including non-league local rivals Kings Lynn – and was still just 23. He ended up having a very respectable career in the game, pulling on the shirts of sixteen different clubs, both league and non-league, but perhaps having the best period of his career at Norwich where he won a Second Division Championship Winners medal in 1986, ending that season with seven league goals from 28 starts – more importantly however, he acted as the foil for City's prolific hitman Kevin Drinkell, who ended that season with 22 goals to his name and a move to Glasgow Rangers not so very far off on the strength of that season.

Dave Beasant, who had made those two unfortunate errors in the game at Stamford Bridge that had seen Norwich win 3-2 after being 2-0 behind was also on the move. Chelsea Manager Ian Porterfield had very publicly lambasted Beasant for the errors he had made in that game, adding that he would never play for the club again (something which he had neglected to tell Beasant first). It must, therefore, have been quite a relief for Beasant to have got the loan move to Grimsby Town that October, away from club and Manager, although, to his credit, Beasant had the last laugh, returning briefly to play again for Chelsea after Porterfield's dismissal and winning the Man of the Match award in his 'comeback' game, as Chelsea beat Arsenal 1-0.

Away from domestic competition, attention turned to England's hiccupping attempts to qualify for the 1994 World Cup. On October 14th, Graham Taylor's side faced Norway at Wembley, but could only manage a 1-1 draw in front of a little over 50,000 spectators – a half full national stadium for a World Cup qualifying match speaking volumes about the nations faith in both side and Manager. Taylor's side had the proverbial good look about it on paper – it featured the likes of David Platt, Paul Gascoigne and Alan Shearer, yet, as has often be the case, chances were wasted on numerous occasions and when Rekdal equalised for the Norwegians with barely a quarter of an hour left it was game over. For Norwich City however, it was very much 'game on'.

October had been a disappointing month for the Canaries, however, with another live appearance on Sky opening their run of fixtures for November 1992, the excitement and expectation started to build again, the opportunity for the players to prove the gathering army of doubters –some of whom were their own supporters – wrong an almost irresistible one. The Canaries had dropped down to 4th place after the weekend fixtures, behind new leaders Arsenal, Blackburn Rovers and Aston Villa, but a win at Oldham would send them back to the top of the Premier League table, just as they had done following their last televised game, at home to Nottingham Forest. The omens, therefore, were good – but, after the upsets and frustration of October, who was going to step up to the mark and make a much-needed difference?

GOSS AND CHIPS

Norwich City breezed into November 1992 with an uncharacteristic swagger not normally associated with Canaries who, according to many in the so-called know, should have 'fallen off their lofty perches by now'. But, regardless of the tired and overused clichés that abounded at the time, the club's position of second in the new Premier League had been gained on merit with some fine results and performances along the way.

A total of 14 League games had been played up to that point, of which Norwich had won eight and drawn three. At the same stage of the previous season, one which had faded out with the very real threat of relegation, City had won just four games and drawn seven – a total of 18 points gained from a possible 42, compared to 27 from 42 a year later. Tangible and very real improvement – but where had it come from?

Many of the players that were winning matches and plaudits for Mike Walker had been regulars in the side that had kicked off the 1991/92 season under Dave Stringer. A total of seven – Bryan Gunn, Ian Culverhouse, Mark Bowen, Ian Butterworth, Ian Crook, Rob Newman and David Phillips – had all been regular starters a season earlier, while the likes of Jerry Goss and John Polston (a Stringer signing) both became prominent members of the first team as the 1991/92 season progressed. In other words, Walker pretty much had the same personnel as Stringer to call upon, with the only additions to the side of any significance being Mark Robins and Gary Megson, both signed in the summer of 1992. So how had Walker overseen such a seismic improvement in his squad's fortunes over such a short period of time?

Dave Stringer, as honest and genuine a football man as you will ever meet, typically, attempted to take some of the responsibility of the team's fall from grace that season himself. In Rick Waghorn's excellent book *Twelve Canary Greats*, Stringer looks back on the closing weeks and months of his tenure as Norwich Manager and admits that the day-to-day challenges of managing a football team and its never-ending demands and routine, had taken its toll on him. He states; "I was filleted to be honest – it had taken its toll on me... they say if you can't change the players, you change the Manager, and I thought it needed someone else to take it on. It gives them a different voice".

Stringer's time in charge of Norwich had certainly been a success. He had guided the club to two FA Cup Semi-Finals in four years, as well as a (to then) highest ever league finish of fourth in the 1988/89 season (when City had also reached one of those FA Cup Semi-Finals), which, at one point, had bookmakers around the country offering odds on Norwich City doing the League and FA Cup double – something that Canary fans are highly unlikely to ever witness at the bookies again! Stringer's Norwich played effervescent football, high tempo, pass and move, pass and move, and it proved effective. He also introduced Chris Sutton to the first-team ranks, a bold move on a then raw 18-year-old that eventually paid dividends, via a cheque for £5 million, a little over three years later. Likewise with Ruel Fox, another player promoted to the first-team by Stringer who went onto bring in big money for the club. He was, in short, an outstanding Manager for Norwich City whose contribution and achievements at the club have been overshadowed by events that followed, certainly under Walker, and, more recently, Nigel Worthington and Paul Lambert.

The defeat to Sunderland in the 1992 FA Cup Semi-Final must have weighed heavily on Stringer's yellow and green heart. The club had been confidently expected to beat Second Division Sunderland at Hillsborough and progress to an eventual Wembley date against Liverpool, but it was not to be. Norwich players involved at the time, who I have met, speak of a post-match dressing room they had not experienced before, nor would want to again. They describe players and staff desolate at defeat, in tears and inconsolable at the loss, one that John Polston recounts in this book; "How we lost that I'll never know... I remember everyone crying afterwards. It was absolutely sickening, to be that close and not make it. We were getting back on the coach, sat down, thoughts were on how that was it, we'd never reach an FA Cup Final now, that was our chance and our only chance..."

That shock defeat, combined with the subsequent loss of form (in the weeks leading up to the FA Cup Semi-Final, Norwich had been comfortably mid-table, indeed, at Christmas time the Canaries had been as high as eighth) must have hugely contributed to Stringer's decision to retire at the end of the season, to 'let someone else take it on' as he said. The team, unquestionably talented and packed with good players, lost nine of their last 11 League games that campaign, as well as that FA Cup Final, with only a fortuitous home draw against Wimbledon in the penultimate game sparing City from going into the last fixture, at Champions Leeds, with the threat of relegation hanging over them. Again, therefore, the question arises... What did Walker do that made such a difference?

Midfielder and scorer of great goals, Jerry Goss, has no doubt about Walker's qualities as a Manager. Goss perhaps best typifies the rise and rise of Norwich City under Walker's brief tenure. He shot to national fame with his goals against Bayern Munich during the club's UEFA Cup run in 1993, as well as fabulous strikes against Leeds and Liverpool in the Premier League that same season. His good form and energetic prominence in the Norwich midfield even had him linked with a move to Portuguese giants Benfica, yet, despite how it seemed, the curious case of Jeremy Goss was anything but an overnight success story.

Goss made his Norwich debut in a Division One game at Coventry City in May 1984, the day after his 19th birthday – eight years before he became a first-team regular at the club under Walker, and nine before his goalscoring exploits against Bayern Munich sealed his place in Canaries folklore. He replaced John Deehan in that game at Highfield Road and looks back on it fondly, recalling; "I just ran around for a bit". His debut match was in a team that featured players like Chris Woods and Dave Watson, players who represented England while they were at Norwich, future big money sales for the club, but players of a different era, Manager, a different game even. During that 1983/84 season, Norwich used a total of 23 players in their 53 League and Cup games, including the likes of Mike Channon and Willie Young, so, if anything, Goss's Norwich career spanned two entire generations of players. By the time that first Premier League season started, a full nine years after Norwich had commenced the 83/84 campaign with a 1-1 draw at Sunderland, Goss was the only survivor of that group of 23 players, all of whom had long departed Carrow Road, and, in some cases, the game. Yet Goss was still going strong.

Jeremy had been signed by City in 1982, as one of the last ever, under the old football apprenticeship scheme, that saw youngsters combining football coaching with some of the more menial tasks around the club – including scrubbing the changing room floors, sweeping the terracing and cleaning the boots of the first-team players. He also recalls being responsible for the established players' lunch order, adding that, if there was a mistake, he would get a "bollocking". That kind of introduction into football for the younger players was hard, mucky and demanding, and a million miles away from what we see in the game today, when even the youngest players in a squad can have their 'baby' Bentley. However, it also sorted the men out from the boys, it was a path that was only trodden upon to the end by those who really wanted a career in the game. And Jeremy Goss did.

Gossy in full competitive flow against Crystal Palace's Geoff Thomas

But the going for him was tough. Following that brief cameo as a substitute against Coventry, Goss only managed one league start the following season, with a further four league appearances as substitute, as well as one start in the FA Cup, against Birmingham, playing alongside Mick Channon! However, if he thought that the following season would bring further first-team appearances, he would have been wrong! The 1985/86 campaign saw Goss spend the entire campaign in the reserves, without even a position on the first-team bench. There was some improvement in 1986/87 however – he made one first-team appearance, in a 4-0 defeat at Everton on December 6th. Interestingly, however, it was the first game in which he played alongside Ian Crook in the Norwich midfield, and, in a further sign of things to come, a side that also included Bryan Gunn, Ian Culverhouse and Ian Butterworth – seeds of future success being carefully nurtured under Ken Brown.

By the dawn of the Premier League, Goss had already spent nearly a decade at the club. Out of a total of 364 League games that he was, feasibly, available for first-team selection for, he started just 68, with a further 20 League appearances as a substitute. Lesser players... lesser men, may have given up, packed it all in, done something, anything, but football. But giving up was not in the Goss vocabulary, he believed in himself and his abilities with a burning desire that was, from 1987, further nurtured under the new Reserve Team Manager at Norwich... one Michael Stewart Gordon Walker.

I had arranged to meet up with Jeremy at the Norwich-based headquarters of the Norfolk and Norwich Association for the Blind, where he works as an Events Fundraiser. Over a long and very pleasant lunch at a near-by hotel, we sat and talked all things Norwich City, and, because I felt that the rise to footballing prominence of Goss co-incided with the appointment of Mike Walker as the club's Manager in 1992, I opened by asking him about the man who gave him nearly as many starts in a season and a half, as he had in the previous nine.

"Mike Walker was terrific in every sense of the word. He believed in me, he gave me a chance; he trusted me and he knew my character. I was fit, I was strong, and he knew that I would never give up, that there was something there that he could work with. I had the passion and the determination for it, there was fire in my belly. Mike had been my Reserve Team Manager, and he must have thought, 'well, I'll build a team around you and those qualities, but it's going to be the first team'. When a Manager has that sort of confidence in you, it makes one hell of a difference. I'd been waiting and waiting, just for someone to give me a chance. Mike did just that, and, as far as my confidence was concerned, I was walking on springs. When someone has that belief in you and what you can do, when they know what your strengths are, how good your mentality on the pitch is and how hard you will work, then you can build on the technical parts of the game. That means working on your passing, your distribution, your tackling, and how you then fit and progress in a team of 11 players. But your must have that foundation. That's the desire, the work effort and the belief. If you don't have that, it's all hopeless. We had that. All of us."

Did, I wonder, it help that there had been some consistency in the way that Norwich played the game and that Mike Walker, like his two predecessors, had been promoted from within' – that everyone knew what sort of football was expected: in the Boardroom, in the dressing room and on the terraces?

"All of the time that I had been with the club and working with those Managers, we had always been a side that wanted to play football the right way. How do you define that? Well, for us it was simple. You encourage the keeper to throw, rather than kick the ball out for a start. Build the move, slowly, and from the back. One thing I always remember was that we were told to always pass the ball below knee height and not to hoof the ball anywhere – that just gives it back to the opposition. But, as players, it was the way we wanted to play. Ken Brown had nurtured what John Bond had started, so it was easy for Dave Stringer to maintain that. The players they brought in, they were all capable of playing that way. Look at the players we got in from Tottenham – Ian Culverhouse, Mark Bowen, Ian Crook and John Polston. They'd all grown up playing the game properly, they all knew how to pass a ball, play the sort of game that was expected at Norwich. Then there was me and the lads who'd known nothing else since they joined the club – Ruel Fox and Chris Sutton – it was coached into them right from an early age."

I wondered if the 1992/93 season had been anything but a 'flash in the pan', and that it had, infact, been the culmination of many years' work from Managers and players alike. Jeremy's answer was emphatic and given with little doubt or need to think.

"Yes, and that's a very important point that people maybe don't always see. All of the things that Ken Brown introduced were 'inherited' by Dave, who kept adding and improving things. But listen; despite all of their hard work and efforts, you can't take anything away from Mike. He brought leadership qualities to the club that were outstanding – he was an inspirational character to us all. He took on what had been set up before him and we all wanted to get behind him, to succeed for him and do whatever it took. And for me, personally, I did not want to let the Manager down."

"Continuity is so important in football. Yes, a Manager will always want to build things around his own team, but the way in which it was to be done barely changed, that Norwich way remained constant, team-to-team, player-to-player. I remember before one game, Mel Machin (then the Assistant Manager to Ken Brown) said to me; "Now, look son, you're the sub today. But you keep an eye on Peter Mendham, you watch how he plays". Then, when Dave Stringer was Manager, the number of subs available on the day increased. But it didn't matter how many subs there were, all of them were always told, 'you watch the lad playing in your position, that's what we want, that's how we want you to play'. Simple. So that sub, if he came on, if he was going to start a game, he knew how he was expected to play. The reserves would mirror the way the first team played. The same formation, the same system of play. I'll give you an example from the early 1980s... Denis Van Wijk, a left-back, was injured... Tony Spearing was reserve left-back, but he came in and knew how to play. Corners, free-kicks, all set pieces, it was all exactly the same, because he's done it in the Reserves. Into the Nineties, it was the same with Rob Ullathorne in the same position. He would have been watching and covering for Mark Bowen. And so on, all around the team. It's so simple. I've heard it said that 'football is an easy game, made complicated by the players'. That's exactly right. I've been on the end of some bollockings; I've seen them, on touchlines, on Reserve Team benches, given by frustrated Managers absolutely pulling their hair out, because it's so simple. You've got to get the ball. You've got to control it. And you've got to give it to someone in a yellow shirt. How easy is that? It's not complicated in any way. That is exactly how Mike told me to play. Get the ball, control it, move it on."

I mentioned that I had preceded our meeting by watching the highlights of the famous opening game at Highbury that season, and that every Norwich goal had been the result of a steady build up, quick, along the ground passing, and, in essence, totally delightful to watch.

"We did a lot of shadow play, for ages. You put your 11 players on the pitch, but have no opposition. You get Gunny on the ball, he pings it out to Mark Bowen at left-back. Where do you move? Who wants it? Who pulls away? Who *has* to pull away as a striker? One striker pulls away, the other comes to receive it. Midfield player. One go as support, one pull away to the furthest side of midfield –in other words, applying things so that, in a game, you know what to do and in every situation when there *is* an opposition. You know where to run, you know where you should be in relation to the ball, wherever it is on the pitch. That's the idea of shadow play. And, once you've got that sussed, you provide an opposition. You put the youth team in, play against them, in exactly the same way. Then you move it into a match; you play that way, in the game, on a Saturday. Every single player knew where they should be and what to do when a player was on the ball, at Carrow Road on a Saturday, in a Premier League game. Simple."

"But not only do you know where you have to be and what you have to be doing, you also know what your team mates are doing. You don't have to look for them when you play the pass into space, you know they should be there, and they know that you are going to make that pass. Four little words, we said over and over again: 'Get it, give it. Get it, give it. Get it, give it.' And that's how I was brought up to play, right from Ronnie Brooks (Ronnie, a former Chief Scout at Carrow Road spent a lot of time nurturing and encouraging the talents of the clubs younger players), Ken Brown, Mel Machin,

Dave Stringer. Get it, give it to a yellow shirt. Control it, move it. Control it, don't complicate it. Don't delay time... if you get caught on the ball, you've waited too long. And I've rarely over-elaborated through my life, because of what was drummed into me. Get it, give it. Get it, give it. Just give it to the nearest yellow shirt! Okay, there's a strategy here. Get it, move forward, and score goals. Don't get it and move backwards. 'Gossy, wherever you are, if you get the ball and Chris Sutton's on – give him it. If Ruel Fox is on – give him it. If there's a cross-field pass on – give him it. Think forward before you think anything else, and, if it's not on, keep possession. If you want to take three or four touches with the ball, keep it. Don't give the bloody thing away'. You're bred to that, 'don't give it away' and 'two touch'."

"When I look back at games, and I don't that often, I note that I'm never in possession for a second or two, I never seem to get the ball and run with it, make a driving run into the box, I'm always elaborating that fact that I have been taught... get it, give it. Get it, give it... and that's what we took into that season, and that's how we were going to play. We didn't deviate. Listen. You've mentioned the Arsenal game. We were 2-0 down at half-time. We came in and Mike just told us, 'get the next goal'. We did and we went onto score another three very good ones. The coach trip back was fantastic; I remember saying to Gary Megson, 'come on son, have a beer, this is fantastic, we've just beaten Arsenal'... most of us were enjoying a few beers by that stage. He said, 'yes, but we want to be doing this every week'. And I just thought, 'we will, we're going to do this every single week'. There was a belief in all of us, the work ethic, the way we played, we believed we could do it. We weren't just happy to be there, merely taking part in the new Premier League, we wanted to make an impact – not just make the numbers up. We'd already shown we could play our part, we'd just beaten one of the teams that were favourites to win the title, not only that, we'd come from 2-0 down, against Arsenal, and at Highbury. So we were thinking, 'we really can do this'. That beer tasted very good on the way back that night."

"When we got back to Norwich, the lads wanted to go out, and although I didn't want to, I went along anyway and it was later that evening I met Margaret, my future wife... What a great day that turned out to be, eh! And a great start to the season, for me personally as well as professionally. But we kept it going, kept that belief. We beat Arsenal, beat Chelsea and then drew with Everton – seven points from nine in what were, after all, three very difficult opening games. And that good start gave us the extra belief to achieve more and win games. We knew we had it in us, but what it did was start to convince others. We were raising eyebrows in this new league, the results were coming in, '...it's Arsenal 2 Norwich 4, that's a big surprise' followed, at some point by, '...but it's a fluke'. It wasn't. We went onto beat Chelsea – Dave Phillips scored one of the goals – he was a good player. Okay, we then lost to Manchester City, which was a shock, but maybe it did us good."

"Reality set in and we had to pick ourselves up and look to bounce back, which we did. And, as we were playing well and winning (following the defeat to Manchester City, Norwich won their next five league games to go two points clear at the top of the Premier League), nobody wanted to lose their place in the team, never mind actually going on and winning the thing, we just wanted to play. Mike expressed it after the Arsenal game, "Well done, go out and have a few beers, but what are you going to be like on Monday? We're going to be training you hard; you're going to be fit. Training on Monday, that's how we'll judge you'".

"In training we used to have what we called 'Terror Tuesdays'. You. Ran. Your. Nuts. Off. We didn't see a football. There'd be a 3,000-metre run, more short and long distance runs, turns, twists. We got Wednesdays off. We deserved that! On Thursdays we'd be in again, and working hard – we had to, we'd had Wednesday off! Then, it was in again on Friday and preparing for the match on the Saturday. You had to be fit. And strong. You had to be at your very best to play and to keep your place in the team. It was the same for all of us, even if you were one of the new players. We'd spent a lot on Mark Robins, but he had to perform and prove himself just like everyone else. Likewise, Gary Megson. A good player, and, like Mike Walker, a leader. I've a lot of time for Meggy, he's a good man. He had a spell at Norwich as Manager under difficult circumstances, but back then, I loved his character, his love for the game. He'd run through a brick wall for you."

Jeremy's conviction and the fire in his eyes as he speaks is astonishing to experience. No wonder the team did so well and exceeded all expectations (except, maybe their own) at that time – if they had all shown that passion and determination, there seems little that couldn't be achieved together. However, there was the odd deviation.

"Yes, there were some surprise results. Silly results. We lost 7-1 at Blackburn, 5-1 at Spurs. We lost both games to Ipswich. Avoidable defeats that made a big difference to the league. If we had won just one of them, we'd have finished second. But we were enjoying ourselves. There weren't any 'big time Charlie's' in the team. We just went out and played. Sky were a big player for the first time that season and we loved being featured in their games with all the fireworks and the dancing girls that accompanied them. When we were warming up for the Sky games, the lads would boot the ball into the centre circle just to get near the 'Sky Strikers'. We'd wander over, slowly, get the ball, a quick 'sorry love', and then have a good look at them!"

"But we could be serious. My attitude at the time was that if I had to go to war, and had to pick some people to come with me, people I trusted and wouldn't let me down – people who I thought the world of – it would be that group of players. I'd run and chase all game, all day, and get into fights, put in that extra shift, the extra tackle, I didn't want to let my team-mates down."

"Many of those players had been at the club for several years already, they were approaching the peak of their game. In every position on the pitch we had a good player, a footballer. Look at someone like Ian Culverhouse. He never used to let people get crosses in. As a full-back, you're judged on the amount of crosses you let in. He didn't let that many in. He was also a great tackler and distributed the ball brilliantly. Mark Bowen was the same. He did it for City and he did it for Wales. He was another leader, another fighter, someone who knew the game. When he spoke, you listened. Ian Crook, same again. We played together in the midfield and I complemented him, he complemented me. We were a good duo."

"I've already mentioned that they were brought up at Tottenham and learnt the game there. Look at the tutors they would have had when they were starting out. They studied the game under Ardiles and Hoddle. People who really knew how to play the game – and they only wanted to play the game in that way. They'd tell us stories of training sessions, of just trying to get the ball off Ricky Villa, who was a big bloke and didn't look as if he would be a skilful player. But they couldn't do it. They'd watch Ardiles, as small and slight a professional footballer as you'd ever see, but could they get the ball off of him? No. Was he too quick for them? Yes. Could he ping out 40-yard passes, using those old Mitre balls? Yes. Ian Crook watched him and that's how Ian Crook wanted to play, like Osvaldo Ardiles, one of the greatest midfielders ever, a World Cup winner? You can't knock that."

"Now, my game, my way of playing, was different – it was focused on someone like Peter Mendham, a workaholic footballer. My asset was my strength and stamina, getting up and down the pitch, supporting everyone. I look back now and realise that I could have done more, that there was more to my game than what people saw or believed. I could have done more, played more. But I was the quiet one, shy, the one who stood back. So it showed with my career. My dad said to me that I held myself back, and the reason for that was that I wasn't 'enough of a bastard'. Perhaps that's why I didn't leave the game a millionaire, why I didn't play for one of the leading clubs, or play 500-plus first-team games for Norwich in the 14 years I spent at the club. Maybe if I had have been a 'bastard', been more of a nasty piece of work, things would have been different? Was my dad right? Well, yes. I know exactly what he meant. When he came to watch me play, he wanted to see me crunch someone in the tackle, Vinnie Jones style. I'd get there, make the tackle – maybe I held back a bit, maybe I didn't dictate situations and games… maybe I wasn't verbal enough? After all, I'd taken some shit in the early part of my career. I was a young player, wanting to earn my place in the Norwich team, ready to play – along comes Mike Phelan, then a few years later, its Andy Townsend. Both played in my position and both were brought into play there and ahead of me. Then it was Ian Crook. At one point, I'd had enough, I went to see Ken Brown and put in a transfer request. It was granted and I was all set to rejoin Mel Machin, who had gone to Manchester City as Manager. I was ready to go and wanted to go. However, at the last moment, it fell through... I think Sir Arthur South and Peter Swales (the respective Club Chairmen at the time) fell out over something, so the deal was off. Later on I had another chance to link up with Mel, that time at Barnsley. I went up there and met with him, then took a look around the ground, and, again, I was ready to leave Norwich. Mel had spoken of his plans for Barnsley and said that he wanted me to be part of them. I went back to Norwich, met with Dave Stringer and put in an official transfer request. However, it was rejected and I ended up being persuaded to sign a new three-year deal with Norwich instead. But it was so frustrating. I hated it. I was the 'nearly man'. I hold a record at Norwich City, want to know what it is? For 18 consecutive games, I was named as substitute. That's a 'nearly man' isn't it? It was pathetic, I had to get away, I wasn't getting, or being given, a chance. Yet Dave Stringer believed in me, just as much as Mike Walker did – I had so much respect for him. He was the Youth Team Manager when we won the FA Youth Cup in 1983. My respect for him is what got me to sign that new deal. Every Monday, I'd be there, banging on his door demanding to know why I wasn't playing... '"Why aren't I in the team, the team isn't doing well... Micky Phelan isn't playing well, Andy Townsend isn't playing well, get me in the team!"' On each occasion, Dave would just look at me and quietly say, "your time will come". And he was right, he knew."

Jeremy has, for me, typified somebody who has stuck at it, worked for his rewards and believed in himself more than any footballer I can name, or, indeed, *anyone* I know, which I told him...

"Well, it wasn't easy, it wasn't easy at all. If I look back at that time now, I'm slightly bitter about it, I have to admit. But you get nothing for loyalty, you just get taken for granted. Ultimately, I signed an improvement to my contract after Sky came into game. Robert Chase looked at me as I was signing it and said, "You're the highest paid player at this club". I looked him in the eye and laughed. Players talk, I knew I wasn't. And I wanted to leave on more than one occasion. As I've said, I was the quiet lad and gave 110% in every training session, every coach's dream. Although there's lots I regret, you know what, I wouldn't change any of it now. Because I did have good times, and I sleep well at night knowing I've not let anyone down. Mike Walker had said he'd build his team around me, that's all I needed to hear, and, from then, I wasn't going to let him down. It made a difference. I remember during pre-season for 1992/93 we we're preparing to play a practice match at Carrow Road, it was a baking hot day in July. I felt a million dollars, I could run a marathon in under four hours and run the 100 metres in under 13 seconds. I was making the runs all over the pitch, getting the touches, getting the ball to Chippy (Ian Crook); running into space... if I lost possession, we lost possession – I'm the first to try and get it back. I'm everywhere. When the

Gossy challenges Everton's Andy Hinchcliffe

game finishes, I was thinking, 'this is where I want to be, I don't want to be anywhere else. I'm a first-team player, I've got the right coloured top on and I'm playing alongside the right people'. And it was a pivotal moment for me, everything was changing, how people perceived me at the club. I was no longer 'young Gossy', there was no more 'your time will come', in and out, in and out. It was now, 'look what he's doing, look what he's bringing to the team,' The established first-team players were starting to respect me, they no longer saw me as a Reserve Team player. I had the chance to stamp my authority on Mike, my team-mates and the fans; physically, as someone who wanted to get out there and go to war with them. I certainly proved I would do that off the pitch, and on more than one occasion. There were scuffles after a few too many drinks, arm-wrestles, etc, but I proved I wouldn't be messed around with. Not anymore. I'd fight for my team-mates and I'd fight the opposition."

Did any such incidents immediately come to mind?

"Yes, a game against Swindon. John Moncur went over and absolutely battered Chippy, knocked him right over. Moncur was standing over Chippy, shouting and screaming at him. I wasn't having that. I went over and battered him back, ran over and knocked him onto the floor. I was ready to kill him, he'd crocked Chippy, who was on the floor injured. So I knocked him over. I wanted to kill him because of what he'd done to my team-mate. Everyone around me could now see, I was a good lad, a good person to have in the team. But that's how we all were. We stuck together. If one went out, we all went out, we were so strong as a unit. I knew that the substitutes were just as important too, lads like Robert Ullathorne, Daryl Sutch and Darren Eadie, quality youngsters. They didn't get many games at that time, but they were good lads. I felt a huge part of the club, making a big contribution. I finally knew who I was, what I could give, what an asset I was. I was protective to everyone around me, even Tim Sheppard (the Physio) and Jock, God rest his soul, the kit man. We were all in it together, even Jock, there, out with us, and we'd all be there, taking the piss out of him, you knew that meant you were part of it and he was. At some clubs it might have been a clique of the 'big name' players going out together... and then the rest of the team. Not at Norwich. It was about *all* of us. Sutty (Chris Sutton) was amongst the goals and getting his name in the papers; I got in the news and the headlines with the Munich goals, but we were all in it together, no big names, just a team. And we could have won the Premier League! We believed we could, no matter what everyone else said. Right up to when Manchester United came to play us at Carrow Road. United showed how much they respected us that night by playing Giggs, Kanchelskis and Sharpe up front – they just sat in the centre circle, pushed right up. We just couldn't get at them, then when they broke, it was like they were going at 100mph, with Eric Cantona playing off the three of them. Three quick players, plus Cantona, three sucker punches, three goals… game over! We couldn't match them. We beat Aston Villa earlier on, we played really well that day, but we couldn't catch Manchester United in the end."

Despite Norwich's third place finish, the football world was quick to write off their chances for the following season. For once, the club were not reckoned to be favourites for relegation, but a mid-table finish was the best that, according to those 'in the know', the Canaries could wish for. Fate and the fixture computer decided that the club's first fixture of the 1993/94 season would be against Manchester United, the Champions, and the new benchmark for all of the other clubs in the league. Norwich lost, 2-0, in a game that was perhaps a little more one-sided than their fans had hoped. However, Goss and his team-mates were determined that the footballing world would continue to take notice of what was happening at Carrow Road.

"Our second game was very important. Lot of pressure on already. And it was at Blackburn, where we'd lost 7-1 the previous season! But we won this time around, and after going behind. That's a big win, against a team that had thrashed us the previous season, and a win after going behind. Again, it breeds confidence. We then bet Leeds 4-0 and I ended up with Goal of the Month for my goal in that game. So, after three games, six points and two away wins and another great start! We were no longer 'little Norwich', we were now making our mark on the game. We had some international players– Mark Bowen, Bryan Gunn, myself… plus others were on the fringes. Chris Sutton was England U-21, Ruel Fox England 'B'. And it all climaxed in the European run, the biggest test of them all. And we passed it again, we proved ourselves again. There were more games like those against the likes of Manchester United, Liverpool, and Arsenal where the Manager would want us to demonstrate that we could cope with the atmosphere and the ability of the opposition. He'd say, 'I want to pick you, but I want to see it in your eyes that you want it… and believe me, we really wanted it and we proved that we wanted it. We mixed with the best and played as well as them, if not better in some of the games. Vitesse Arnhem, Bayern Munich, Manchester United at Old Trafford, Liverpool at Anfield. Norfolk, Norwich… we were on the map of the footballing world."

"I wanted it more than I wanted water, I was desperate for it. Winning was all that we wanted. That's the mentality Mike Walker drove home, all the time. Players respond to Managers who have gone out and done it themselves, as Paul Lambert had done. He won the Champions League, but not only that, outside of the perceived 'comfort zone', he did it in Germany. That man is a winner. We wanted to win and we knew exactly what our roles were. Before a game, I'm told; "Gossy, you stick to Roy Keane, he'll be cunning but don't let him onto the ball, keep close to him, mark him…" So I did just that. I knew exactly what my role was, and, therefore I didn't need to worry about anyone else. All I've been told to do is look after Roy Keane. That's all.

It's like being in the Army, you listen to your leader, your Captain. We go out onto that pitch and we obey orders. And that football pitch, it can be a lonely place. You can't always communicate with your team-mates as they're too far away. It can be you, the ball, your little area of grass. You have to know exactly what you have to do, you have to know your job."

"We didn't go into the following season still thinking about what a great time we'd all had, 'haven't we done well, we can now rest on our laurels'. No, it was more a case of 'let's do it again'. And that's what we set out to do. Pre-season training then, Denver, Colorado, for the hardest training sessions of my life – but I was as fit as a butcher's dog – the strongest I'd ever felt. The belief was there, the confidence was there. Look at how we played during that Leeds game at Elland Road, which is never an easy place to go to. But we were full of confidence, right at the top of our games, all of us, with so much time and space on the ball in that game."

There's an old adage that says that when you are doing something well, you make it look easy. It is especially true of sportsmen and women. Think of someone like Lee Westwood, the effortless beauty of his golf swing, or the sheer fluidity of movement from Rebecca Adlington in the swimming pool; like Westwood, she makes it look as easy as walking. That Norwich side did the same in some of their football matches at the time, the lead up to, and execution, of Goss's goal in the game at Leeds is a perfect example. Ruel Fox had so much time to place his cross that, if you watch the game highlights, you can see him stop, look up, and place his cross into the penalty area, much like a considered and expert sniper, with all the time in the world on his hands. Goss admitted to me, however, that the cross hadn't been intended for him, but for Mark Robins and that he had pushed him out of the way in order to get to the ball. Such hunger is the essence of a winner.

The pending campaign in the UEFA Cup was a new experience for the football club and for nearly all of the players. What had been Goss's impressions of European football?

"Well, in the very first game, against Vitesse, we struggled initially. They played a sweeper and we didn't quite work out how to best play against it. At half-time, Mike said, 'don't watch them, get into them'. So we did, and Efan, John Polston and myself scored. Good signs... goals from a defender, midfielder, and striker. But we could do that; we were scoring goals from all over the shop. The second-leg was tough though... the referee was on their side and they battered us. Foxy got done so I squared up to the geezer and had a fight with him! But that's how we were and how protective we were towards each other. But we got a 0-0 draw, job done, next round, Bayern Munich. We were confident, as always, 'oh, we'll beat them, bring it on', but Mike had to remind us that there were a few League games to play first. At Bayern, before the first match, they couldn't get us off that pitch. We were training there the night before the game in one of the greatest stadiums in the world, and we wanted to stay out there. John Deehan was shouting at us;

'Come on lads, get off the pitch, get to bed!' But how could we be expected to just pack it in and go to bed?"

"Of course, that game is now part of the club's proud history and everyone knows the result, the scorers, how the goals went in. But, maybe one thing people don't know happened before the game itself, when we were out on the pitch having a walk around. We'd picked up our programmes and were getting focused, anyway, while most of us are outside, Chris Sutton decided to pops to the loo in the changing room. While that was all happening, Jock was laying out the playing gear. It was one of the biggest games in our careers, as it was for Jock, so he has made that changing room look absolutely pristine. It was fantastic, all of our kits were laid out perfectly, and he'd finished off by straightening out the folded up towels. It was towel, shorts, socks, top, T-shirt, plus strapping for the players that want it. He's even laid out two pieces of tape so that I could cover up my rings. Jock's attention to detail was outstanding and the dressing room looked amazing. Anyway, as Sutty came out of the loo and went to wash his hands, he grabbed the nearest towel, and with that, all the kit on top, ended up falling on the floor, which was typically clumsy for Sutty. Anyway, just as that happened, I walked back into the changing room at the same moment that Jock saw what Sutty had done – he went absolutely ballistic. He was glaring at Sutty and shouting at him, 'You ****, you ******* ****, I've spent all ******* night getting this changing room ready and you, you big ****, look what you've ******* done!!"

Sutty's just stood and laughed at him and said, 'Jock, settle down son'. And because he was still drying his hands on this towel, Jock rolled up his sleeves and started attacking him. By that stage everyone had come back into the changing room to find Chris Sutton and our kit man rolling around, fighting on the floor of the Bayern Munich changing rooms! Unbelievable, and all before the biggest game in the club's history. Eventually John Deehan grabbed Jock, led him out and calmed him down so that Mike could give the team talk... fantastic, great days!"

Jeremy, like many of his one-time team-mates, has settled in the Norwich area. It does seem as if, even after hanging up their boots, the City and Norfolk remains very special to them?

"Tim Sheppard used to say, 'when you sign for Norwich, you sign for life'. Norwich has a great ground, fantastic facilities at Colney, and as a player, being able to live ten minutes from the ground, ten minutes from training and ten minutes from some glorious countryside is fantastic. Some players at other clubs battle for an hour and a half in heavy traffic just to get to training. Some take that long just to get to their ground, then all get on mini buses to head off together to a park where they'll do their training. Norwich is the place to live and chill out – it's a cosmopolitan City."

Jeremy Goss relates his stories and opinions about football, both then and now, with the same passion and fire in his eyes that Norwich fans grew used to seeing as he strode the turf at Carrow Road, Old Trafford, Anfield,

Highbury... oh yes, and the Munich Stadium. Walker had clearly seen the desire to succeed at the highest level in him that his two predecessors had maybe overlooked. Walker had lit the yellow and green touch paper... then stood well back.

The result was the perfect foil in the Norwich midfield for the gifted Ian Crook. In giving the pair the responsibility for running the Norwich midfield, Walker had created quite a cocktail. Goss was energetic, all fire and brimstone, hard running, energetic, driven and passionate about his game, his team-mates, his club. Crook, in contrast, was laid back, considered, even languid – but what a player. Goss confided in me that he thought that Crook was "the best player ever to wear a Norwich shirt", high praise indeed – but one in which he will not be alone in having. They dovetailed perfectly, the 'evidence' of their being able to perform in tandem immediately evident in that opening game at Arsenal and from then on in.

Crooks' team-mates were certainly not adverse to giving the ex-Tottenham midfielder the praise his ability merited; Canaries goalkeeper and future Manager Bryan Gunn has very fond memories of his colleague's abilities, and on more than one sporting stage!

"Ian 'Chippy' Crook, what a player! Straight out of the Glenn Hoddle mould and one of the main reasons that Norwich City FC were a successful side in the late 80s and early 90s – he made us play and pass. I'm sure that he would be the first to admit that he was not the ideal physical identikit for a central midfielder, but he had the skills and endeavours to be a top player. He was more than good enough for NCFC with his pinpoint passing, his accuracy from set-plays, his psychic relationship with Mark Bowen, plus his humour in and around the dressing room were some of his City highlights – but we also remember his unique diet that included polo mints, a can of coke and a fag! He must have got that from Ossie Ardiles!"

"Chippy was always a keen golfer and at the end of the 1994/95 season we had a players' day at Thetford Golf Club. Ian ended up as my partner and we had arranged to play Carl Bradshaw and Mark Bowen. The previous night we attended a sporting dinner in Norwich, and over the course of the night, the bets came flying in, which, after a few drinks, got higher and higher. We started at £5 for the front nine, £5 for the back, £5 for the match and it was also £1 for birdies. By the end of the night it was upped to £100 for each corner and £5 for birdies. The next day, even when everyone had sobered up, nobody was willing to back down on the bets. Well, to cut a long story short, I picked the right partner on the day and Ian played a blinder as we won the front nine and were leading the back nine as we played the 16th, a great par three. Ian hit a six-iron to within ten feet, and then putted in the birdie to win us the match, 3 and 2 , plus £305. Mark and Carl were none too happy with Chippy that day, saying he was a bandit and he had a dodgy handicap, but once again he showed his skills with the ball, a little white one that time!"

"When I took on the manager's role in January 2009, Ian was one of my first phone calls, to ask if he would join my coaching staff. He was always interested in coaching and had built up a great reputation in Australia, so I was delighted when he accepted and he certainly proved his worth as an important member of the club's coaching team moving forward."

Crook duly took his place in the Norwich midfield for the tricky visit to Oldham on November 9th, with Goss missing the game due to injury (he didn't return to the first team until the New Year) he was accompanied in midfield by Ruel Fox and David Phillips, Walker opting to play Ian Culverhouse in the sweeper position and Daryl Sutch filling in for Culverhouse at right-back. In effect, a 1-4-3-2 formation, which was a brave move, but one Walker clearly felt compelled to take, with the Canaries having conceded eleven goals in previous two away fixtures.

The game was a personal triumph for Norwich striker Mark Robins. He had scored six goals in Norwich's opening eight League fixtures, but, following his brace against Chelsea back in September, had gone a further six games without scoring. Walker, to his credit, had kept his faith in the former Manchester United man, who repaid him with a hat-trick in Norwich's 3-2 win – those three points putting the club back on top of the Premier League pile where they remained until the end of January!

The first goal against Oldham was typical Norwich, but had a rather unlikely source in terms of the build-up play. Ian Culverhouse took a short throw in, getting an immediate touch back from Ruel Fox before passing again, this time to Darren Beckford. Beckford's delightful back-flick then found Culverhouse again, with time and space to cross from the right where a criminally unmarked Robins headed home after just fourteen minutes. Andy Gray, co-commentating on the game for Sky with Ian Darke, summed it up perfectly; "Super Norwich move and very typical of them." So it might have been, but it was hardly typical of Beckford, bought as a target man and renowned for his physical strength and power, rather than his ability to conjure up the sort of pass more normally associated with Crook. As it was, Beckford's performance that night clearly impressed the watching Oldham coaching staff, for Beckford only made a further six appearances for City that season (being substituted for Chris Sutton in four of those, so the writing clearly on the wall for the ex-Port Vale man) before moving to Boundary Park in early 1993 for £300,000. He was, perhaps, a little unfortunate at Norwich. Upon signing him, Beckford was described by then Norwich Manager, Dave Stringer as "The answer to the Norwich supporters prayers". At £925,000, a club record at the time, he needed to be – but things never really worked out for the striker at Carrow Road. Under Stringer he memorably scored a hat-trick for Norwich in a 4-3 Carrow Road win, however, it is still the little back-flick that helped set up that opening goal for Norwich in the Oldham match that most Norwich fans still remember him for.

Robins netted his third goal late on, personal glory for himself, and for City, a place back atop the league – all in front of his watching father, a high ranking official in the local police force. That victory at Oldham was the first of four consecutive League victories for Norwich. Impressive as it had been (although it had not impressed the Sky 'expert' at the game, Carlton Palmer, who was dismissive of the Canaries throughout the programme – but maybe he wasn't used to watching football?), it was overshadowed by one of the club's best performances of the season at the end of the month. With Norwich due to play at Aston Villa, fellow contenders and formidable as an attacking force with Dean Saunders and Dalian Atkinson as good a front pairing as any in the Premier League (they had scored 16 goals between them as Villa, after only two wins in their opening eight fixtures, had climbed to third place in the table) the game had been selected as the feature match on *Match of the Day* and was touted as a 'real test' to Norwich's title winning aspirations.

The heat was back on. The club had been called to prove themselves time and time again already that season, with every victory regarded with suspicion ("it can't last") and every defeat as a sign that the bubble had burst ("told you so"). But this game would be the stiffest test so far, tougher than that early trip to Highbury, or the proverbial cold night out in Oldham – indeed, it might, mused those in the know, end up being another Blackburn – only for Shearer and Wegerle, read Saunders and Atkinson.

Like a BBC Natural History Unit covering hunting lions in the Serengeti, the *Match of the Day* camera's arrived at Villa Park for the long-awaited kill... only to be disappointed as Norwich took the honours by three goals to two. The Canaries took an early 2-0 lead, but Villa pegged it back to 2-2, the goals coming either side of half-time. With nearly 30,000 fans, most of them frenzied Villa supporters, scenting victory, the stage was set for a hero, and, for Norwich, it was a most unlikely one – Daryl Sutch scored the winning goal two minutes after Garry Parker (who was to miss the most open of goals in the return match at Carrow Road) had scored the Villa equaliser. Sutch, unassuming and unknown, even to a lot of Norwich supporters, had the game of his life, making one goal and scoring the winner, which is a typical example of the maxim endorsed by Jerry Goss, that City were a team, with every member of that team able to play his part and do his job. Sutch had certainly done his on that chilly November afternoon in Birmingham – job done, game won, and the Canaries were five points clear at the top of the Premier League. The question now being asked of them was no longer "it can't last" but "will it last?" People were beginning to believe the impossible just might happen.

The Tottenham connection

The list of professional footballers that have represented both Norwich City and Tottenham Hotspur is a formidable one. Even going back a short while, to 1980, the list of those who have, in one way or another, be it playing or coaching, represented both Canary and Cockerel, totals 69 different names, and even then, someone, somewhere, may have been missed off the list!

Naturally, some of the connections are not particularly strong or long lasting ones. Who, for example, remembers the name of defender John Purches, who spent some time as a youngster with both Norwich and Tottenham in 1998/99, but who failed to impress and ending up at Barnet? Or Lee Kersey, a one-time Tottenham trainee, who played just one game for Norwich reserves following his release from White Hart Lane? Then there's Steven Borrill, Tess Bramble and Roy Darbo, and plenty more like them... young players who, eager to seize a chance, any chance, to have a career in football, who travel from club to club, keen and eager to prove themselves, to earn a full-time, professional contract, but who, inevitably, tumble down the leagues and out of the game. The list is legion and a very high percentage of the names noted will have done just that, footballing waifs and strays who come and go, and who are never noted, neither destined to make a career in the game.

There are notable exceptions of course. John Bond parted with just £50,000 in order to sign Martin Peters from Tottenham in March 1975. Peters was a huge success at Norwich, helping his new club to firmly establish themselves in the First Division, and ending up being voted the club's Player of the Year in both 1976 and 1977. Such was his form at the time, there was even talk of an England recall, which, sadly, failed to materialise – England Manager Ron Greenwood surprisingly opting for Liverpool's Ian Callaghan (18 months older than Peters) as his preferred experienced option in midfield. Such was the success of Peters' time at Norwich, that he ended up making more appearances for the Canaries (232) than he had at Tottenham... he also remains the only player ever to have represented Norwich who has played, let alone scored, in a World Cup Final.

Norwich signed another ex-England international from Tottenham in 1978. John Bond had identified Martin Chivers as the striker who had both the experience and physical presence to play alongside the emerging Kevin Reeves in the Canaries attack. Chivers had been languishing in Swiss football with Servette and, at 33, must have thought the chance of leading the line in an English top-flight side had passed him by. He made an immediate impact, scoring against Southampton on his debut, Norwich winning 3-1; playing in a City side that included one-time White Hart Lane team-mates Peters and winger Jimmy Neighbour. Unfortunately for Norwich, two years of playing in the Swiss league had dulled Chivers' hunger for the game, making just 11 League starts for Norwich, scoring four goals before heading off to semi-footballing retirement at Brighton.

Successive Norwich Managers had seen the need to sign players from Tottenham. Perhaps the most obvious reason for doing so would have been the similarity in the footballing philosophies of the clubs. Both Tottenham and Norwich have long been renowned as "footballing sides", where passing and precision takes precedence over pace and power. Thus, those schooled in the ways of White Hart Lane, would, logically, fit in well with the way that Norwich played the game. On a more prosaic basis, travel and relocation for those players moving from London would not have been too excessive either – those Tottenham players living in and around Hertfordshire and Essex's leafy suburbs would not find Norwich too cataclysmic a move. Indeed, there might not have been any need to move at all.

Plus, of course, there is the very real fact that the financial disparity that dominates the game in this modern era was nowhere near as obvious in the 60s, 70s and early 80s. If Norwich wanted to buy an equivalent of Peters today – successful at the highest level, honours, multiple England caps, early 30's – a Frank Lampard or a Stephen Gerrard perhaps – it simply wouldn't happen. The transfer fee alone would have been prohibitive, as would the wage expectations, not to mention the fact that the player and his agents would trot out the tired old line about only wanting to "play for a club that can offer Champions League football", meaning, of course, the income, lifestyle and kudos that goes with it. Back in 1975, however, none of those factors would have played a part in the efforts of Bond to sign Peters for Norwich. The transfer fee reflected his worth as an older player, one who Tottenham, rightly or wrongly, thought was coming to the end of his career, while, as far as wages were concerned, Norwich may well have been able to compete with, or even exceed what the player had been earning at Tottenham. And, as far as playing in Europe was concerned, Peters had very much "been there, done that", so the attraction of playing midweek ties against the likes of FC Wacker Innsbruck or R.W.D Molenbeek may have lost their glossy allure... that's assuming Tottenham even qualified for Europe in the first place. They may well be serious Champions League contenders now, but, back in the mid-70s, they had consecutive league finishes of 11th (1974); 19th and one point from being relegated (1975); 9th and only one point above Norwich in 10th (1976), and, in finishing bottom in 1977, were relegated to Division Two – the same season that Peters played all 42 league matches for Norwich and was voted City's Player of the Year. It could therefore be argued that, on joining Norwich, his career was on the up again, preventing it from stagnating at a troubled and struggling Tottenham.

So Peters remains perhaps the best-known player to have made the move from the hurly-burly of North London to the quieter highways and byways of Norfolk, but Tottenham remains the club which most people recognise as the one which Norwich have benefitted most from in terms of purchasing players. This 'tradition' continued into the 1980s, with, in three successive years, Ken Brown successfully raiding White Hart Lane for bargains and returning with plunder of unquestionable quality in Ian Culverhouse (1985), Ian Crook (1986), and Mark Bowen (1987).

Those three purchases, evidence of Brown and his staff's ability to spot potential and talent where, perhaps, nobody else saw it (Dave Watson anyone?) are, arguably, three of the most successful signings made by any Norwich Manager, as well as three of the finest players ever to have played for the club. The facts speak for themselves. Culverhouse was signed for just £50,000 (that sum again!) having made only two first team appearances for Tottenham. He went onto make 369 for Norwich, playing in all but one of their League matches in the first Premier League campaign, as well as gracing both the Munich Stadium (where he completely overshadowed his fellow right-back, Bayern Munich's much lauded Jorginho) as he played a full part in Norwich's UEFA cup run. How much was he worth to Norwich during his time at the club?

Likewise Crook, who I have already written about... but any excuse to mention him again! In four years at Tottenham, he made only 20 league appearances, his route to the first-team being denied to by the experience and skills of Glenn Hoddle and Ossie Ardiles, and what better tutors? Norwich paid £80,000 for Crook, who made 418 appearances in his two spells at the club, as well as a short time coaching at Carrow Road from 2009/10. Under Mike Walker's management Crook enjoyed a relatively free role in the Norwich midfield, 'minded' by the tenacity and energy of Jerry Goss alongside him – Goss's brief being to feed Crook the ball, then Crook duly opening up defences and finding passes that most players could not even visualise. In this author's opinion, it is a footballing crime that Ian Crook didn't win a full international cap, a crime made even more heinous when it is considered that, when Crook was in his pomp, players like Andy Sinton, David Batty and Carlton Palmer did play for England and even played in a major tournament (the 1992 European Championships), leaving players of the calibre of Crook at home. No doubt had Crook been French, Spanish, Dutch, German, or just about any other nationality in Europe, he would have been a full international. The folly of our national side and a succession of inadequate managers.

By the time Bowen arrived at Carrow Road joined his former team-mates at Norwich in 1987, the club having paid £97,000 for the services of the Welsh left-back, he had made just 17 appearances for Tottenham in the four seasons spanning 1983 to 1987. At the end of the 1987/88 season, his first at Norwich, Bowen had made 29 appearances for the Canaries, and had made the left-back position his personal property by the time Dave Stringer's first full season in charge at Carrow Road (1988/89) had kicked-off. Bowen ended up making 399 appearances for Norwich, and is now, like his team-mates, a respected footballing coach, although he is the only one of the trio who has (at the time of writing) not had a spell back at Carrow Road in that capacity.

The contribution that these three players made to the club, both on and off the pitch, during Norwich City's remarkable Premier League campaign of 1992/93 was remarkable and cannot be understated. It is true to say, as Jerry Goss emphatically states, that it was, most of all, a team effort – a squad minus the big stars and their egos, and one which stood together as one, the yellow and green sum being more important than its individual parts.

Culverhouse, tactically astute and as intelligent a footballer as you will ever meet, was primed by Walker to play as a sweeper for his Norwich side. The position of sweeper, or libero as it is more generally known, was an alien enough footballing concept in England when Walker introduced it at Carrow Road, let alone at Norwich. To play the position requires exceptional ball control and passing ability, it also demands responsibility and discipline, it is a 'fluid' position that is not as restricted positionally as others might be (indeed, libero is the Italian word for 'free'), however, the player in this role still needs to be aware of the positioning of his team-mates, so he can never 'roam at will'. The rigid, disciplined ways of English football, with its obsession for the 4-4-2 formation, does not, even today, favour any sort of libero based system, yet, here we had, 20 years ago, a man who had been sacked as Manager of Colchester United, introducing it to a club that had been brought up on the traditionally physical defensive qualities of Duncan Forbes. No wonder Walker's players were initially mystified at the way and manner he wanted them to be playing – Culverhouse's defensive colleague, John Polston, describing it as; "Some formation that I don't think anyone knew, or had ever heard of before." Not in England, maybe!

Walker clearly knew enough about Culverhouse's game to select him as his libero when the game and tactical plan demanded it. Did it work? The fragility of Norwich's defence in the 1992/93 season suggests otherwise, the Canaries conceded 46 goals in their 21 away league games, those that would have most likely seen Walker employ his then radical 3-1-4-2 formation. However, that defensive nous, and the ability it gave Culverhouse to read the game, to see the moves and find the players that had space, also meant the side had a lot more attacking flexibility – especially with Bowen able to push forward, almost like an orthodox left-winger. The end result for Norwich was a total of 30 goals scored in those 21 away League games, more than Champions Manchester United's 28 and runners up Aston Villa's 21. Indeed, it was the joint highest away goals total in the division, one the Canaries shared with Blackburn Rovers.

Along with the mercurial Crook, the three ex-Tottenham men had developed an understanding that was fashioned together by Brown, honed by Stringer, and peaked under Walker. It seems remarkable that none of them were given a chance at White Hart Lane, however, that fact is surpassed by their longevity as Norwich players. Norwich, known as a 'selling club' retained their services throughout the successes that both Brown and Stringer's side had, as well as through Walker's year and a half with the club, which included that third place Premier League finish and UEFA Cup campaign.

Other players left the club in that time – the likes of Townsend, Fleck, Sutton and Fox to name just four – however, Culverhouse, Crook and Bowen pretty much saw out their footballing careers at Norwich, the opportunity of a big move never seeming to come their way. In the case of Culverhouse and Bowen, maybe it was Norwich's perceived defensive frailties that put clubs off from wanting to buy them, the 'establishment' of English football preferring defensive rigidity to the flair that they offered. More fool them if that was the case, for Ian Culverhouse and Mark Bowen were made for Norwich City just as their contemporaries at the other Premier League clubs were not. Could you have ever seen Lee Dixon and Brian Borrows, or Steve Staunton and Francis Benali, in a Norwich City shirt? Me neither. Culverhouse and Bowen 'belonged'; their ability as footballers without doubt, their capability of being so much more than mere 'defenders' ably demonstrated in Walker's thrilling side. They were as right for Norwich at that time, as Darren Huckerby and Grant Holt were to become.

Another ex-Tottenham man featured strongly in Norwich's 1992/93 side. Like Bowen and Culverhouse, he was a defender, and, again, like them, he was not a 'traditional' defender, mired only in the ideals of stopping both play and opposition. John Polston was signed by Dave Stringer in 1990 for £300,000, the fee seeming comparatively high, but certainly not so when you consider that Tottenham, maybe at long last aware that Norwich had a tendency to 'sting' them in the transfer market (the combined fee for Culverhouse, Crook and Bowen was £227,000!), had originally asked for £750,000! Had that fee been agreed then it might have meant that Norwich never secured the services of Polston, a centre-half by trade, but with his Tottenham upbringing, one who preferred to play the ball rather than the man. Polston ultimately displaced the rather more combative Paul Blades at the heart of the Norwich defence, forming a reliable partnership with another centre-half who was more creator than destroyer, Ian Butterworth, the duo ending up as Mike Walker's chosen pairing in the centre of the Canaries defence. Like his fellow ex-Tottenham team-mates, Polston spent the peak years of his playing career at Carrow Road, and his total of 263 appearances would have been far higher had it not been for a series of niggling injuries while at City, not least the one that came directly from the boot of Mick Harford. John ultimately left Norwich for Reading in 1998, where he has settled. So it was in Reading where I met the former Canary, curious to find out more about his spell at Norwich's feeder club, as well as his time at Carrow Road.

COCKEREL
TURNED CANARY

We started our chat talking about the present, rather than looking back at John's time at Norwich straight away. I had learnt, through his personal website, that he was working as a Personal Fitness Trainer, a fact that quite a few of his ex-teammates had found amusing when I had told them – John was, apparently, not always the best of trainers, and the phrase 'poacher turned gamekeeper' was the general feeling amongst them!

John, who is a very easy going and pleasant chap, reflected on the 'accusation' for all of a second, before laughing and feigning surprise that they had done such a thing. Unlike many of his contemporaries, he had remained in the area that his last move had taken him, finding that his work as a trainer, along with what he called 'other bits and pieces' had made the decision to stay in Berkshire an easy one.

"It made sense to settle here, as much as I loved living in Norwich, we had a house in Thorpe for eight years. But we've been down in Reading for 14 years now, the children are settled... mind you, the cost of living down here is a bloody nightmare! But I don't see us moving away now. People in Norwich still remember me and I am still asked about the goal I scored against Aston Villa in that great season we had – I think it lingers in the memory for a lot of people because a lot was made of the fact that my son had been born the same day. Looking back, that's quite scary; he's nearly 19 now! Was it really that long ago? It was an odd situation, I spoke to my wife after that game and said that; "We won 1-0, and you'll never guess... I scored the goal!" I think she must have fallen off the bed when she heard that. It was a very eventful and slightly weird day or so."

John Polston berating someone for not doing their job properly

"There were film crews all over the place and the story made all of the papers; it was a mad couple of weeks. I suppose if it had happened now, I'd have had people camped out on the doorstep and been expected to put all of the details on Twitter, which is not my cup of tea at all."

Looking back to the beginning of John's professional career, I wondered if he, like so many of his Tottenham team-mates, had ever found it hard to accept, even now, that they had proven themselves at the highest level in the game, yet had not been given the opportunity to do so at White Hart Lane? To remind him of that time, I had brought along a photograph of him clad in a Tottenham kit.

"Yeah (looking at the photo and smiling broadly) it was hard. You have to remember that at that time, Tottenham had a lot of big names. I was with players like Ian Crook, Mark Bowen, Ian Culverhouse, all a little bit older than me, but, like me, players who'd come through the youth team and into the reserves. And yes, you could tell that they were good players, along with players like David Howells, Vinnie Samways and Danny Maddix, who were all in my youth team. From that side, I reckon about seven or eight of them must have gone on to play in the Premier League, or, at least, made a good living from the game, which is an unusually high number. But we had good Managers and Coaches, people like Keith Burkinshaw and Peter Shreeve, so that helped. I was working my way upwards with them and got into the first-team squad for the first time when I was about 17, alongside people like Taff (Mark Bowen) and Chippy (Ian Crook). And, like I said, they were a little bit older and, as I was making that move towards the first-team myself, they were already getting a sniff of playing in the first-team or had played a few games. But it was so tough at Tottenham at that time. You think of all the players who are ahead of you – Glenn Hoddle, Richard Gough, Clive Allen, Gary Lineker, Graham Roberts, Tony Galvin... then Gazza came along. To get into that first-team, with that sort of quality, was virtually impossible for a young kid at the time. But I made my debut, knowing I had to play exceptionally well or hope for an injury somewhere to get the chance of retaining my place."

"As far as those older, more established players are concerned, I was in awe of them. Not like today, when the youngsters go into the first-team dressing room and they're all so chirpy... it's a different world now. Back then, you'd go in and... well, you still had your jobs to do, boots to clean. I think I cleaned Clive Allen's and Paul Miller's. So you kept your head down, you didn't say anything or speak to any of them unless they spoke to you first – you just focused on your job. It was scary. Getting on the training pitch with them for example, the respect I had for them was unbelievable, they're on a pedestal. I just wanted to play alongside them, I was not thinking of the money, just wanting to play. When Tottenham first signed me as a pro, I think they offered me about £10 a week. I said; 'Yes, thank you very much'.

There was no negotiation, I took what was offered. I was just happy to be there and amongst those players. Money was never an issue; I played for the love of the game. But do I regret not playing the game now, with all of its rewards? Well, to be honest, no I don't, not at all. I miss the day-to-day thing, the training and the banter, but not so much the playing. I've a good career now, but I do miss the daily banter."

Once again the 'b' word crosses an ex-professional footballer's lips. I've heard it so often, said so many times, and accompanied by wistful looks and far-away expressions passing over their faces. I put it to John that was it that, the day-to-day camaraderie, with good mates, that most of the ex-pro's missed more than anything, including the lifestyle?

"Yes. Remember though, you're spending a lot of time together. Training, every day, week in, week out. Travel, going away, going out, you're doing all of that together. You all make some good friends along the way and become part of a tight-knit little group, and, the tighter that group becomes, the better you play as a team. It helped that we had big characters in the group."

"Gunny for example, Flecky too. The other ex-Tottenham boys were big characters for me as well –they were never big shouters, never the clenched fists – but I had the utmost respect for them because I knew them, knew they were really top players. They were seasoned pros when I arrived at Norwich, so I was still the young pro to them. I ended up playing a lot of games at Norwich alongside Ian Butterworth, but when I arrived at Norwich, I was teamed up in central defence with Paul Blades. We made our debut in the same game (an opening day win against Sunderland at Carrow Road on August 25th 1990) which we won 3-2. But I didn't play particularly well in those first few games. After Sunderland, we went to Southampton and lost 1-0, I scored an own goal... A classy header at the near post, which was a good start! We then had a home game against Crystal Palace, and lost again. I didn't play at all well that day so that was it; I was dropped for the next game. But I don't blame the Manager, I'd had left myself out to be honest. I then had to go through a spell in the Reserves, which was a chance to get myself together, settle into the club and area more."

"Mike Walker was in charge of the Reserves then, and we had a good side under him. Gossy was playing for them then; Mark Walton was in goal. Good lads. I got some games with them and was playing well, eventually getting back into the first-team just before Christmas – I never really looked back after that. And I got to know Mike, so the transition to the first-team and playing there under him was fairly easy. I had enjoyed playing for Mike in the Reserves. He told you like it was, if you played well, he told you, if you played badly, well... So that time in the Reserves under Mike was invaluable to me. But, if you end up playing in the Reserves for a while, especially after a big move, you do start to wonder if you may have made a mistake. By December (1990) when I wasn't back in the team, and although I'd been playing well for the Reserves, I did begin to wonder. I eventually regained my place because Paul Blades got injured. My second game back was at Sunderland, Roker Park, we won 2-1, which was a good result. In the end I think I got an award at the end of the season (following his selection for that game in Sunderland on December 15th, John played in Norwich's remaining 21 League fixtures that season, ending the campaign with 27 League starts), something like 'Most Improved Player' or similar!"

Once you were back in the side you soon showed everyone that you weren't the typical big, clattering centre-half, either?

"No, that was never my way. I liked to make a tackle, but, even so, I wasn't a giant centre-half (and indeed he is not, John is 5'11"). I was comfortable on the ball, I could read the game and pass the ball well – they were my main attributes. We liked to play from the back and everyone was comfortable on the ball, so it was natural for me to play that way. Get it, control it, pass it, move on. And, of course, two of my team-mates were ex-Tottenham as well, so we all liked to play. Taffy on the left, Cully on the right, and a mixture of myself with either Ian Butterworth, Rob Newman or even, for some games, Chris Sutton. A good mixture with some decent partnerships. Gunny was an ever present too – he was there for eternity, wasn't he? We had a really good understanding at the time and we all got to know each other extremely well. We were never a defensive team though, Mike Walker's ethos seemed to be 'however many they score, we'll score more', and he picked teams that led from the front, not the back. Soon after Mike took over, we played a formation that I don't think anyone knew of, or had heard of before. We played three centre-halves, with a sweeper. The three at the back were me, Rob Newman and Ian Butterworth, with Ian Culverhouse sweeping. Mark Bowen would be on the left and Ruel Fox on the right. Chippy was in the middle with Gossy. That was the basis of that formation and we played it in the year that we came third. Although we conceded some silly goals, a ridiculous amount that saw us ending the season with a negative goal difference, we also scored loads!"

"I'm not sure where we got that formation from, maybe the trip out to Denver, Colorado in pre-season! At first, we were all thinking, 'what's going on here?', but we stuck with it and got used to it, eventually. We used it quite a bit in away games, but I don't think we ever played it at home, we stuck to that flat back four then. We didn't really need the system at Carrow Road, as we were expected to attack in home games anyway. But it worked when we used it. Cully read the game really well as sweeper, and that was the base on which the system was built. In any case, I don't think Norwich fans would have wanted it in any other way, they like to see the ball played from the back, and the formation we had then more than allowed for it. John Deehan made coaching sessions very enjoyable, it was light-hearted with plenty of joking around; he was good to have about the place, you could talk to him. Mike was a little more distant, he'd be friendly with the players, but he was still the Manager. But the two worked well together and, when they went their separate ways, it was never the same for either of them. I think that, ultimately, when Dixie (Deehan) became Manager, he found it quite hard adjusting. He did change the style of play a bit and we tended to hit the front a bit earlier than we had under Mike. We had Gary Megson doing some coaching by then who was very organised, led from the front too, and had a big influence on how we were playing. He's gone on to have a good career in management."

Another ex-Norwich Manager who John would have played under was Martin O'Neill, somebody whose impact and influence has been considerable at the clubs he's managed. It is often forgotten that he had a short spell at Norwich, however, as brief his Carrow Road tenure was, he still made an impression on John.

"Martin O'Neill? Honestly? (grimaces) I couldn't actually stand him, I really couldn't. From day one. I probably didn't do myself any favours, I'd just come back from a hernia operation and I wasn't fit at all when I turned up for pre-season. The thing was, though, I'd been putting that operation off, I'd needed it since the previous Christmas, but, because we were struggling, I was needed to play. Anyway. I finally had the operation that summer, but the operation requires decent recovery time that needing to be taken into consideration. However, I think he just looked at me and thought that I was the worse trainer in the world. So no, I just didn't like him, neither as a person, or his training methods. I thought the training was so off the cuff, he'd say things like, 'go and run around that tree and then that tree then come back', I was all running sessions, which were not enjoyable. Then, of course, you're not going to like the Manager if you're not in his team, but I know there were a few who were in the team who didn't warm to Martin either. But you can't argue with his track record or ability as a Manager. He's in that Brian Clough mould; he looks for a reaction from players. If he puts you down, he wants a reaction from you to make you perform on the pitch, that's O'Neill's way. Steve Walford took the training for Martin, I quite liked him, and John Robertson got involved too, but that was more a case of just kicking a few balls about on the edge of the pitch in his old suit. Paul Franklin was there too, but I'm not certain what he did, really. I just didn't enjoy the whole set-up, it was my worse time at Norwich, if I could have left, I would, without a doubt. But, like I said, if you're playing, you're more likely to be on the Manager's side. And I wasn't playing, I was in and out of the side. (John started just six out of the 21 league games that Martin O'Neill had as Norwich Manager, plus three appearances as a substitute – this was after starting in 38 of the clubs 42 league games during the previous, 1994/95 campaign – more appearances than any other player that season). Having been a constant starter in the Premier League, then, all of a sudden, I wasn't featuring, just the odd game here and there. Then in one match, O'Neill played me in the left-back position... I thought I was being brought in as a left-sided centre-half, but no, I was picked at left-back, which he had even explained to me! That's how unorganised it was, he picked the team and just let you work the rest out for yourselves. No socks that I didn't play well that day... me, a left-back... Seriously?! God only knows what he was thinking about."

"O'Neill didn't stay at Norwich for very long of course, and I remember the day he left. We were up in Leicester, before a match against City and I'd gone along as part of the squad. There'd been some whispers about Martin circulating, however, on the morning of the game, we were all called into a meeting. Steve Walford and Paul Franklin spoke to us, they just said, 'Martin O'Neill has left the club, we'll be taking the side today'. They didn't say why or anything like that. Anyway, when they said that, all the players got up and, as one, shouted "Yesssss!!!" then started clapping and punching the air. It was unbelievable, all of the players, in unison. Walford and Franklin took that game (Norwich lost 3-2 after being 2-0 ahead; one of the Leicester goals coming from a certain Iwan Roberts) and, afterwards, they left too – Gary Megson then took over."

John's honest assessment of Martin O'Neill had surprised me. Maybe O'Neill had 'inherited' some of his more left-field traits from one of his own ex-gaffers, Brian Clough? I suggested to John that I would not be the only person surprised at his opinion and experience under O'Neill who had been, and is still, from a fans' perspective at least, regarded as one of the most popular Managers in the game.

"People's perception of him baffles me! Everyone I speak to, they all say, 'oh, we love Martin O'Neill'. Well, you just ask some of the people at Norwich when he was there for their opinion. Some players had cause to like him even less than I did... Gossy would be one, also Ashley Ward. Wardie played under him, did well for him, scored some goals – but he still got rubbished by the Manager and I think Wardie took it personally. It seemed to be part of his 'put you down' mentality, see how you react. Some people could take it, others couldn't... that six months was the worse of my career, I hated it. Of course, nobody knows what might have happened had he stayed. We were going very well, up in fifth place when he left, but although we were well placed, I think that some people fit a club and others don't. Martin had a great time at Leicester, likewise at Celtic, he also did some good stuff at Aston Villa when he was there and now he has a great chance of doing well at Sunderland. But if you speak to some ex-Norwich players, Spencer Prior for example, they would probably tell you how much they liked him and enjoyed working under him (Prior and Darren Eadie, who talks of his admiration for Martin O'Neill in this book, both went on to join their former Norwich Manager at Leicester). Some players did, some didn't, but that's football. You go through your whole career in the same manner, liking some people, not liking

Spencer Prior with BBC Radio Norfolk commentator Roy Waller

others. Besides, not like the Manager who isn't picking you softens the blow when you're not playing!"

Expanding on that, and thinking of how you all, almost without exception it seems, wanted to play well and perform for Mike Walker, I wondered if, conversely, a group of players could actually 'decide' that they didn't want to play for a certain Manager any more, and that he really could 'lose the dressing room'?

"Oh yes, it happens, without a doubt. Everyone has to like the Manager to a certain degree, either that, or you should at least respect him, especially if there is a great camaraderie at the club. It's a very tough job, and one that was never for me. By the time I finished playing, I'd fallen out of love with the game a bit. I'd left Norwich and signed for Reading, and was looking forward to that, getting fit and ready for a new season at a new club, under a new Manager. I hadn't played too much towards the end of my time at Norwich, so I was really focused on that, on playing, not managing. Ask any ex-player who is now a Manager: they'll say nothing compares to playing. And I wanted to carry on playing and took the opportunity to do just that at Reading."

"Anyway, about two weeks before I was due to start there, I was at home and playing with one of my children who had asked to go on the back of my bike while I was riding it. So, off we went around the block, with me peddling away in my flip-flops, but after a little while I thought 'what on earth is the matter with my foot?' because it wasn't half hurting! I'd only gone and pulled a ligament in my foot while riding the bike! So there I was, starting pre-season training at Reading in a fortnight and I'd injured myself. Not only that, but the contract I'd signed for them didn't take effect until July 1st, so I was worried that, if and when they found out, they'd cancel it. Naturally, I was very worried! I got on the phone to Tim Sheppard at Norwich (Tim was then the club physio) and said, 'I've done something to my foot, can you have a look?' So I went to Carrow Road where he examined it and gave me some treatment for a couple of weeks. I had to tell him to keep it quiet, as I didn't want Reading finding out. Then, lo-and-behold, on July 2nd, when I'd officially joined Reading, I rang the Manager, Tommy Burns, to tell him that I'd been out running and had done something to my foot and that they'd given me treatment at Norwich and a cortisone injection to keep me going. So that was it, I told them I'd done it whilst out running on my first day at Reading and I ended up missing all of pre-season training there, as well as the first month of the season."

"But as soon as I was fit, Tommy had me in the first-team and I made a winning debut, things went well. He then wanted to push my fitness along and play me in the Reserves, however, I knew I wasn't fit enough to play another game so soon, I needed another week of training to gently get myself fully match fit again. But, of course, you can't say to the Manager, 'I don't want to play' – so I did and ended up tearing my cartilage. By the end of the following January, I'd only played one game in a year, it was a nightmare. I just could not get fit, it felt as if my legs had gone, I couldn't play, couldn't run – God knows what the people at Reading were thinking about me. I certainly wasn't the player they'd seen at Norwich; my knee was in a state, lots of wear and tear and I didn't have any pace... Okay, I wasn't the quickest player, but I could keep up with most. It hit me in training, I was thinking, 'how is he running past me?' My lack of pace was being exposed more and more, there were lots of young lads at Reading, they worked us hard and I struggled, my legs had well and truly gone. I did eventually get match fit for the following season, but then I injured my groin... it was all so stop and start! I think I played about 20 games that season, but then, in my last year, I struggled with my knee again. By that stage Alan Pardew had joined the club along with Martin Allen as his Assistant Manager – during that pre-season, they took the squad over to Arborfield to do an Outward Bound course... OH-MY-GOD! They were the worse three days of my life. We worked so hard; they had us carrying logs, doing assault courses, the works. It was unbelievable. I felt my knee start to go again on the assault course, and, a month or so into the season, it had gone again, only this time it was really bad. I'd had enough by then, that was pretty much four years on the treatment table, and I just wanted to play. So I decided to pack it all in, get away from the game and do something different. I remember that last day so well, I went into training, shook everyone's hand and just went home. That was it. The end."

"I got home, sat on the bed with Jo and bawled my eyes out... (long pause) ... all of a sudden you're not a footballer. As a young pro, aged 17 or 18, you think you'll to play forever, it's all you know. But to be fair, I did have a bloody good run, but, even so, when it all stops, just like that.... (pauses again, clear emotion in his voice)… it does hit you hard. You think, 'what am I going to do?'. I did a bit of coaching, but then, within a month, I'd gone from playing football to sitting in a classroom, which was a real challenge. The course I was on ran over three months, time that I spent back in the real world, working with, and alongside some very down to earth people. I enjoyed it, different people from different backgrounds. I even enjoyed all the writing – the only time I'd ever done that previously was when I signed autographs, so it was like going back to school"

"I thoroughly enjoy what I'm doing now, and one of my jobs is at a school and involves football again at a Japanese school near Slough, funny enough I sent them my CV and they got back to me within a day! I've even done some coaching out in Japan with them too."

As well as bringing his football career to a halt, it was also an injury that kept John out of the Norwich side that played in the San Siro tie against Inter Milan… which must have been gutting for a first-team regular.

"I remember picking up that injury… We were at training ahead of the return in Germany, when Ade Akinbiyi tackled me… And when Ade tackled you, you felt it! And it wasn't a very good tackle either, to say the least. So I turned up for the game, knowing I wasn't fit, knowing I couldn't play, but still intent on doing a warm up, just in case. I even did a little jog up a corridor before we got to the San Siro, but I was clutching at straws. In truth I could barely walk, I was limping, but so, so desperate to play. As it was, we had a lot of players missing from the side that night, so I wanted to be in the side. But I had no chance. I look back now and think, 'what a game to miss'. Mind you, I didn't play in Munich either! I got a tweak in my groin then, I think I probably could have played, but ended up missing a lot of games afterwards as a result. I was there, of course, but missed out on playing. I did get to play in both games against Vitesse Arnhem though."

I told John about Jerry Goss had commenting about how well Vitesse had initially played at Norwich and how the side had struggled, at first, to break them down.

"That's right. Vitesse played very well in the first-half of the game in Norwich. In fact, it was unbelievable, and a real shock to our systems. It was 0-0 at half-time and we all came in, sat down, looked at each other and thought, 'Okay, what are we doing here?' I can't remember what Mike said to us, but we got it together for the second-half, played really well and got to grips with them and how they were playing. We stepped it up a gear and deservedly ran out as winners. Efan Ekoku scored, so did Gossy… and can you remember who got the other? Yep, I got the third! A little tap-in. That's something most players can't show on their CV… playing in and scoring, in competitive European football. At the time you think it is great, but you move on – it's only now, when I look back, that I realise what I've done and exactly how much part of the history of Norwich City Football Club that will always be. I scored against Ipswich as well, a cross from Keith O'Neill then a glancing header; we won that game 3-1. It was always nice to get one over them. We had a mixed record against Ipswich under Mike though, they had a good team at the time and it was always tight against them. But they were really good games to play in because we had some good players too; Keith, Darren Eadie, Andy Johnson and Craig Bellamy."

I asked if Craig Bellamy, even at that very early stage of his career, was as 'lively' a character as he has become – a reputation that grew with him as he advanced his career at clubs like Newcastle United and Blackburn Rovers? There is a well known story at Carrow Road about the youthful and uber-confident Bellamy being locked in the toilet on the coach going to one away game after annoying everyone else on board.

"Oh yes. He was a good player, but a pain in the arse on the training pitch, a right little pest. He was always trying to nutmeg you, that and shouting "nuts!!" He may be annoying, but he was a top player then, and he's a top player now. When I was selling my house in Norwich, I had a phone call, from a guy who told me that he was Craig Bellamy's agent, and that he was interested in buying our house. I was thinking, 'Craig, if you want to buy my house, you ring me up, you speak to me.' But that was Craig all over, but he's a good lad. I've been lucky, playing with and against some very good players. At Tottenham, Glenn Hoddle was unbelievable. Gazza was amazing too, as was Ian Crook. Richard Gough, he was a top centre-half, and although I didn't play too many games alongside him, he was a quality player and a really nice guy who always helped the younger players. At Norwich, you could see that Chris Sutton was going to be a top player, straight away. He must regret saying 'no' to the opportunity of playing for the England 'B' team that time, as I think he'd have gone on to play a lot of games for England – he could have made it as either a centre-half or centre-forward. Good times and good players."

"So, you could see things coming together, even though the season before the Premier League started wasn't the best – we still got to the FA Cup semi-final... but how we lost to Sunderland I'll never know. I think we must all look back on that, even now, and think, 'how did we lose to them?'. We'd played well in the quarter-final, beating Southampton, so I think, maybe, on some level, and not consciously, we thought we were already there? I don't remember too much about the game, but I remember their goal – everyone crying afterwards. It was absolutely sickening, to be that close to the Final and not make it. We were getting back on the coach our thoughts were on how that was it, we'd never reach an FA Cup final now, that was our one and only chance. In fact I don't think any player from that side ever went on to play in an FA Cup final? (John is correct). It was shocking really, we should have won, and we kept the bad run going after that defeat, only really making ourselves safe by drawing at home to Wimbledon in the second-to-last game. John Fashanu was playing for them, he had a soft spot for Norwich, and I don't think he was trying that hard, thankfully!"

"So, it was a pretty bad end to that season, struggling in the last few weeks and losing the FA Cup semi-final. I think it was the last straw for Dave Stringer, so he left and Mike Walker took over. Even then, we had a pretty average pre-season, we didn't play at all well and just weren't at the races. We might have been a little conscious of how hard the first few fixtures of the following season were. We were looking down on them and it was, 'Oh my God, Arsenal first match, then Chelsea' – both really tough games. At 2-0 down at Arsenal we are getting completely outplayed, but second-half, after Mark Robins came on, we got the ball rolling, which set the scene for the rest of the season. Robbo was on fire and we scored some great goals in those opening matches – but in that first game at Highbury we had come off at half-time feeling so low… So to be on such a high at the end was unbelievable. We took that vibe into the Chelsea game, we had no fears by then. But I broke my nose in that game. I was on the half-way line, standing alongside Mick Harford. The ball came in and I just tried to nick in front of him and head it away, but, as it bounced up, he's tried to pivot round and get his boot on it. But I still got there first meaning he absolutely smashed me with his right foot, which knocked me out cold. I was stretchered off and out of it – I remember waking up at half-time in the dressing room; a few of the lads were looking across at me. Anyway, the looks on their faces when they saw me was like, 'Ooooh, look at his face!'. I'd broken my nose and my teeth – so I looked a right old state when I woke up the next morning… I couldn't open my eyes, which had become two slits."

"Mick Harford was one of the hardest men to have ever played professional football – a league above pretenders like Vinny Jones. There was no messing with Mick, he did what he did and he did it well. As a striker, he was amongst the very best, and, as an opponent, well, when Mick Harford hits you, you stay hit to put it mildly… and that day he'd hit me hard. There was no intent, but I was clobbered. I had trouble with my teeth for a while afterwards, but I soon got back playing again, in fact, my first game was the return fixture at Chelsea when they had Flecky and Mick up front. Anyway, I was standing on the half-way line again, first goal kick of the game, Mick just looks across at me and goes, 'you alright then?'. So I said, 'Oh yeah, cheers Mick, thanks very much.' He then says, 'how've you been?', I said 'alright'... and that was it, we got on with the game. Bit of a weird situation, but Mick, he was as good as gold. We were late for that game and had to change on the bus and went straight out and played, we didn't have a warm up or anything, it was ridiculous. Consequently, they were 2-0 up in half an hour, before Dave Beasant helped us back into the game and we eventually went on to win – we were still on a real roll. Mind you, as confident as we were, we were soon brought down to earth; getting done 7-1 at Blackburn a few weeks later. I remember that one particularly well, as I wasn't playing (laughs). I was on the bench, but, with about 20 minutes to go, Mike Walker turned to me and said, 'go and have a warm up'. Shearer was on fire, he'd got two and we were 5-1 down, so I looked at him and said, '...sorry?', But he said it again, 'go and have a warm up'. I went off and thinking, 'Oh, I don't need to be going on here', but I started my stretches, still thinking, 'No, I really don't want to be going on here.' Then they scored again and it was 6-1… I then thought, 'Jeez, I do NOT fancy this'. So I headed off to one of the corners to continue my warm up, right out of the way, not wanting to go on. I looked across just once and could see Mike and John Deehan both waving at me, they were telling me to come over and get ready to go on… but I wasn't having any of that, so I ignored them and carried on with my stretching. And I stayed there for the next 20 minutes, just stretching, then, with only a few minutes to go, I decided to head back, thinking, 'well, they won't put me on now'. When I got back, they said, 'what have you been doing, we've been calling you to come back, you're not going on now, don't worry about it'. I just did not fancy facing Alan Shearer that day, I thought, 'let the rest of them deal with that'. But it was a freak result, just one of those games and we showed we were a decent side by winning the next match. I was back in the side by then and had a good run, we all did, all peaking at the same time. We had a good philosophy and played some really good football, and, when you're on a roll like that, you think you can beat anyone. We had a little blip at Manchester United, but we soon picked it up again. But I don't think we ever felt under any real pressure, even though we were still pinching ourselves a little bit. I don't think we were disappointed that we hadn't won the Premier League, no. we were delighted to have finished third. We were a good group of players who all got on well, playing good football and scoring good goals – it was a snowball effect. Things would have moved onwards and upwards....."

I interrupted John at that point by mentioning that all the momentum, all the good work, all the belief and confidence that the players must have had in themselves and their team-mates must have been shattered by Mike Walker's decision to leave the club to take over as Manager of Everton?

"Yes, God only knows what the Chairman was thinking. I've spoken to Mike since then, and I don't think it was about money with him, he just wanted a bit of time and security with his contract. Why on earth they wouldn't they have given it to him? Of course, finances were a factor, they always are, but he wanted security first. Once he'd left, the dynamism of the

Gary Megson congratulates Mark Robins after his Wimbledon winner

team changed, people began to leave the club, players were sold and new ones came in, things changed very quickly. Let me tell you a little story about Mike, something that shows what a good man-manager he was."

"Mike knew how to treat players, that was his big strength. Well, on one occasion when we were all out, we had an 11pm curfew. Anyway, Gossy stayed out later in a bar somewhere, but all of a sudden he said he just turned round and there was Mike Walker, right up close to him and in his face, just standing but saying nothing. Gossy said he thought he would kill him, but Mike didn't have to say anything and Gossy certainly didn't hang about – he shot off to bed knowing he'd be punished the next day. The way Mike dealt with it was hilarious though… He punished Gossy by making him run and Gossy loves running, in fact, he's one of the best runners I've ever seen as a footballer, he was amazing. So, Mike made him run and ran him into the ground. Gossy knew he'd been in the wrong, he'd taken his punishment, but Mike had treated him like a man."

With the departure of Walker, the momentum that the club had gathered began to slow. Players began to question, as was to be expected, the club's ambition, and, within a short time, quite a few left the club.

"The major problem was, we sold all the goal-scorers. Ruel Fox, Chris Sutton, Mark Robins, Efan Ekoku. Yes, we conceded less, but we couldn't score. We didn't have anyone who could score regularly, which really cost us. But it can't detract from the fact that we can all look back at those great memories, and time spent with really good players, good mates – it had been an amazing 18 months together. My time at Norwich was full of wonderful up's and not so good down's, but overall, the memories are very fond ones. I love going back to Norfolk and Norwich and whenever I do, people talk and reminisce, which I enjoy. It's great to be part of the club's history. Whenever the players all meet up it's just like old times straight away, the stories, the laughter, the banter; it all comes out again quickly and easily. Great times."

John is such a laid back, friendly and happy-go-lucky person, and like so many of the Norwich players of the time, he came across as someone who loved the game, who enjoyed playing football and the education, experiences and friendships it brought him. He is, perhaps, the least well known of the famous quartet that the club signed from Tottenham between 1985 and 1990, yet his contribution should not, in anyway, be underestimated, nor his footballing abilities forgotten. Typically, with Ian Butterworth unavailable for Norwich's first-round, first-leg game against Vitesse Arnhem in the 1994 UEFA Cup match, Mike Walker named John as his Captain for the club's first ever competitive match in Europe – quite a tribute to both Polston's leadership skills and popularity amongst his team-mates – especially given he was selected to lead the side ahead of other possible candidates for the job as Gary Megson and Jeremy Goss. John took the job, and the game, in his stride, helping Norwich to a convincing 3-0 win… and scoring a goal in the process! And the ex-Tottenham quartets were all selected to play in the Canaries fixture, against their old club on Boxing Day.

There is a saying amongst Norwich fans that the club starts to come down (as in the league table) at about the same time as the Christmas decorations, but that season was proving to be different. The Canaries dominated much of the Spurs game with Crooks' probing sparking many Norwich attacks, however, despite Norwich giving Tottenham a lesson in how to play football, the elusive goal that would have won the game never arrived and the game ended 0-0.

Indeed, December turned out to be a disappointing month for the club. Out of the five games played, Norwich won only one, a 2-1 home win over Wimbledon on December 5th, a game that Walker's side was fortunate to come away from with the three points. Successive defeats against Manchester United and Ipswich Town (the club's first home defeat of the season) followed, prompting thoughts that maybe the old Christmas decorations gag was going to be a reality after all, however, the point against Tottenham, and the one that followed at Leeds, held back the doubters and the Canaries ended the year three points clear at the top of the table. Ironically, it was to be a future Norwich City Manager who would ultimately topple them from their lofty position at the top.

The understudies

Norwich fans of a certain vintage (and over) can trip the names of the established first-team players in Mike Walker's successful side off the tips of their Norfolk tongues with the ease of a people who have seen many-a-hero grace the Carrow Road pitch; starting line-ups that lure gentle nods of approval when their footballing merits are discussed. Walker's starting XI picked itself most of the time, rather like the great Leeds United team of the 1960's and 70's, you could reel off your ideal starting line-up with no problem or pause for breath.

Likewise the flair sides of the John Bond era, the solid team that secured a first-ever promotion to the top flight under Ron Saunders in 1972 and Nigel Worthington's Championship winning side of 2004. Great sides, great players, although there is little room for debate or manoeuvre on which was the best side. Everyone has jotted the numbers one to 11 down on a piece of paper, a school exercise book, a jotter at work, or even the proverbial back of a cigarette packet, now in these modern times we are able to share our 'dream' XI with others online and trigger even more debate. We can now continue this obsession with picking the side and doing the Manager's job for him buy using computer simulations, not only that, but we can do a better job of it too – who, for example, has won the Champions League while "managing" Norwich City? Well I certainly have.

- *Norwich's FA Cup side of 1958/59? Ron Ashman, Barry Butler and Terry Bly.*
- *Saunders promotion winners? Kevin Keelan, Duncan Forbes and Ken Foggo.*
- *Bond's swashbucklers? Martin Peters, Ted MacDougall and Phil Boyer.*
- *Worthington's Champions? Adam Drury, Iwan Roberts and Darren Huckerby.*

If asked to select three players from each of those sides, some will agree with my selections, others will partially agree, while many more will vehemently disagree with all of my choices, citing their own and explaining why. It is one of the delights of football, to be able to endlessly debate, argue, pick and choose, agree, or disagree. The debate however, does have its restrictions. It is limited to the 'names', the players who played every week, familiar faces, known quantities, 'must' picks. It does not take into consideration those players on the fringes of the first team and certainly not those for whom a place on the fringe of the first team would be personal and professional triumph, so remote did their chance seem.

The obvious names in Walker's squad are well known, revered, respected, indeed, many of them are members of the Norwich City Hall of Fame – Carrow Road immortality. But there could only ever be 11 of them out on the pitch at any one time. Three members of the squad started every one of Norwich's 42 League games that Premier League season: Bryan Gunn, Mark Bowen and David Phillips, while Ian Culverhouse started 41. Following that illustrious quartet, there are a further four players who made over 30 League starts: Mark Robins and John Polston (34 each) and Ian Crook, Ruel Fox and Chris Sutton (32 each). And so on and so forth, players personal tallies being affected by a number of parameters – form, injury, suspension, and arrival at, or departure from the club during that season. But they are the first-team players, the names, the fans favourites. The talent.

And then, as in the world of Theatre, there are the understudies. Players who rarely see the light at the end of the first-team tunnel, those who train every day and have to be ready, with little or no notice at times, to take their place in the side, to step in when needed and, in the words of one Manager, to "do a job". Praise indeed. "Do a job". Not very motivational. Often, when the players on the fringes appear in the side, the talk amongst spectators is not of them, but the player who they have replaced, and how he is going to be missed. Again, hardly the most motivational introduction to a rare first-team opportunity. It's not unknown for a fringe player to start a game, or to come on as a substitute, and for the spectators to hurriedly refer to their programmes in order to see who the player is – when did we sign him, is he any good? The glamour of professional football outside the first-team.

Norwich City used a total of 22 players during the 1992/93 season. In other words, you could write your first choice starting line up down on that scrap of paper and still have room for another team. We all know who the 'players' were that season, this book is about them, but it seems right and fair to remember Jerry Goss's words, that football is a team game, and that those players who might need to slot into the side for a short spell, maybe even as a substitute in one game need to be acknowledged as well. So, taking that number as a benchmark, who were these unheralded players that contributed less than half a dozen starts that season?

There are six in total. The "Daddy" of them all is Colin Woodthorpe, a Dave Stringer signing from Chester City in 1990. Woodthorpe was a more than capable left-back, who found himself behind the consistent and un-prone to injury Mark Bowen, the undisputed first choice at the club in that position. He made just five first-team League starts during the 92/93 season, as well as two substitute appearances. Needless to say, with Bowen an ever-present that campaign, Woodthorpe didn't, when selected, even get the chance to play in his preferred position. His first appearance came in the game at QPR on March 3rd, one of the away fixtures, which saw Walker play the sweeper system, with Ian Culverhouse stepping into the libero role as he frequently had done that season. Woodthorpe slotted into the centre of the Norwich defence, playing alongside Chris Sutton, with Daryl Sutch and Mark Bowen taking up the right and left-hand sides of the defence respectively. It was a make-shift solution for a Norwich side missing Butterworth, Polston and Newman, all of whom could have played at centre-back, and it yielded a makeshift result, Norwich losing 3-1.

With Polston fit and back in the side for Norwich's next game, Woodthorpe retained his place for the team's next four games, only this time he was played in midfield. For three of those four matches, Walker's much-changed side (Goss, Newman and Butterworth all missing and Sutton remaining in central defence) impressed, winning three on the spin following the QPR game, including a credible 3-0 victory at Nottingham Forest, the game that saw Forest Manager Brian Clough kick then Norwich Secretary, Andrew Neville, in a fit of post-game pique! That impressive win was followed by a 3-0 reverse at Wimbledon however, and, with Goss available for selection again, Woodthorpe's season ended at the very less than salubrious surrounds of Selhurst Park.

Woodthorpe may have been a peripheral figure for City that season, but, on the whole, his career at the club did include some highlights. He scored in Norwich's 3-0 win over Liverpool in 1991, played in the FA Cup semi-final against Sunderland in 1992, and, in 1993, played at the San Siro, when Norwich bravely went out of the UEFA Cup. His selection in that game was due to injuries and suspensions to a number of established first-team players, but he and the team performed admirably, drawing praise from the Inter players, management and fans after the game. Woodthorpe didn't look out of place, not even at the San Siro, and went on to make a total of 20 first-team league appearances during that 1993/94 season before moving to Aberdeen for £400,000 and, at the time of writing, he is the Assistant Manager of Colwyn Bay in the Blue Square Conference (North).

Just behind Woodthorpe in the 1992/93 'fringe player' stakes is midfielder David Smith who joined Norwich as a trainee in late 1987. Smith made five league starts that season, plus one as a substitute. His peers in the Norwich youth team included Andy Johnson, Lee Power, Robert Ullathorne and Daryl

Sutch, all of them, like Smith, going onto appear in the Norwich first-team at some point, albeit with varying degrees of success. He invariably filled in when either Gary Megson or Jerry Goss was unavailable, and, in two of his games that season played alongside Woodthorpe, the win at Forest and subsequent away defeat to Wimbledon. Smith also played in Norwich's 1-1 home draw against Arsenal on March 3rd, a game that saw the Canaries without Ian Butterworth, Jerry Goss, Ian Crook, Gary Megson and Rob Newman. Smith duly partnered his old youth side team-mate Daryl Sutch in the Norwich midfield that evening, and it is credit to them that Norwich largely controlled the game and would have won had Ian Wright not been afforded space just the once (once was usually enough with Wright) to secure the Arsenal equaliser. And like Woodthorpe, Smith left Norwich at the end of the following season, having only made an additional five league starts that campaign, joining Oxford United for £100,000, where he went on to make nearly 200 appearances.

Next on the list of unsung squad members from the 1992/93 season is one of Smith's youth team contemporaries, the afore-mentioned Andy Johnson. Johnson made just one first-team start that campaign, plus one as a substitute, in what was only his second season at the club as a full-time professional. However, despite those modest statistics, he is the best known of all six players referred to in this chapter, because of what he's gone on to achieve in the game.

Johnson signed professional forms with Norwich prior to the 1990/91 season, making his debut for the Canaries in a 2-0 defeat at Sheffield Wednesday on April 20th 1992 at the age of 17. He also played in the club's last game of the season, another defeat, this time 1-0 to eventual Champions Leeds United at Carrow Road. Always confident in his own ability, Johnson would have therefore approached the following season confident of asserting his claim as a first-team regular, however, with Mike Walker rich in midfield options, the youngster didn't get his chance until Norwich entertained Manchester City on February 20th when he came on as a replacement for another member of that youth team squad of a few years previously, Lee Power. Johnson impressed in his cameo role, but didn't make another appearance until the team's last game of the season, a trip to Middlesbrough that had possible European qualification riding on the result.

His opportunity had arisen due to both Jeremy Goss and Gary Megson being unavailable, Johnson taking his place alongside Ian Crook in the centre of the Norwich midfield, the provider, worker, young apprentice to the wily wizard. He would have known exactly what his role was and how he was expected to play – as Goss explained in this chapter. Anyone coming in for an established first-team player would have studied that player, how he carried out his duties on the pitch, who he marked and what role he took at set pieces. Goss and Mike Walker would, therefore, have had no qualms about giving Johnson his first start in that last match, one in which Norwich needed to get a point to guarantee third place (and a UEFA Cup slot) providing Arsenal won the FA Cup the following weekend! The stakes were high, but Johnson thrived on the pressure and responsibility. He didn't start the game particularly well – an over-eagerness to please probably, rather than nerves, and, in Norfolk 'n' Good, Kevin Baldwin, nervously watching laments the selection of Johnson, "...Johnson was finding it difficult to get into the game. Everything seemed to be passing him by, and it was generally agreed that he should be substituted."

With the score at 2-1 to Middlesbrough and news that Blackburn, Norwich's rivals for a UEFA Cup place were winning, the mood at Ayresome Park was grim amongst the Norwich supporters. Two goals were to change the season around though, firstly Efan Ekoku struck and then, gloriously, an unlikely hero in Johnson, whose volley gave Norwich an unexpected lead. The details are, of course, academic: the game ended 3-3, Norwich finished third and secured their place in Europe when an ex-Canary, also called Andy (don't you love the symmetry?), one Andy Linighan, won the FA Cup for Arsenal. The point to make of course is that, in the last game of the season, Andy Johnson had arrived as a Norwich player. There was little doubt that summer amongst Norwich fans that he was going to be one to watch.

Johnson eventually secured himself a semi-regular first-team berth from the very start of the 1995/96 season, with Martin O'Neill giving him a run of 16 consecutive starts from which Johnson scoring four goals. First team appearances were slightly more sporadic when Gary Megson replaced O'Neill, but, after Mike Walker's return to the club in the summer of 1996, Johnson reclaimed his place, making 24 starts before being sold to Nottingham Forest, his debut for Forest coming four years after his first Premier League start at Norwich. Johnson went on to have a decent career in the game, playing at the highest level for Forest and West Bromwich Albion, as well as winning 15 caps for Wales. So, although the part he played for Norwich City in the 1992/93 season was a very small one, as things turned out, it was hugely significant.

Efan Ekoku, like Johnson, a scorer in that crucial game at Middlesbrough, is the fourth player within the squad who made less than six League starts for Norwich during that record breaking season. He is the best known of this fringe player group and, for that reason, we will lightly skip over his career on this occasion as the facts speak for themselves. Efan, of course, was the scorer of Norwich's first ever goals in competitive European football, as well as a plunderer of four goals in a memorable 5-1 win at Everton in September 1993. He joined Norwich from Bournemouth with only six games of the 1992/93 season left, and would undoubtedly have made more appearances, scored more goals and had a bigger impact, had he been at Carrow Road since the start of the season. However, it is often forgotten that he played a part, albeit right at the end of that campaign, his three goals in four League appearances (three as a sub) a sign of great things to come from him during the following season, when he scored 12 from 20 League starts.

Jason Minett's one appearance for the Canaries that season came from the bench as he replaced Lee Power during the 3-1 defeat at QPR on March 3rd, the game that saw Woodthorpe's first start. As well as being his first appearance of the season, it was also his last for the club – his previous two appearances for Norwich, also as a substitute, were consecutive games at the beginning of the 1990/91 season, a 3-0 defeat at Leeds United on September 1st and, 3-0 again, a week later at home to Crystal Palace. Jason joined Exeter City in 1993, and also had a spell with Lincoln City.

Mark Walton, like Minett, made just the one appearance for Norwich City in the 1992/93 season and had the unenviable job as being understudy to City goalkeeper Bryan Gunn – and with Gunn playing in all of the Canaries League games that season, Walton's one appearance came in the League Cup, a second round, second leg tie against Carlisle on October 7th which City won 2-0, courtesy of two goals from Chris Sutton. And that was it. Out of 47 league and cup games played that season, Walton appeared in just one, proving to be the ultimate understudy to a peerless master.

The circumstances behind Walton's appearance in that singular game are ones which he would not have wished for, however, as Gunn was on compassionate leave because of his daughter's serious illness, which tragically led to her death a few days after the Carlisle game. Typically, Gunny, a man with the heart of the Scottish Lion Rampant was back in the City side that beat QPR barely a week after Francesca had passed away, and remained in the side for the rest of the season. So, while Bryan played on, Mark continued in his shadow, working and training hard, keeping up his fitness, yet remaining a vital member of the squad. I tracked Mark down in South Wales and invited him to share his memories of his time as a professional footballer and to ask just how frustrating it was to have been not to be playing week in week out that season.

SECOND
TO GUNN

Keen as I always am to find out why the person sat in front of me managed to become a professional footballer, while I never did, I started by asking Mark what he felt had been the defining moment at the start of his career, that instance that might have made him aware that he was going to have a career as a top flight player?

"I was just 18 and at Luton Town when I was made aware that there was a 'goalkeeping crisis' at Colchester United – they had Graham Benstead on loan from Norwich, but he was not able to play in Cup games. Ron Howard, who was the Chief Scout at Luton back then called me into his office and asked if I wanted to play for Colchester in the League Cup. Yes please! Mike Walker, who was in charge at Colchester, came to pick me up from Kenilworth Road and I played against Fulham the following night. I ended up staying at Colchester for three months, by which time we were top of the League – then Mike was sacked! The following season, with me now a Colchester player I discovered that Norwich were looking for a keeper and was I interested? Mike was of course working there by that stage, which made the decision a no brainer! Colchester wanted to keep me though and actually offered a contract that was better than the one Norwich had proposed, so, in the end, the deal had to be settled by a tribunal, which was held at Watford's ground in July 1989.

I was nervous that they would ask for, and get, more than Norwich were prepared to pay, but, luckily, it didn't come to that and the deal was done at £75,000. Of course, it was a massive step up from playing at a lower level to a club that was regarded as one of the elite, and it was obvious to me just how much of a change there was on my first day at the club – a day I remember very clearly. The first team squad were away in Scandinavia, so

I was at training with the young professionals and apprentices. I was shy, nervous, and not really sure if I was good enough. I quietly slipped into one of the apprentices changing rooms and got changed, not really certain of my status, or where I stood in the squad pecking order. A week later the first-team squad returned, and I was surrounded by big names and big players in my estimation; people like Andy Townsend, Robert Fleck, Dale Gordon, Andy Linighan and Bryan Gunn, with even more outstanding players to back them up. It was during that early stage that Jerry Goss got changed next to me – he was recovering from a hernia operation at the time and we struck up an instant rapport – we then became room-mates on away trips and are now life-long friends. The training was a different world to what I had been used to and it was a very steep learning curve. Having said that, David Williams was the best coach I ever had the pleasure to work for, or with, and his impact on Norwich City should never be underestimated. In my eyes he should have taken more plaudits for the club's success than anyone."

"I owe Mike Walker a huge debt of gratitude as he basically taught me from scratch and helped develop me into a solid keeper with a sound technique. We used to put in a tremendous amount of time after training, just focusing on getting fitter and better. I loved training in a sandpit, which was constructed for the keepers, and enjoyed some very gruelling sessions, which were both stimulating and challenging. In truth, Mike was very hard but very fair. I worked hard and I lived hard, but he never judged me, and, I think, deep down, he knew that I would not overstep the mark in any way towards him or football."

"As for Gunny? Well, he was very good to me too. As an established keeper on the verge of the Scotland side it put him in a very strong position within the club, but he was always very generous, offering gloves or kit that he didn't want, which was always greatly received. But we were total opposites! I needed to train hard daily to keep up to the demands and standards, while Bryan had a knack of doing enough to get by, and produced great performances, which were bloody frustrating for me as a young upstart! We mixed at training and at weekly team bonding sessions. I always found him good company and, again, he was always very generous to me. I think there is genuine warmth towards fellow goalkeepers, as they are the only ones who really understand the demons you go through and how solitary it can be at times. But I always wanted to replace him and wanted him to struggle in games, hypocritical maybe, as I wanted Norwich to win, but then football is a strange life. I have *total* respect for Bryan, any man who comes through what he did as a father and husband deserves more praise than anything his football achievements gained him."

Despite the granite-like presence of BG in front of him, Mark still had opportunities to make his own mark (terrible pun intended) at Carrow Road, when injury to Gunn gave him the opportunity to have a run in the team

Mark Walton and Jeremy Goss celebrate the FA Cup win over Southampton

at end of the 1991/92 season, in doing so, it would appear, giving himself a great opportunity to retain his place for Premier League campaign that would follow. How did he look back a run in the team that which included the fateful FA Cup semi-final date with Sunderland?

"My run of games in 91/92 was fantastic. To be truthful, I was ready to play. I was experienced enough and had enthusiasm and commitment to the club. Like many at the club at that time, I ate, drank and slept football, nothing else was important apart from knocking the froth off a few beers and enjoying life. Bryan had a serious back injury, so my first game was against Southampton, and then a midweek FA Cup game against Millwall – we won both. In the Millwall game I saved a penalty just before half-time, but we actually won the game quite comfortably. That sent me on my way, my confidence grew and the confidence of others in me mirrored that. Looking back, which I try not to do too often, there were some fine players in that side, and you only tend to appreciate them when you are in the heat of battle – but there were no big stars at the club and everyone respected each other. Obviously there were personality clashes, like at any workplace, but they were few and far between. The spirit at the club, whether it was during training, on trips to games or tours, was fantastic – there was always a willing partner to go out and have a beer with, which usually developed into almighty piss-ups, but there was never any bad behaviour, just boys enjoying one other's company and letting off steam… along with some healthy banter. The humour in a dressing room is very black, very sarcastic, and very personal and funny. I miss that."

"The Cup run was a highlight obviously, after beating Millwall, we knocked out Notts County with ease in the next round, before two very tight, physical games against Southampton, who we saw off in a replay at Carrow Road. The build up to the semi-final built from there – it was almost impossible for me personally imagine, that the lad from the council estate in Merthyr Tydfil, actually had a chance to walk out at Wembley. I remember my dad telling me he couldn't make the semi because of work commitments, but he would be at Wembley… no pressure then! I don't remember much about Sunderland game apart from the fact that we didn't play as well as we had in the previous rounds."

"There was despondency in the dressing room afterwards, and I remember people crying. I was fairly good post-match but remember breaking down in a churchyard when we stopped for a beer in a pub. I remember Gossy, and, I think, Gerry Peyton (another keeper who was on loan at Norwich from Everton at that time) coming to console me, along with John Polston. When I got home, I rang my dad and broke down again, sobbing while I sat at the top of my stairs talking to him. And some fans think players have no passion when we lose. Luckily, we soon had the Premier League to think about, and I remember how it was all heralded with great enthusiasm and publicity –

the start of something special. There was a wider interest, and, for the first time, players, and the game in general, were really being scrutinised, which, I think, has led to far higher standards. I loved being involved in the games against the top teams and players who, only a few years earlier, I'd been watching on TV with my friends. It was surreal, to be in a tunnel alongside them, then taking them on and finding out some were not as good as their reputations suggested. By then, Mike had taken over from Dave Stringer. Dave was a good man and had gone through the wringer with some bad results, but he was a gentleman to the last. In fact, I believe he was above being a bastard, which is exactly what the majority of Managers are! And Mike didn't change much in what we did.'

"The pre-season tours always seem to included a frenzy of games along with some major drinking, sorry, I mean 'bonding' sessions! These always started out with a 'quiet beer' but rarely ended as quietly. I remember one trip to Finland, where our hotel was next to a river and had a nightclub and casino downstairs – hence some wayward behaviour! Two of our more prominent players were caught riding baker's bicycles back to the hotel at 5am, another climbed down a drainpipe to get back *into* the casino!"

"As far as I was concerned, the new season offered me a chance of securing a starting place in the team, but when the new season began, Mike opted for Bryan. I was obviously gutted about that as I'd played against Colchester in pre-season, while Bryan played against Southend. Mike said later that he thought Gunny looked better on crosses, that's why he got the shirt ahead of me. Disappointment was an understatement! However, there are two ways to deal with that sort of thing: move on or sulk. I moved on. I had three friends who came down from South Wales for that opening win at Arsenal meaning there were a fair few celebratory drinks consumed in Arsenal's free bar afterwards – my mates headed back home merry! That result and the performance set us up for the season... okay, it may only have been the first game, but we were fearless in the way we approached games and everyone seemed happy with the way we were playing. There were no disruptive influences in the changing room or at the club either, which made for a buoyant, laid-back atmosphere in whatever we did. Most of the players went to *Strikers* for lunch, the pub on the Carrow Road complex, where there was a chap called Sandy, who charged you £2 whatever you bought."

"The overall feeling from my time at Norwich was that it was a happy club. I had great team-mates who were totally relaxed in each other's company. I guess there must have been a few tensions, but I was blissfully unaware of any. I loved my football and I loved Norwich, and, for me, it is still 'my club'. The camaraderie of the dressing room was fantastic, indeed, while I don't miss playing one bit, I do miss the changing room banter, with all the characters, those shared triumphs, the disasters, but above all, the amazing sense of humour."

"I don't know how much players are allowed to unwind with the lads these days, but some of the stuff that we all got up to 'off duty', although crazy in many ways, certainly helped contribute to the club's success. Home or away, we were always enjoying ourselves. I vividly remember a mammoth trip to Istanbul, which included an overnight stay and one almighty piss-up with around 30 dignitaries. We then flew to Romania, before having a three-hour boat trip to play a game where we got stuffed four or five-one. I also recall Lee Power ordering 40 vodka and oranges, then bringing them to the tables – Robert Chase's face was a picture! On some of the away trips the team coach resembled a disco on wheels at times as good results were always celebrated – although by some players more than others admittedly! I remember Mike Walker, Lee Power and Gossy with their shirts off, punching each other in the stomachs to see who had the best abdominal muscles and the best punch. That made for great viewing I can tell you!"

"Of course, it's an old cliché, but because we played hard, we were worked hard too. We got weighed every Monday and Friday, which was the bain of my life as I was one of the larger lads! One way around it was the dehydration trick, a favourite of Rob Newman, Gunny and I. I would have lunch on the Thursday, followed by a long sauna in the evening, then go 'nil by mouth' until I weighed in the next morning. Then I'd order sausage rolls and pies from the Trowse bakery, which my apprentice would go and get for me. As a result, the changing rooms at Trowse smelt like a baker's oven."

"We also celebrated birthdays with cream cakes after training, always nice if you had a sweet tooth. The reserves used to play on Friday nights of course, and, if some of us were needed for the first-team squad the next day, we'd have to make our way to wherever they were staying after the game. Can you imagine that now? The club would provide a car and we'd have to get to the hotel as soon as possible. I remember that the 'three Amigos' (Mark, Rob Newman and Gossy) had to get to Crystal Palace one evening, but we stopped at the Old Ram on the A140 outside Norwich and had a beer or two, before getting to the team's hotel at about 3am! Charmer (Rob) came on as sub after about 15 minutes, and almost immediately got hit in the face by the ball and promptly hit the deck, with all the other subs absolutely pissing themselves in the dugout. Another time, for an away trip to Sheffield United for last fixture of the 1990/91 season, we travelled up from the Post House hotel in Norwich – I was ready, parked up and a bit tense as it was a big game for me, but not everyone was as tense! Flecky (Robert Fleck) was sat on the mini-roundabout just outside the hotel, eating a Chinese takeaway. He then debagged and showed me the new tattoo he'd just had engraved on his arse – a little devil I believe!"

"Later on, after a nice communal dinner at the hotel in Sheffield, I went for a walk with Gossy, which was not an unusual thing to do, as it killed the boredom. We were joined by Flecky, David Phillips and Ian Butterworth and, as we walked, we passed a small, nondescript pub… we all looked at each other… as if to say 'should we walk past or not?' Obviously we went in for a few and were joined by Peter Elliott, the Olympics middle distance runner, which was very unexpected, but most enjoyable. After that game we went to Marbella for an end of season jolly, which was also lively and enjoyable. Gossy and I made a pact that we would not wash for the entire trip, which became an endurance test, one that would test our sense of self-consciousness in what was a very nice four star hotel. I buckled after four days, but to his credit Gossy won with flying colours, in fact he went the entire trip without even brushing his teeth!"

"They were great times and it looked as if City would go onto even bigger and better things. So, for me, it's so sad that my time at Norwich ended in pain, frustration and anger. The first year of the Premier League had been incredible, with some great games and, more importantly, fantastic results. It was an achievement, one that will never be replicated due to the financial disparages that exist in the game now. But at the time I thought nothing of it – I was young and had no perspective of success or appreciation of it. I remember being offered an extension to my contract by Mike Walker and I turned it down because I didn't believe it was as good as the deal offered to the two other young players that had been offered extensions. As a result I was dropped from the squad to play Middlesbrough in the last game of the season, but, typically of my life and career, that wasn't the end of the drama."

"I was scheduled to play in the reserves the following day at Spurs – I'd arranged with John Faulkner, the Reserve Coach, to be picked up on the A12 at Marks Tey, near to Colchester at a specified time. No bus arrived, as it had gone down the A14 to London instead! I had a mobile phone with me and managed to get in touch with John Deehan at the first-team hotel to inform him of the situation and he told me to get a taxi there. Luckily, I was absolved of the blame, however, even if I had left immediately, I would not have got there until half-time, so I left and went home. The reserves went on to lose 10-0 and I think Lee Power played in goal. No further contract negotiations took place, but I returned for pre-season training and went on tour to Colorado, which was a privilege. The club, meantime, were looking to sign another keeper, which turned out to be Scott Howie. So I knew my time at the Norwich was over and I ended up training with the youth team until the following March. It's the harsh reality of being a professional footballer, you're here one day, gone the next. That wasn't a good time for me. I'd been amongst a great team of lads, involved in some great games and playing at some great stadiums. Then all of a sudden I was training on the third field at Trowse, which had a slope and was full of molehills with all the 16 and 17-year-olds. Then Mike Walker left for Everton and John Deehan took over. He gave me a free transfer, in effect, sacked me, within a couple of weeks. I'd enjoyed incredible highs and lows, but that was an ignominious end, those last six months were a blur, a downward spiral of anger, frustration, drinking and loneliness. Players left, the club drifted, and, in my opinion, it lost its soul. The rest is history! I had a short spell with Bolton soon after leaving Norwich, but only for about six weeks. I then ran into a drama and a half in Hong Kong, followed by a spell near Norwich with Wroxham. I eventually resurfaced at Fulham and won a couple of Championships there, during the Keegan and Wilkins era, before moving onto Brighton. My career finished at Cardiff City, which was a great club to play at home and so close to my home town."

"After leaving football I lived in Australia for 18 months, which was a great experience, then returned home to help run a restaurant. I now work for Cricket Wales and deliver Cricket in schools, which is very rewarding. I'm off to University for a year, which should be another great experience. But, although the parting of the ways wasn't a good time for me and a lot has happened since I left Norwich, not least the times I had at my other clubs, I still look back on my time at Norwich very fondly – as I said earlier, City are still 'my' club."

Mark typifies that old adage about football being a *squad* game, rather than a team game. His input, playing wise, during the 1992/93 season was minimal, yet his place as a valued squad member, team-mate and friend cannot be under estimated. I've already written about how the team at that time was greater than the sum of its individual parts and Mark's presence in the squad was as important as any other players'.

Admittedly Mark was unlucky to have been at Norwich during a time when Bryan Gunn was at the top of his game, but Mark was clearly a more than capable goalkeeper, a fact backed up by the medals and recognition he won at Fulham under the leadership of Kevin Keegan and Ray Wilkins – experienced men who knew a good player, or goalkeeper, when they saw one.

As far as I'm concerned the story of Mark's life in the game is far more interesting than those of star names like Gerrard, Lampard and Rooney – he was a footballer's footballer and the game needs people like Mark.

Norwich saw the New Year in as Premier League leaders, a position that had been seen as a temporary aberration when they had won the televised Sky match back in September ("Canaries Flying High", "Lofty Perch For Canaries" etc), but nobody expected us to be there four months later – yet that's exactly where we were! Countless excuses had been made for City's position at the summit, one being that it had been attained by default because of the Champions Leeds United's poor results, as well as unexpected defeats for challengers Aston Villa (including that home loss to Norwich) and the fact that the Manchester United and Liverpool juggernauts were not quite firing on all cylinders. However, the Canaries were top and, if they were still there in another four months, they would be Champions, but there were four tough January League fixtures to successfully navigate past first.

The first of which was a return trip to Hillsborough, the scene of the Canaries' FA Cup capitulation, looked winnable. Norwich had already taken three points from Arsenal, Chelsea and Aston Villa, so there was every reason to suggest that another three point haul would be coming from The Owls who were struggling at the wrong end of the table and the fact that Norwich had already beaten them at Carrow Road.

Prior to the Wednesday game however, Norwich had gone for four games without scoring a goal. To attempt to alleviate that problem, Walker kept faith in the strike partnership of Lee Power and Mark Robins, but the robust attentions of Wednesday's defence saw the pair struggled again and Robins ended up getting injured too. The game was won by Wednesday when future Canaries' Manager, Nigel Worthington, scored shortly before half-time, the result knocking Norwich off the top of the Premier League for the first time since October.

City drew the next game 1-1, at home to Coventry, before the first of a series of 'must win' encounters between then and the end of the season, at home to Crystal Palace. With Robins out, Walker opted to replace Darren Beckford with Lee Power, who slotted in alongside Chris Sutton – the changes had excellent results. City won 4-2 with Power scoring twice, alongside Sutton and Goss. More to the point, City had achieved the result without the midfield promptings of Crook.

A tricky trip to Goodison Park followed, with a fixture against an Everton side looking for their fourth win on the trot. And typical Norwich, so disappointing in the game they were expected to win against Sheffield Wednesday, they were back on form against Everton with a superbly executed 1-0 victory thanks to a Sutton goal – a win that no doubt had the Goodison Park suits discussing Mike Walker's name for the first time.

So Norwich waved goodbye to January back on top of the pile, but predictably, the sports headlines were not of City's victory on Merseyside, but the fact that Manchester United and Aston Villa had both lost. Yes, you guessed it, the Canaries were back by 'default' again!

The way we were

So onwards into February with Norwich City leaders of the Premier League. Historically, as I already mentioned, it was not unusual to see a 'lesser' clubs at the pinnacle of English football. However, such instances are usually exclusively restricted to the first few weeks of a new football season when the tables are somewhat of an oddity, an indulgence of newspaper sports editor or TV producer, who feels the need to show some kind of pecking order even if all the teams have played just one game. For the small fry, the sunshine and optimism of early season was *their* time to pounce, but February is a short, cold month usually cluttered with cup matches, and inevitably, the month that the big clubs made their move and the 'lesser' ones to stand aside. It was the way of things.

The Division One League table on September 10th 1988, for example, showed Southampton leading the way after three games, with Millwall proudly sitting in fourth position. But it was a different story at the end of that season – Arsenal were Champions, with Liverpool runners-up. Millwall finished in tenth place, Southampton in 13th. Perhaps the most extreme change of circumstances occurred in the 1974/75 season, when three games in Carlisle United were the early pace-setters in Division One having comfortably won their first three games – away to Chelsea and Middlesbrough, plus a home victory over Tottenham – without even conceding a goal. Inspired by their midfielder Captain, Chris Balderstone, who also represented England at cricket, Carlisle were the talking point of the back pages and *Match of the Day* alike, however, they then proceeded to lose ten out of their next 15 League games and found themselves in the bottom three by mid-November, where they resolutely remained, eventually being relegated in last place with only five wins to their name all season.

On similar form, shock 92/93 pace-setters Norwich (despite finishing the 1988/89 season in fourth place) would have been in a similar position to Carlisle's by February, but instead, and breaking with all tradition, the Canaries remained at the very top. So, the likelihood of City being relegated (Ladbrokes had them at 5/2 for the drop at the start of the season, remember?) had all but evaporated, in fact, the odds on becoming Premier League Champions was shortening week by week, although it should be said that Manchester United, Aston Villa, Arsenal and Liverpool remained as more likely Champion possibilities than Norwich, even then.

Naturally enough, it was still a relatively new experience for Norwich fans to be approaching the St Valentine's Day stage of the season with their side still possible contenders for English football's elite league. The Club and its supporters were far more use to the anonymity of mid-table, or below, to accompany the Bovril on damp Saturday afternoons; days spent wondering who our possible relegation rivals were playing, and who had games in hand over who, rather than dreaming of European qualification. For example:

February 1972 – Norwich were in the middle of their first ever season of Division One but were finding the going tough. The Canaries first League fixture of the month was a home match with West Ham on February 10th. Norwich had already gone ten games without a victory before that game, a run that had seen them slip from sixth in the table (following a 2-1 win at Leicester on October 21st, David Cross and Graham Paddon scoring) to 17th at the time of the West Ham game, just four points off a relegation place. Desperate to put the appalling run right, and cheered on by a Carrow Road crowd of just over 32,000, Norwich huffed and puffed but couldn't bring the house down – the Hammers won with a solitary goal from Bryan 'Pop' Robson.

Because of a run of postponements due to the poor weather at the time, Norwich only played one more fixture that month, another home game, this time against Newcastle United. Saunders fielded two new signings; the competitive midfielder Trevor Hockey, signed from Sheffield United (in an exchange deal that, strangely, saw forward and fans' favourite, Jimmy Bone, head in the opposite direction) and left-sided midfielder Colin Suggett, procured from West Bromwich Albion. However, despite the addition of those two new faces, Norwich lost 1-0, thanks to a goal midway through the first-half from Malcolm McDonald – City slipping to 20th place in the process.

The Canaries eventually won a game on April 14th, defeating Chelsea 1-0 at Carrow Road. They had gone 19 League games without a win, obvious relegation form, or so you would think. Two more successes after that, at The Hawthorns and Selhurst Park, saw the Canaries survive by the skin of their beaks, with their victims in those two games being the two sides that went down. Norwich survived in 20th place, and, in doing so, became the last team to avoid relegation by finishing in that place, the 'three up, three down' rule for promotion and relegation being introduced the following season.

February 1977 – February 15th saw Norwich capitulate to one of their worst *ever* defeats in the East Anglian derby match against Ipswich Town; a post-Valentine's day massacre. Nearly 35,000 packed into Portman Road to see Ipswich win 5-0, with Norfolk-born Trevor Whymark doing the most damage by scoring a hat-trick. Ipswich were title contenders that season, the victory lifting them to second in the table. Norwich, by contrast, had a season of mid-table mediocrity, ending that match in 12th place, and the season back in 15th. John Bond's team put the misery of that derby defeat behind them in their next match however, turning over Coventry City 3-0 at Carrow Road, with goals from Viv Busby (2) and Kevin Reeves.

February 1981 – February 7th saw the Canaries travel to The Dell to play Southampton, already marooned in the bottom three of Division One and on a roll of five defeats in seven games. This month and year perhaps, perfectly typified the way in which early-season optimism among Norwich fans can soon be reversed, albeit in a very extreme manner! The first game of the season, back in August, when the grass was green and hope sprang eternal, saw a 5-1 demolition of Stoke City at Carrow Road, a win that briefly and gloriously sent John Bond's side to the summit. However, rather than wait until Christmas, and accompany the decorations on their way down in that traditional City manner, Norwich decided to do it as soon as that opening day win against Stoke was out of the way instead. Four defeats on the trot had them in the bottom three by September and, between then and the end of the season, the highest position Norwich 'enjoyed' in the table was 17th, attained after a 1-0 Carrow Road win against Ipswich (them again) on April 20th. But back to the Southampton game.

By that stage, Ken Brown had succeeded Bond, and the side he selected to play The Saints was full of attacking flair, including names like Barham, Fashanu, Royle, Paddon and Goble. However, Southampton had a few useful players in their own line-up – Kevin Keegan, Mike Channon and Charlie George to name but three. The south coast outfit won 2-1, with George among the scorers. Norwich were relegated at the end of that season and their February form was a major factor – following the defeat at Southampton, the Canaries lost their next two games without scoring a goal – going down 2-0 at home to West Brom and 4-0 at Birmingham City. Some redemption was gained on February 28th with a 3-1 home win over Brighton, a victory precipitated, no doubt, by Martin O'Neill, signed from Nottingham Forest, who was making his Canaries debut that chilly February afternoon.

February 1985 – Four years later, relegation was the last thing on the minds of Norwich fans as they braved the wintry elements for what turned out to be the club's only League fixture of the month. Poor weather, and a proverbial monsoon of postponements in early 1985, meant a fixture pile-up at the end of that season as games were re-arranged. The back-log included

Norwich having to play two games in three days at the beginning of May, however, prior to the Forest match, Norwich sat in 10th place in Division One, with a place in the League Cup semi-finals already assured. Disappointment, therefore, when Forest won thanks to a single Peter Davenport goal. But, as the fans trailed home after the game, attention would have turned to that pending semi-final, matters of the League largely forgotten. A pity. In their 16 League games following the defeat to Brian Clough's side, Norwich won just three games, and, in the end of season farce that left Coventry City still with three games to play (following Norwich's final fixture) armed with the knowledge of realising exactly what they needed to do to survive. The Sky Blues, perhaps inevitably, won all three games, including a 4-1 victory over Champions, Everton, in their last game – the minds and bodies of the Everton players clearly already on the beach, duly sending stunned Norwich down to Division Two.

February 1989 – One glorious exception to those seasons where mediocrity bordered relegation possibility, and a sign of things to come perhaps, was Dave Stringers superbly crafted side of 1988/89, which featured familiar names that would go on and become key players in Mike Walker's side four years later – the likes of Gunn, Culverhouse, Bowen, Butterworth and Crook. The foundations of Walker's defence had been built, the fulcrum of his midfield already in place. That February saw four league games played and three victories, which included Charlton (2-1); Derby County (1-0) and, gloriously, Manchester United (2-1). For the entire month, Stringer's side sat in second place in the table, a Fifth round FA Cup victory over Sheffield United (3-2) adding to the sense of excitement and expectation at Carrow Road. Norwich ended the month second in the League, five points behind leaders Arsenal (with a game in hand) and seven points ahead of third placed Millwall. Hence, at that time, genuine odds were being offered on the Canaries winning a League and FA double. Sadly for Norwich, a run of six League games between April 1st and May 1st saw two draws and four defeats – two points from a possible 18 and any dreams of glory crushed.

In football, of course, history and 'tradition', though frequently lauded, counts for nothing, despite the success of Stringer's side just four years earlier, and to coin a phrase, the reaction of most football supporters to Norwich's fourth place finish in 1989 was "meh". They'd finished fourth, so what? They hadn't won it. Arsenal had, in the last game of the season, with the last kick of the game. And Liverpool had finished second. More to the point, Chelsea and Manchester City had been promoted. So Norwich had finished fourth? "Meh". That is, of course, my personal opinion. In truth, of course, the club had a magnificent season, one worthy of much acclaim and tribute. Fourth place and an FA Cup semi-final, isn't that what fans of Arsenal, Liverpool and Tottenham, for example, will consider, if not success, certainly satisfactory during the 2012/13 season? Especially as it would mean Champions League qualification and a trip to Wembley!

Norwich got neither that campaign; their place in Europe was denied to them because of the continuing ramifications of the ban on English clubs following Heysel, while their FA Cup semi was played at Villa Park, a ground where they had already had a League match that season. There is no doubt, in my mind, that the achievements of Stringer's side has been cruelly underplayed and uncelebrated, simply because, in the end, the club failed to win a trophy, and, unlike now, there wasn't a multi-million pound European Champions League reward for finishing fourth.

So why has the club's achievement of finishing just the one place higher in the 1992/93 season (and only a 4th round of the FA Cup appearance) merited more praise, more attention, and, indeed, is seen as being a 'one-off', when, just four years earlier, a precedent had been well and truly set? Three words. The. Premier. League.

As I wrote in an earlier part of this book, the goal of the Premier League was to change football in England, and on a seismic level. Can anyone argue that hasn't been achieved? Regardless of the fact that some, much of it maybe, may not be seen as being good for the game, or healthy for it on an overall basis, the game has changed. But that change didn't take two decades to emerge, it started on day one. The Premier League was, immediately, the only place to be. It was everything. So how well did City maintain their lofty grip during February 1993?

February 1993 – The Canaries first match of the month was that tricky trip to The Dell. Southampton had been bobbing along in mid-table without really bothering anyone, indeed, they had been as low as 19th in mid-January. Their best result to that stage was a 2-0 win over Arsenal in early December, but then they had always been a tricky proposition at the Dell. And so it was to prove when Norwich were in town, two goals within the first half-hour of the (no) contest from Richard Hall (born in Ipswich) and Micky Adams settled matters early on, and insult was merely added to yellow and green misery when Nicky Banger made it 3-0 with a little over ten minutes left. It was Norwich's joint second heaviest defeat of the season so far and was a massive blow as even City's sternest critics had expected them to see off the Saints.

Prior to the home match against Manchester City that followed, the Canaries found themselves, by their own high standards, languishing in third place, five points behind leaders Aston Villa. Double relief, therefore, when Robins opened the scoring just before the half-hour, with his first goal in eleven weeks. Admittedly, some of that time had seen him out with an injury, but, none-the-less, he remained Norwich's goal-scoring focus. Then, a minute later, a delicious one-touch pass by Fox set up Power for Norwich's second. An early second-half strike by Canary-to-be, Mike Sheron, got City back into the match, but, following Robins' return to form, the result was never going to be in any doubt and Norwich celebrated their first victory over Manchester City for 12 long years; Mick McGuire and John McDowell had been the goal-scorers when they had last been beaten, also at Carrow Road, back in April 1981!

Blackburn Rovers followed in a live televised match, Norwich's third date with Sky that season, with the record standing at played two, won two. The game was an excellent choice for Sky – both sides were in the top five, while there was also the chance for either Norwich to seek some sort of revenge for the 7-1 mauling they had endured at the hands of Rovers earlier in the season, or, perhaps, just perhaps, Blackburn would go goal-crazy again? In the end, neither came to pass and the nation were precipitated into their Sunday afternoon naps by a dire 0-0 draw, enlivened only by the falling snow and the introduction of the fabled orange ball, which was arguably the brightest thing on display. Norwich, in securing a point and keeping a clean sheet against their October nemesis, had maybe proved a point, but a point was their sole reward and they remained in third place. Aston Villa were seven points in the distance, still on the summit and with a far superior goal difference, obscenely superior in fact – Villa's being +17, with Norwich's, (no thanks to that result at Blackburn) a resolute but symmetrical 0, which was only two better than that of Wimbledon in 16th place.

Witnessing the unfolding events of the season and the club's impressive ascendancy was a Norwich fan who, in time, would rise to the heights of his own chosen profession, one that has its very own 'Premiership'. Ed Balls was working on the staff of the *Financial Times* at the time of the launch of the Premier League, but his calling was to be in the political world, with a position as an economic advisor to Gordon Brown to follow in 1994, the first step of a swift, impressive rise up the ranks of the Labour Party, that ultimately saw him appointed as Shadow Chancellor in January 2011.

CORRIDORS OF POWER

Two Ed's; Norfolk born and Norwich fans... Ed Balls MP and the Author

Ed Balls MP is now the most senior Canaries supporter (of many) in Parliament and was delighted to meet with me to chat about his support of all things Norwich City. An astonished PA confessed to me that, when he was made aware of my enquiry, he had said, "yes, get him in as soon as possible", a privilege that is doubtless denied to many a journalist and media man of greater prominence than me! It turned out to be a very interesting afternoon, although, as you'll discover, Ed's fondest memories of the Canaries are of a much earlier vintage. I began by asking Ed, who, like me, is very proud of his Norfolk roots, how long had he been a Canaries fan?

"Since before I can remember! I was actually due to be born on February 18th 1967, which was the date of Norwich's fourth round FA Cup game against Manchester United at Old Trafford. Well, that caused a bit of a debate in the family and, in the end, it was decided that my dad should go to the football, so he went. As you can tell, it was a different era then! A special train had been laid on from Thorpe St. Andrew to Manchester for the game, so my dad and uncle went, accompanied by Ian Gibson (who became the MP for

Norwich North in 1997), they all enjoyed the game and duly came back again, but I wasn't born for another week anyway, so it's a good job he went up to Old Trafford really. Interestingly, a few months ago, I finally got to see the goals from that match. They're on *You Tube* and someone sent the link to me. So, I've been a fan ever since I can remember. I lived in Norwich until I was eight, then we moved to Nottingham, but my family are all from Norwich, and my parents are back living there again now."

"The first game I went to was during the 1973/74 season, and it was a big one, against Leeds United. They had a great team at that time – Harvey, Bremner, Lorimer, Jordan were all playing. I remember we were sat on the edge of the 18-yard box, about five rows up. I remember at one point, David Harvey (the Leeds keeper) came right up near to us on the side of the pitch to get the ball. I don't remember very much about the match at all, but I do remember that! The week before then, I was taken to see March Town play Wisbech Town, along with my dad and uncle. It was a test to see whether or not I could survive a game. My second game was Norwich against Ipswich on Boxing Day that season and, if my memory serves me right, Billy Steele scored for us (Ed is nearly right, Steele, who was making his debut that day hit the crossbar with a thunderous shot before Ted MacDougall poked home the rebound). Another game I remember well was in April 1976 against QPR, who were in the running for the title and we beat them 3-2, which ruined their chances of winning it. That team from that era is the one I regard as 'my' team."

Just like Ed, we've all got our favourite City 'team', a team that you particularly relate to, or remember because of a defining factor which is usually chosen during an important stage of your life – in fact, its rather like having a favourite Doctor Who.

"I remember the players *so* well from that era – Keelan, Stringer, Forbes, Paddon, Suggett, Boyer. But my favourite player was Ted MacDougall. He didn't do an awful lot though, apart from score goals. I liked Kevin Keelan as well. At school we all used to pretend we were him when we kicked the ball, because when he did, he'd flick his left foot up as well. Kevin 'the Cat' Keelan.... (a distant, sentimental look had appeared in Ed's eyes at that point). I go as often as I can now, my dad and uncle have season tickets in the Barclay, so if one of them can't go, I get first refusal. It's a great ground and match experience now, especially when I compare it to how it was when I went to my very first game. Another game I particularly remember, for the atmosphere at Carrow Road, was the first-leg of the play-off game against Wolves. It was brilliant. The same for the home-leg in the UEFA Cup against Inter Milan. Mind you, it was different in the return-leg at Wolves that season; I went to that one alone. I wasn't an MP then, but Ian Gibson was. He had a ticket for the game but there was a vote in the House that night, so he had to go to that instead, giving me his ticket before I set off on the train.

Meanwhile, the Westminster Canaries at this time, Ian Gibson, Charles Clark (then MP for Norwich South) and Phil Webster (then Chief Political Editor of *The Times*) headed off to the Sports Bar in Leicester Square to watch it. I rang them from the ground to let them have a taste of the atmosphere, which was incredible, really fierce. And when Wolves scored, it was wild. But we always knew that, deep down, we were going to do it and get through to the play-off final, which I went to that as well. Of course, there wasn't a happy ending that time around, but we got there by winning the Championship a couple of years later. Looking back at that season, the Boxing Day fixture against Forest stands out still – I was in the Gunn Club before the game when the rumours began ricocheting around the place, which originally started when the car park attendant rang a mate to say that Darren Huckerby had been booked into the car park and was on his way – that was the first we knew of him signing, and then, of course, he went out on the pitch before kick-off with Delia."

"Looking back to that first Premier League season, however, my favourite memory is probably that first game at Arsenal. I went along to it with my dad and brother, but we couldn't get tickets for the away end, so had to go in with the home fans. We were sat opposite the main stand at Highbury and I remember the controversy about their mural, and the fact that, amongst all the supporters faces that had been painted on it, not one of them was black. Anyway, before the game, parachutists come in and tried to land on the centre circle, but one of them overshot the landing area and went out of the ground, beyond the mural and onto the building site. That was rather symbolic of Arsenal's afternoon! Okay, it looked as if it was going to be a very bad day at 2-0 down and everyone in the stand we were sitting in was happy apart from us. When Robins scored to make it 2-1 we stood up and cheered, but as we were still losing, nobody seemed to mind, but by the time City had scored their third things had got pretty tense! We had loads of Londoners yelling at us about being cider drinkers, which is, of course, what you'd expect, what with Norwich being stuck out in the West Country! Anyway, at that point we decided we'd better quieten down, so when we scored our fourth, we just hummed 'On the Ball City' to ourselves instead!"

Passionate and noisy Norwich supporters celebrating amidst an army of Gunners typifies Canaries fans, who remain determined to show their love for the team, no matter where they are, or who they are. With that thought in mind, Ed also mentioned one particular fan who garnished quite a reputation for her support at the time, demonstrated, as it was, very publicly on Sky Sports.

"Talking of Delia, on the night of 'Let's be 'aving you', I was at the club as her guest for dinner. We were playing Manchester City and had gone 2-0 up, only for the visitors to claw it back to 2-2 at the break. When half-time arrived, she turned to me and said "they're not singing like they did against

Middlesbrough a few weeks ago" when, of course, we'd been 4-1 down and fought back to 4-4 and it felt, to Delia at least, that the fans had willed the team on to earn that unlikely point. But, for this game against Manchester City, she clearly didn't feel it was the same! Anyway, Delia then added, "They're not doing it!". But nobody knew that she'd slipped off and headed onto the pitch, and I think she must have forgotten that the game was live on Sky because her appearance wasn't set up in any way at all. She just felt that if the fans reacted in the same way that they had in the game against Middlesbrough, we would won the game"

I then asked if Ed owned a Norwich shirt that he wore to matches or around the house during 'down' time perhaps... But obviously not in any sordid, David Mellor-esque way!

"Not at the moment, no, but I remember my first kit very well. I got it about 1973 and the socks were completely yellow, with no green braiding on them at all. The shorts were green with two yellow lines on each side, while the shirt was yellow with green edging around a round collar and, of course, the badge. The club then switched to Umbro, then to Admiral and it all became a bit fashionable. Mind you, I still have two of the older shirts, the Norwich and Peterborough Building Society one (Ribero, 1992-1994) and the Digital Phones one (Xara, 2001-2003)."

It couldn't have been easy for Ed to get to games in recent years when you consider his workload and the expectations of the electorate for their politicians to always be seen at, or involved in, their work, either at Parliament or in their constituencies?

"It can be a challenge sometimes, like the Millwall game in 2010 for example. We had an important vote at the House that night and nobody was let off from attending! I still went to the game though, along with Clive Efford (Labour MP for Eltham and a Millwall fan), but we HAD to be back in the House by 10pm. We had the initial vote at 7pm before taking the train to the game – me in the Norwich end, Clive in with the Millwall fans. We knew that the absolute latest we could leave in order to get back in time for the vote was 9.35pm, so we booked a cab and left the match with Norwich winning 1-0. However, Millwall equalised after we'd gone, which was a bit of a blow!"

Ed's own parliamentary seat is representing Morley and Outwood in Leeds, so I wondered if there had been, or were, any expectations from his constituents that he should do, what might be perceived as the 'right thing', and be seen supporting Leeds United?

"I have attended a Leeds game – big mistake! Delia asked me if I wanted to attend the game at Elland Road last season, so I went along and sat near to them and the others in the Director's Box, visibly in with the Norwich supporters. Now, you have to remember that, geographically, Elland Road sits about 100-metres from the edge of my constituency, something I hadn't thought about when I agreed to go along. Anyway, Leeds scored first and about 29,000 home supporters stood up to celebrate. The Norwich fans, including me of course, didn't. Then Norwich equalised and 29,000 Leeds fans are sat, in silence, apart from the MP for Morley and Outwood, who is up on his feet, clapping and cheering a goal *against* Leeds. I suddenly thought 'for God's sake, what have I done, how can I be so stupid?' I couldn't *not* stand up, I'm a Norwich fan, but at the same time, there were thousands of people looking at Delia, with me near to her, all thinking, 'what's HE doing?'. I got loads of abuse from Leeds fans, 'how dare you' etc, terrible! It's the only game I've ever been to where the scores have been level (2-2) and I've wanted the final whistle to blow – if Norwich had got a winner, I'd have been lynched!"

I wondered if Ed's wife, a fellow politician (Yvette Cooper, MP for Normanton, Pontefract and Castleford) shared his passion for the beautiful game?

"Yvette has got used to me getting quite dejected about football over the years, especially in the 90s when things weren't always going terribly well at Norwich. I'd look for the result, see we'd lost and she'd just say, 'well, what did you expect?' But no, she isn't a fan as such, she just went through those years smiling sympathetically at me whenever Norwich lost. Mind you, in the last couple of years or so, she's been silenced, which is a nice change, as it was quite destabilising for the family whenever we City were down in the third pier. Another time when we were able to celebrate as City fans was the previous time we were promoted back to the Premier League in 2004, again, against all expectations. Of course, we have performed very well on our return to the Premier League in 2011/12, but it felt different back then compared to this time around. I didn't feel that the 2004/05 team was quite strong enough for the Premier League, and our two big signings, Helveg and Jonson, didn't look quite right. City didn't really have a goal threat until we signed Dean Ashton. If we had forged the striking partnership between Ashton and Leon McKenzie earlier, who knows? But we *nearly* survived that season and we needed to win at Fulham in the last game to stay up. I went to Craven Cottage and sat six rows back directly behind the goal, so we were watching the match through the net. And I just remember watching that net bulge in front of me, what a thoroughly bad day, with the team looked as if they had fallen apart. It feels so different now. The whole set-up now is different at Carrow Road, it's fantastic. But, however well we are doing, there does seem to be this deep Norfolk pessimism surrounding some of the games especially from my dad and uncle, which I don't understand."

Another Carrow Road highlight is the day I got to play on the pitch, and although I'm out of condition, I still play for the MP's team sometimes. Ian Gibson had arranged for a political team to play against a team of Norwich City All Stars, which was great, but we didn't play in the 'real' goals, which was a bit disappointing, but at least I can say that I've scored at Carrow Road! I love being around the club and the stadium. I stayed at the Holiday

Inn Hotel overlooking the ground during Sky's coverage of the Labour Party leadership contest, which was held in Norwich two summers ago, and when the booking was made, I requested a room with a view of the ground, and although there was no match on that week, I just want to be able to wake-up, open the curtains and gaze at the pitch!"

I could empathise with Ed on that point, having often stayed at the hotel myself and have made exactly the same request – I wholeheartedly agree, there doesn't need to be a game, just the opportunity to gaze out onto the green of Carrow Road is enough for me – the slightly eccentric behaviour of a besotted supporter. Ed Balls is clearly a big City fan, but would Ed ever consider taking his involvement with the club a step further, as Delia Smith and Stephen Fry have done, or to a similar level as his Parliamentary colleague, David Milliband, has at Sunderland? His answer was; "I think I'd have to consider anything that was asked of me as I'm sure it would be a pleasure..." so watch this space perhaps!

Chatting to Ed in his office at Portcullis House in London had also been a genuine pleasure and, as we talked, it was easy to forget the surroundings, the security, the sense of history and political power that is encapsulated within in the building, which included the very clear sounds made by Big Ben every quarter of an hour. Ed may be a high-profile politician, but, for the hour or so that we together, we were just two Norwich fans chatting and reminiscing about the team we care so much about. I was, and remain, grateful to Ed and his Westminster team for taking the time out for him to be able to contribute to this book.

February 1993 saw several clubs make moves to remove their Managers – at Stamford Bridge, Chelsea Manager, Ian Porterfield, he who had so openly criticised Dave Beasant following their home defeat to Norwich back in September, was fired on February 15th with the club wallowing in 11th place. Having already poached Fleck, brows were briefly set to 'furrow' mode in Norfolk – would Ken Bates now launch another Carrow Road raid? Was Mike Walker seen a possible replacement for Porterfield? Thankfully Bates stayed away from Norfolk as Chelsea's stellar ambitions to build for a glorious and long-lasting dynasty at Stamford Bridge was reflected in their appointment of former Bournemouth, Torquay and Southend Manager, David Webb. What must have Fleck thought? Although the former City favourite looks back fondly at his time at Chelsea, and describes Webb as a "decent and honest guy", he also admits to being puzzled at Webb's decision to play him as a right-sided midfielder in one game.

Porterfield's former club, Sunderland, had also gone shopping for a new Manager earlier in the month, replacing the sacked Malcolm Crosby with Terry Butcher. Just nine months earlier Crosby had led Sunderland to the FA Cup final by virtue of *that* win over City, but ultimately it counted for nothing, for as great an achievement as it was for the Black Cats, the club demanded to be in the Premier League and it didn't look as if Crosby was going to take them there.

February was also the month that the Premier League's first sponsor was unveiled. The £12 million cash injection came courtesy of the Bass Brewery, but in the guise of Carling, who agreed to pump a frothy fortune into the game in a four-year agreement. Lager and football were obvious and suitable bedfellows, it was, after all, the liquid refreshment of fans and players alike and, without wishing this to be a plug, if anyone suspects that the footballers of the 90's were all tee-total, I suggest they read the autobiographies of both Mark Ward and Paul Merson to see just *how* excellent a choice of sponsor the Premier League had made!

Carling would now be looking to see who the first winners of their new plaything would be – would the ribbons on the Premier League trophy be blue and white or claret and blue? Nobody seemed to think there was much chance of them being yellow and green anymore. But City's ambitions were certainly not finished yet... one of the Canaries' games in April is still hailed as one of the finest ever been played at Carrow Road, by fans and players alike.

Take me to your Leader

Depending on their age, most Canaries fans will have a specific name which springs to mind whenever the position of the Norwich City Captain is mentioned. For those who bathed in the glory of the run to the FA Cup Semi Finals in 1959, there has only ever been one Captain of the club.

Ron Ashman was at Norwich for nearly 20 years, making his debut in 1947 and going on to appear in 662 games for the club (including a run of 192 consecutive games between 1950 and 1954); 590 of which were League appearances – a club record for an outfield player that is unlikely to be broken. Originally a centre-forward, Ron eventually settled as a left-sided defender, and, as well as captaining the side in those triumphant FA Cup successes against Manchester United and Tottenham (a Cup run that ran to 11 matches, when a team can win it in six!), he also had the honour of holding aloft the club's first ever major trophy, that being the League Cup in 1962, after City beat Rochdale over two legs. Along with Kevin Keelan, Ashman went on to appear in 17 successive seasons for the club (to put that into some sort of perspective, Adam Drury, Norwich's current longest serving player at the time of writing, would need to be still lining up for the Canaries in the opening game of the 2017/18 season to match that achievement!), also, if that was not impressive enough, he scored in 11 successive seasons for the club as well as being an ever present in five solid campaigns. In short, for many years, he was Norwich City, the living, breathing, tough-tackling, gentlemanly, life and soul of the club, the sort of devoted player that so many teams seemed to have at that time, yet are so rare in today's with the modern easy-come, easy-go attitude of so many professional footballers. Then, having retired as a player, Ron then served the club as Manager from 1962 to 1966.

Ashman was a comic book character come to life, a comparison that is not meant, in any way, to belittle the man or his character, indeed, I make the comparison with due reverence. Throughout the 1950s and the following two decades, the popular comics of the day all featured stories about men, granite jawed, loyal, strong and decent, one for whom values and morals came above all other things, along with clean and healthy living and exercise. The list of these characters is a long one. I grew up reading about Roy Race and his footballing exploits, which often bordered on the miraculous, but somehow, always seemed believable. He stoically led Melchester Rovers to trophy after trophy, with victory often coming at the expense of teams rampant with players of dubious character, he of the pencil-thin moustache or the sneaky latino, smouldering star of the 'crack' (they were always 'crack'!) Italian or Spanish sides that Roy, thanks to his love of fair play and decency, would inevitably overcome. And there were others – Alf Tupper, the 'tough' of the track; described by Simon Turnbull of the Independent as "The welder-cum-world-beating runner from the grimy grim-up-north backstreets of Greytone. After a hard day slaving under the bonnet of a truck, Alf would stop off at Aunt Meg's cafe for a steaming mug of tea and a fish supper, hitch a lift down to London, get to the White City with a minute to spare and overcome his customary mid-race tumble to pip some toff, or Eastern European hulk, on the line. 'I've run 'em,' he would cry as he breasted the tape..."

The creators of Race, Tupper, and others like them, could have used Ashman as their template. His background was by no means exceptional; he was born in the small Cambridgeshire town of Whittlesey in 1926, thus a Fenman by birth, honest, proud and true, qualities he took into his life and game. He was a bakery worker, enjoying his football with an Eastern Counties Air Training Corps team when Norwich came calling. Ashman put duty first and became a Bevin boy, determined to contribute to the war effort, moving to Nottinghamshire to fulfil his duties, with Norwich permitting him to combine his work with playing for Peterborough United, then a non-League team. He duly served throughout the war, before accepting professional terms at Norwich in 1946.

So there was no nonsense about Ashman – he knew where his priorities lay and carried out his duties to the very best of his abilities whenever he was asked, and until he was no longer required to continue. In 12 Canary Greats, Terry Allcock, describes his former team-mate as "A good pro... tremendous work ethic... and always very physical..." You knew where you were with Ron Ashman!

If it seems a little odd that I am devoting time and words to a figure from Norwich's distant past, bear with me. The purpose of detailing aspects of Ashman's life and time with the club is done in an attempt to draw parallels with those who shared the honour (as he would have seen it) of being Captain of Norwich City football club in later years, specifically the man who had been given the honour under Mike Walker during 1992/93.

Cup runs aside, Ashman captained Norwich at a time when they were considered a relatively unknown outpost and was Captain of Norwich during one of the worst seasons of our entire history, when the club finished bottom of Division Three (South) in 1957, following a run of 25 League matches without a win, not to mention a First Round FA Cup exit at the hands of non-League Bedford Town. Yet, just two years later, Ashman led the club to within 90 minutes of an FA Cup final place, as well as finishing fourth in the 'all new' Division Three (without the 'South' bit)! One year later Norwich were promoted, the year after that they finished fourth in Division Two, with only a run of five defeats in their last ten League games preventing Ron from leading Norwich to Division One for the first time in their history, some eleven years before Duncan Forbes achieved the feat. There was also that victory in the League Cup in 1962.

For any team to have experienced such a dramatic turnaround in its fortunes, over such a short period of time, you have to look to the effect of the Captain on and off the field of play. Ashman dragged Norwich up by their bootlaces, demanded the same high standards from others that he produced himself and was not shy to let his team-mates know if they had not performed accordingly. Ashman would have related to Canaries' defender Joe Hannah, who, after an appearance that he deemed to be unsatisfactory, 'punished' himself by walking home after that game – the trudge from Norwich to Sheringham being a distance of about 25 miles!

Ashman was therefore Norwich's leader, and, quite possibly, the club's greatest-ever Captain. He led by example having earned immense respect from his team-mates, men who would all have referred to him as 'Skip' or 'Captain', in much the same way that modern players refer to their Managers as 'Boss' or 'Gaffer'. In short, it was an era when the role of Captain really meant something to the supporters as well as the players as it marked you out as a leader of men, someone to look up to, the man in charge. Was it so very different, three decades on from when Ashman lifted the League Cup aloft and was carried, like some triumphant ancient gladiator, up upon the shoulders of his team-mates?

Norwich's Captain for the Premier League's inaugural season was Ian Butterworth. Comparisons between him and Ashman can be drawn if you look hard enough, despite the 30-year divide that separates their playing careers, as well as the enormous changes that had occurred in the game between Ashman's time and Butterworth's arrival at Carrow Road. For a start, they were both defenders (Ashman a left-sided one, Butterworth a centre-back, or 'stopper' as Ron would have said) although Ian Butterworth, as a player, was anything other than an old-fashioned 'stopper'. They also had connections with Nottinghamshire – Ashman had worked as a wartime Bevin boy in the county, whilst Butterworth had joined Norwich from Nottingham Forest. And both had a spell as the Manager at City – Ashman for three and a half years, Butterworth for one game. However, in all other aspects, the differences between the men, their careers and their time spent in the game are stellar. Ashman may have led Norwich to unexpected successes in the Cup, but that had been as a lower division side, where such achievements were secondary to the team's existence. Butterworth, on the other hand, prior to the Premier League opening fixture for Norwich at Arsenal, had already played in another two FA Cup semi-finals, as well as a team that had finished fourth in Division One, as opposed to bottom of Division Three South! The same role, the same club, but certainly a very different game.

I met up with Ian to talk about his recollections from the time he spent at Norwich, and from a career that saw him make nearly 300 appearances and play under four very different City Managers.

THE CAPTAIN

started by saying how I thought it was sometimes overlooked that Butterworth, along with some of his team-mates, had played in more than
just one good Norwich team, having also contributed to the success of
the Canaries under both Ken Brown and Dave Stringer.

"Yes, in the season I signed for Norwich (1986/87) we finished fifth
under Ken and then fourth two years later under Dave Stringer – we should
have qualified for Europe on both occasions. I joined on loan originally, Ken
signed me from Nottingham Forest and immediately put me into the side
for my debut at Aston Villa, alongside Steve Bruce. We won 4-1, which was
a great start! I played three more games before going back to Forest, but I
wasn't getting a game under Cloughie, and although I played to the best of
my ability when I *was* picked, I was having a bad time. I just wanted to play,
so when Norwich put in a bid of £160,000 for me at the beginning of December, I moved on. I was delighted to make the move permanent, although, I
didn't really appreciate how long it took me to drive to Norwich when I had
been there on loan! I remember travelling along the A47 with Ken Brown and
Nigel Pleasants (the Club Secretary at the time), and remarked to them; 'This
road just goes on forever, doesn't it?' Ken just looked at me and said; 'You'll
get used to it!' And I did get used to it, along with all those long coach jour-

A captain and a gentleman... Ian Butterworth

neys that were to come. Ken put his faith in me and I played regularly, Brucie (Steve Bruce) was here at the time, as was Shaun Elliott, who got injured, so I initially came in for him – I ended up playing alongside Brucie for just over a year and really enjoyed it. We had a decent season or so together and, during my time at Norwich, City had top-flight finishes of fifth, fourth and third. That was good going. Remember, we were a small club, we didn't pay massive wages, neither could we attract the very top players, but the crowds were good."

Ian started his career alongside Stuart Pearce at Coventry City and, while at Highfield Road, played in a game many Canaries fans would rather forget.

"Yes, I was in the Coventry side that won against Everton and put Norwich down! We had to win our last three games to avoid the drop at the expense of Norwich, which we did! Mind you, Everton had just won the League, and drafted in several reserves on the day, but we wanted that win. It was a really hot Sunday morning and we played well, got the win and put Norwich down. Everybody thought Norwich had done enough, but we proved them all wrong. Of course, the authorities have since changed the way the fixtures are played at the end of a season, and rightly so."

"Although I am a real traditionalist when it comes to football, it *was* an exciting time when Sky arrived on the scene in 1992 and started to put the money in – they were showing a lot of games and had a lot of choice. Clubs started spending the money on new players and improving their grounds, so there was a lot happening. When they covered the first Sky game at Norwich, we met Richard Keys and Andy Gray, who I think they did a fantastic job over the years. I liked Andy Gray, his analysis was always very good because he could relate to the ordinary football fan when he was talking about the game."

I mentioned the opening game of the Premier League season to Ian, at Arsenal. I'd raised it with his team-mates, all of whom had said how they felt the eventual result and the nature of the win had been a pivotal in defining both the side and season. What were his thoughts on that game?

"Coming in 2-0 down at half-time, what do you do? It was the first game of the season, you're away to Arsenal and they've got a two-goal advantage. But had been a pretty even game though. Well, we weren't exactly being walloped and had simply made two defensive mistakes – given away two free-kicks and conceded two goals, so Arsenal had their tails up. We chatted at half-time and all agreed that we had to go back out and get the next goal as it would be a vital one. We knew we'd come back into the game sooner or later. Anyway, Robbo scored with a header and it all snowballed from there. Then, all of a sudden, from being so flat at half-time, it was *us* who had our tails up and we were already looking forward to our next game on the Tuesday night. When your confidence is high, you can't wait. We were at home to Chelsea and we won again, despite going behind again. We kept going and then won the big Sky game against Forest, so we had a really good start and were soon clear at the top. With that impressive early run, then being clear at Christmas, I always thought that was the time we should have brought in a couple of new players, that's always the time to do it, it can make such a difference. We got Efan (Ekoku) in March, but that was a bit late, we should, perhaps, have pushed the boat out a little earlier, it might have helped push us across the line. I'm not saying we would then have won the Premier League, but we would have been a lot closer, I'm sure."

Thinking back to the start of the season, what was the reaction of the players to Mike Walker being appointed as Manager?

"We all knew Mike well, as he had been Reserve Team Manager, so most of the players got on with him OK and knew how he worked. So it was a smooth transition, he already had our respect and it progressed from there. We were happy with his appointment and he changed a few of things, as Managers always do. Gossy is the prime example perhaps, he'd played very few games for the first-team under Dave Stringer, but Mike soon elevated him to the first-team, and he really prospered, playing well and scoring some important goals. Remember, five or six of us had been together for quite a while by that stage, so we all knew each other's games, our respective strengths and weaknesses, so Mike knew what needed to be done."

"What we did improve upon that season was the pace of the side, we were quicker up front with Foxy and Chris Sutton – then Efan came onboard – none of them were slouches! All three of them worried teams, so we'd suck the opposition into us a bit, then have the option of hitting them fast on the break, or knocking the ball over the top and running at them. We had belief in ourselves, in how we played and our Manager. We were going out, playing and enjoying ourselves. We got caught out a couple of times, but, for a small, provincial, club, we did very well. We got lots of attention and media coverage – can you imagine what it would be had we won the title?"

"Certainly the extra pace that Mike brought to the side made a big difference, although if you wanted to be a little bit cynical, a little bit critical, maybe we did tend to over-play at times previously. But Mike and John Deehan were a good team and we flourished under them because of their characters and how they wanted the game played. Mike was more of a leader and motivator, whilst Dixie was very much more connected with the players on a day-to-day basis. But in the end, it's the Manager who has the final say in everything, and you do what he decides, we all knew that. So it was a good partnership, with Mike always having the final say. I learnt quite a bit about Managers while playing for Cloughie at Forest – he was a one off wasn't he? I think your opinion of your Manager changes when you play for him regularly. Then, as you get a little bit older and a little bit wiser you start to think like them – looking back at events that have happened and you realise why a Manager did this or changed that, and you start to work out why they said or did something."

"However, I don't think that, contrary to what some people say, you should automatically become detached from your players when you become a Manager, you need to have a real connection I feel, you've still got to have an element of interaction. You've got to be able to interact with people in order to work well with them and to help them improve as players, especially as a coach. I've also learnt a lot through my involvement in the game since I stopped playing having been a coach for twelve years at Hartlepool, Darlington and Cardiff, plus some time at Norwich. I've also done some work for the FA, alongside Stuart Pearce with the England U-21s. I just love being involved in football, it's like a drug! I've been in football since I was a school kid and want to stay involved, it's all I've ever known and, as I always say, it's better than working. You experience such incredible highs and lows – one season can be brilliant and you're enjoy every moment, the next and it can go horribly wrong."

"I think the Premier League been good for football, although you can argue that too many foreign players have come into our game, but some of them have been great players, and we all want to see top class football or play against the best in the world. Maybe the Premier League is recognised as being so big and important that many English players regard it as being more important than the national side, not to mentioned the absurd £200,000 a week wages that some enjoy. Can playing for England really be as important as that? There are certainly players now who I consider to be putting their club careers above the England team, saying they no longer wish to be considered, or is that because of the England Manager? Or is it down to the way young footballers who look at the England team's history in recent tournaments of only getting to the last eight at best. Are we really better than that? Should we get further and achieve more? Is the lack of success down to the players and the Premier League?"

"So, maybe the only thing that the Premier League has achieved really, is to hand clubs vast amounts of extra finance – even the clubs that get relegated receive parachute money, which doesn't create a level playing field for the other clubs. The Premier League now dictates the whole game and, quite often, the rest of football gets forgotten. The grassroots of the game in this country are the lower divisions and non-League football, which is too often overlooked – a lot of people just want to watch or talk about the Premier League. But there are a lot of good players and Managers outside the Premier League, and I wished more money could filter down further because the gap is getting bigger."

"But being in the Premier League is undoubtedly the pinnacle of the game in this country and, understandably, every club wants to be there, as do the players. It's particularly good for a club like Norwich as there's a real feel good factor in the City and throughout the community when they're doing well, And the Premier League seems recession proof – it just gets stronger and stronger and the wages get bigger and bigger – the money the players are on now, even squad players, is extraordinary."

Talking of money and salaries, I understand that City had a very good bonus structure in place at the time you were at the club.

"Ah (laughs), you've heard about that from the other lads, have you? Well, as Captain I had to go and negotiate that with 'Chasey' (Robert Chase) on behalf of the lads. We had written down lots of figures on a piece of paper, which I presented to the Chairman. Anyway, Chasy has a very good look at it, before saying; 'Yes, yes, this all looks very good…" he then paused and looked at me, before continuing, 'But you're having this!' To be fair, he was quite good in that he offered, although the wages were low but incentives were high. And that was that, if a player didn't agree, if they wanted more money, they'd have to go elsewhere! In retrospect, I think the system in place worked well, for one thing it meant that the club didn't have too many financial worries at that stage because of the new players that were brought in or the wage structure. Yes, Robert Chase had his faults, but we had an excellent bonus system, which was forward-thinking enough to have included us playing in the UEFA Cup, as well as just winning matches. Remember, we weren't a big City club, and although our wages were decent, they weren't high by any means."

"But, we did get rewarded for winning and, in that period, we won a lot of games. If we won one it was so much, two a little bit more, and if we won five on the trot, we were laughing. So we did a lot of laughing! We had a great bunch of lads at the club who all got on well, which is important. And because of all of those long journeys, it was great to get a result at one of the big clubs – okay, we did get a few drubbings here and there, but those trips back down the A1, the A17, the A47 always took ages, but they were great fun for the lads if we'd won."

"And we often got good results at the big stadiums in matches where we were just expected to make up the numbers – we certainly didn't go down 4-0 every time. I remember winning 2-0 on the night Gary Pallister made his debut at Old Trafford in 1989, where we had also won (2-1) the previous season – Micky Phelan and Andy Townsend scored (Norwich also beat Liverpool 1-0 at Anfield during that 1988/89 season). I also remember losing 4-1 at Liverpool during the first Premier League season, but only because I scored at the Kop end – I didn't score many! So we rarely got a drubbing from the bigger clubs and Mike Walker gave us the belief we could win games, so we went out and enjoyed them, knowing that we *could* win, which was our main objective."

Do you think that the success the club achieved during your spell at Carrow Road has worked against the club in more recent times – that people have expected more than is maybe realistic?

"No, I don't think that, I certainly didn't feel any pressure to live up to all that whilst I was on the coaching staff here, none at all. I also had the one game as Caretaker Manager (at Exeter on August 15th 2009, Norwich drew 1-1). I would have liked to have had the chance to do more, but I got caught up in everything that started to happen at the club at the time, then Paul Lambert came in and brought his own staff, you accept it that's football, that's life. I would have liked the chance to do more, but it's history now, but it was disappointing as I would have liked to have been the Manager here, but things didn't work out. That challenge is over. But I really like Norwich as a place and I have lots of fond memories of living there – my children were born there and I still have lots of friends in Norwich."

Given Ian's varied moves and experiences within the game, especially since he turned to coaching, I wondered if he was still enjoying the professional life, was he still in love with the game?

"Yes. I'm really enjoying working with the FA at the moment , where I've been after I left Cardiff, doing in-depth match and player reports. My database of players is growing all the time from watching at least three games a week, and, just lately, I've been focusing on the U-21 players. I also came to Norwich to watch Henri Lansbury, Kieran Gibbs and Ryan Bertrand when they were on loan here, as well as doing some on-going scouting for Stuart Pearce the Olympic Games in mind."

"The first part of 2012 has seen me take on another new role in football, albeit an unusual one, and that's the TV show I am doing in Turkey. We're looking at lots of young footballers in much the same way as X Factor does with singers and groups, with the winner of the show getting the opportunity to go on a year-long development programme with Liverpool. I got that job through the League Managers' Association in London. I'm the sole judge, so I get the final say on who goes through and who doesn't, I'm just like Simon Cowell! Ultimately, however, I want to get back into coaching and management in the UK, and hope to do some more scouting for the FA prior to the 2012 European Championships."

Who was the best player he had ever played against?

"I'd pick two, but for different reasons. Firstly, Graeme Souness, as he was such a great leader and Captain, and secondly, Ian Rush, as a phenomenal goalscorer. Rush was like a magnet to the ball in the area, but he also worked tirelessly in chasing the ball down and testing defences – he was so sharp, so quick. But when you are playing in the Premier League, a week doesn't go by without you having to test yourself against one of the greats, or an outstanding player in the opposition that you really look out for. At Norwich it just was like that in every game, but we acquitted ourselves and had players like Pols (John Polston) and Rob Newman –we did well, including in Europe. One of my biggest disappointments from my playing career, though, was not playing in our game against Inter Milan at the San Siro. Along with Ian Culverhouse and Ian Crook, who both missed the game too, I was ab-so-lutely GUTTED!."

Did Ian ever think that playing in those big games could have got him noticed by a bigger club?

"Yes, I thought my performances were good enough to get noticed and meritted interest in me from bigger clubs, but I was settled – Norwich were, and remain, a stable club. If you're settled, you don't really want to move anywhere, and although there were one or two rumours about me at one point, certainly earlier in my time at Norwich, when I could have left the club and moved on. But I was happy, it's a nice place to live in, the kids were growing up, so we were content, enjoying ourselves and having a good time. And, as I have said, and I'm sure the other players will tell you, we enjoyed playing there, going out and giving it a go, but doing it playing football the proper way. I certainly tried to be more than the typical centre-half and to play with the ball at my feet, but I was neither big nor physical, so I *had* to try and play. Look at someone like Crooky, he was a great passer; Gossy would run all day, so we all had our strengths and the team played to them. Players have more of an athlete's look about them these days, in all positions. I thought I was tall at 6' 2", but some of the younger lads now are 6' 4" or 6' 5". But you need to be an athlete, you need to be fit and strong. There are lots of games and you need whatever recovery time you can get. And then there's the travel time!"

"People often overlook the travelling time, but we used to have some right coach trips at Norwich. Infact, at many of my clubs, the travelling has been an issue. I was at Darlington for two years and the trips down to Torquay and Plymouth were huge – six and a half hours plus on the bus, you play the game, then travel all the way back again! We did fly to some games while I was at Norwich too: to Oldham for a Sky game where Mark Robins scored a hat-trick and to Everton which really paid off as we did them 5-1. Efan was different class that day, his pace just tore Everton apart, although I haven't come across him again since he left Norwich. But a lot of the lads still live locally and I still see them. We all try to keep fit, too, no ex-Pro wants to be fat and 50!"

Ian played in successful Norwich sides for Dave Stringer and Mike Walker, I wondered which team and Manager might have emerged victorious had they ever played one another?

"It'd be close. A lot of us could play for both sides of course – certainly the defence. Hmm, who to choose? Fleckie or Mark Robins? I'd say Fleckie. Andy Townsend, Micky Phelan or Gary Megson? It's tough, they're both good sides. It was always enjoyable, and, under Mike, we had such belief and confidence. Even when we lost 7-1 at Blackburn, we knew it was just a one-off, a fluke. We proved that by beating QPR in the next game. We had a great mix, the older players like myself, Gossy and Gary Megson, and also the younger ones who were coming through like Sutty, Ruel Fox and Lee Power. They were all good lads, with lots of energy and enthusiasm. We all got on and that showed on the pitch, we did well, we won lots of games... and of course, the banters always better when you're winning!"

Norwich City celebrate Tony Henry's own goal during the Oldham win

One thing that came across loud and clear during our conversation was Ian's passion and love for the game. Ian's involvement in football has continued since his playing retirement and, unlike so many players in the top flight, has not shirked from taking coaching jobs with lower division clubs, which include stints at Darlington, Bristol Rovers and Hartlepool before his brief return to Norwich, and that one game as Caretaker Manager.

So, back to March 1993, a month that coincided with one of Ian's infrequent spells out with injury, the Canaries' defender missing out on all seven of Norwich's Premier League fixtures during the month. Thankfully, City's record over these seven games was fairly respectable, with four wins, one draw and two defeats. Both losses came in London, with QPR triumphing 3-1 on March 3rd, while Wimbledon prevailed 3-0 at Plough Lane on March 20th, Dean Holdsworth scoring twice.

On a more positive note, three of the wins came in consecutive matches; 1-0 at Sheffield United on March 10th (Fox); the same score at home to Oldham three days later (admittedly fortuitously via a Tony Henry own goal) and 3-0 at Nottingham Forest on March 17th (Robins, Power and Crook) – the one draw coming at the start of the month, with Arsenal's Ian Wright earning a late point at Carrow Road in a 1-1 draw.

The highlight of the month however, and, quite possibly, of the season, was the visit to Carrow Road of fellow title chasers Aston Villa on March

24th. The game had everything and was a *real* end-to-end thriller, which was described, in suitably lyrical tones, by Kevin Baldwin in *Norfolk 'n' Good* as follows... "Both teams performed with exceptional skill, speed, strength and subtlety. The passing and movement were mesmerising..." Which it was! Dean Saunders had a goal disallowed, while Garry Parker missed the most open of open goals in front of the Barclay before, with less than ten minutes to go, a very unusual goal scorer popped up in the Villa penalty area and scrambled the ball home past a desperate Mark Bosnich. John Polston's timely intervention created, quite possibly, the loudest cheer at Carrow Road that season, and, with previous results not being entirely unfavourable to Norwich, the night ended with City back on top of the Premier League with just six league games to play. Next up? Norwich City versus Manchester United, April 5th 1993. Be there!

Canaries and Devils

So, for Norwich City, it had come to this. The FA's blueprint for the future of English football, its "whole new ball game", the dancing girls, fireworks and wall-to-wall coverage on Sky, the glitz and glamour, the excitement and expectation, the drama and its cast of celebrity characters – Cantona, Sheringham, Shearer, Strachan, Beardsley et al – had come down to a title decider at Carrow Road, Norwich. The country bumpkins, the original (and best) tractor boys, the eternal pride of East Anglia, the City known for its mustard and proximity to the Norfolk Broads, against the nation's favourites, the glitz and the glamour, every fans' 'second' team. Devoid of a title since 1967 and, according to many, unjustly denied the last ever First Division Championship by Leeds United the previous season (the only thing anyone had ever liked about Leeds that year was Eric Cantona, and he now played for the Red Devils, so that had worked out well); Manchester United had kept pace with Norwich for much of the season without really threatening to pull away and leave the Canaries choking in their thoroughbred wake. Now, however, they had a chance.

The meeting at Old Trafford earlier in the season had been a curiously static affair. It wasn't as much that United did enough to win; more that Norwich had done just about enough to narrowly lose. The game saw Eric Cantona make his full debut, in a side packed with attacking talent from the likes of Lee Sharpe, Mark Hughes, Brian McClair and Ryan Giggs, who were all in the same starting XI as the enigmatic man from Marseilles – five of the best offensive players in the country at the time, and all with yellow and green in their sights. Mike Walker, fresh from winning the Manager of the Month award for November, decided to counter fire with fire and picked an attacking line-up too – Crook pulling the strings in midfield with the pace provided by United old boy Robins and Fox – aligned to the physical force of Darren Beckford, who had been surprisingly selected ahead of Chris Sutton.

It had, on paper at least, all the makings of a classic. And clearly having been instructed to take the game to their opponents, Norwich started well, with Crook's influence in the centre of the pitch proving invaluable. It was therefore unfortunate for Norwich that their play-maker had to depart with a calf muscle injury after barely ten minutes, and although City had a midfield replacement on the bench in Megson, with due respect, it was like replacing Michelangelo with Rolf Harris and still expecting a half-decent job on the Sistine Chapel roof. "Can you tell what it is yet?" "Nope, but it looks like a comedy kangaroo".

This is not to denigrate Megson, as his experience and big game know-how had been exactly the reason Walker had fought so strongly to sign him the previous summer. An endearing image of Megson's time at Norwich, and a demonstration of his value to the club, came as early as that first game at Arsenal – when Norwich scored the first goal to get back in the match, amongst the celebrations, was the figure of Megson, fist clenched, grounding his excited team-mates, demanding more of them. It was only after Robins had sealed the victory with Norwich's fourth goal that Megson allowed himself to be drawn into the 'here and now', and he leapt onto Robins with a broad smile on his face – his job done.

So perhaps Walker had that in mind when he named Megson as substitute for the game against United? He would serve a dual purpose – come on if we are losing and drive us forward in much the same way he had at Highbury – or, with the game looking won, make a cameo appearance and slap down any signs of complacency as the seconds ticked away. He was a good option to have on the bench, but to come on after barely ten minutes, replacing perhaps the most important player in the Norwich side? Hmmmm, not so good. On the day Megson did what he did best – hurrying, worrying, snapping and stealing – but with the United midfield featuring a younger Paul Ince, he had to work hard to win that particular battle, never mind influence the game in the way Crook could.

With barely any back-lift or change of glance, Crook could change a game, the angle of attack, the ebb and flow of a football match. United had to respect him and the influence he had on any match. Ince had, no doubt, been expecting a hard afternoon trying to read Crook's intentions, so it was as much a relief for him as it was a blow for Norwich when his willowy figure departed the scene prematurely. As far as Ince was concerned, Megson was an older version of himself – he not only knew what Megson would be doing, he also knew what he'd be thinking – perhaps even before Megson had thought it himself. In that time after Crook's departure therefore, the game began to ebb away from Norwich, their element of surprise had gone, and, in a game full of metaphors, City's stealth fighter had been replaced by a Hercules transporter, he did the job, but wasn't really capable of carrying out much collateral damage.

It began to show. Half-time was approaching when United carved out not one, but two good chances to score, the first coming from Cantona. Worry-ingly, as United began to chip away at the Norwich defences, little squabbles began to break out in the Norwich ranks; the Canaries were rattled in their cages, something that, without doubt, Alex Ferguson would have pointed out to his side at the interval.

United broke the deadlock just before the hour mark – a typically inquisi-tive cross from Lee Sharpe took an unfortunate deflection off of Daryl Sutch and fell, invitingly, to the feet of Mark Hughes. In such circumstances, maybe referees should just stop play and award the goal, because Hughes, in his pomp, didn't miss those sort of opportunities and so it proved – 1-0 to United.

Walker then brought Sutton on to replace Beckford, but the damage had been done, and the game was lost. Norwich had acquitted themselves well however, a narrow defeat at Old Trafford was certainly no disgrace, and the players could hold their heads high, and so on, and so forth. What wasn't mentioned in the wake of that loss was just how well the team had per-formed at the self-titled Theatre of Dreams in recent seasons.

February 1984
Manchester United 0 Norwich City 0
United had been second going into this match, while Norwich were still licking their wounds from a 3-0 defeat at Forest in their preceding game. United, with the likes of Wilkins, Robson, Muhren, Stapleton and Whiteside were overwhelming favourites to win and maintain their challenge for the title under Ron Atkinson, however, Ken Brown's side performed magnificently to secure the point, with John Devine outstanding.

December 1986
Manchester United 0 Norwich City 1
It gets better! Nearly 45,000 at Old Trafford (a big crowd at the time up there) attended for the obligatory post-Christmas stuffing of some unfortu-nate bird, but were left crying into their left-overs when Kevin Drinkell scored

in a 1-0 win for Norwich – their first at Old Trafford in 16 visits! A day earlier, United had won at Champions Liverpool.

October 1988
Manchester United 1 Norwich City 2

There were all sorts of things "wrong" with this result! Firstly, Norwich went into the game as Division One leaders, having won six of their opening eight games. United, in stark contrast, were in mid-table. However, parity seemed to be restored when United, through that man Hughes, opened the scoring. The fabric that holds the time/space continuim together had previously been ripped asunder when United were awarded their obligatory "come on ref, help us out" penalty, only for McClair to see his effort saved by Gunn. The carnage continued. Norwich equalised with just over five minutes remaining, through a long-range drive from Phelan (surely sealing his pending move to Old Trafford where, of course, he remains to this day) I wonder if he ever thinks "what if I had never scored that goal for Norwich here?" That was followed, a minute later, by Townsend's winner. Dave Stringer's side thus prevailed, and to add insult to United injury, won the return match at Carrow Road the following February by the same score.

August 1989
Manchester United 0 Norwich City 2

Another League success for Norwich at Old Trafford, but the result was no longer so shocking. Familiar scenes at Old Trafford saw Bryan Robson departing the scene with an injury, and while last time out Norwich had defied the footballing gods with Gunn saving McClair's penalty, in 1989, the Canaries were awarded one of their own. Fleck converted and, with Dale Gordon having opened the scoring in the first-half, it seals another City victory. Not a particularly happy debut for United's £2.3 Million record signing, Gary Pallister, who was given a veritable run-around by the effervescent Fleck.

So, at that stage City's Old Trafford form had been rather favourable, although the Canaries' golden spell in the 1980s had not been a one-off by any means. As far back as 1967, and as a Second Division side, we had gone there for an FA Cup Third Round match and won 2-1 – the goals coming from Don Heath and Gordon Bolland. An extraordinary result, but one which remains in the shadow of the more famous Carrow Road victory over United in 1959. So there would have been optimism for Walker and his men prior to that first meeting of the season in 1992, and for good reason. Norwich were the form side that had recently run up five consecutive League wins over the Old Trafford outfit. Norwich City didn't go into the match as favourites, naturally, they rarely do, but there was certainly more of an air of expectancy than simply of hope. And perhaps it was that factor that ultimately led to a performance that lacked some of the sparkle of previous visits? Did Walker's side, unfeasibly for a Norwich team, feel the pressure of being expected to win at Old Trafford? Probably not. Walker's side may have been full of self belief and confidence in its own abilities, but they wouldn't have gone to Old Trafford in any other state of mind than that of being totally committed and motivated. Norwich would have gone there to win and with a plan in place to make that happen, and pivotal to that, would have been the influence of Ian Crook. His early loss meant a sudden and unexpected change to the Canaries pre-game plan and also the sudden departure of lady luck, which was best exemplified when Mark Robins' goal-bound effort was kept out by Schmeichel's feet.

In all of those aforementioned Old Trafford highlights, Norwich had got points that, while extremely welcome, were neither expected, or, in the bigger scheme of things, critical to the bigger picture. But this time, by their own standards, City had fallen short. There would be a reckoning of course, but few outside of Norfolk (or even inside the county if I'm honest) thought the return match at Carrow Road would take on the importance that it ultimately did. A group of players within the confines of Carrow Road would almost certainly have been amongst those who felt that the title race could go to the wire – and it would be them and Manchester United who were still fighting it out for the glory, four, long months later as it turned out.

Bryan Gunn played in all three of the Canaries League victories at Old Trafford in that five-year spell between 1984 and 1989, keeping a clean sheet on two occasions, and, notably, saving that Brian McClair penalty, which he cites in his excellent autobiography, *In Where It Hurts*, as his second best ever penalty save. So which was his best? That, apparently, came against McClair again, a year earlier, when Norwich narrowly lost 2-1. Gunn also played in that single-goal defeat in December 1992, as well as the "title decider". Indeed, Gunn played for Norwich against Manchester United a total of 18 times (16 League, two FA Cup), a period that saw the Canaries secure those five successive League wins, plus two more in the FA Cup.

A respectable record, but then we are talking about a special person, both as a goalkeeper and as a man – somebody who represented the club as a keeper, as a coach and as the club Manager (amongst other responsibilities) for nearly a quarter of a century between 1986 and 2009. Gunn's playing time at Carrow Road saw him serve six Managers: Ken Brown, Dave Stringer, Mike Walker (twice), John Deehan, Gary Megson (twice) and Martin O'Neill - so to say that he'd witnessed a handful of ups, downs and controversies in his time at Carrow Road would be an understatement.

I met up with Bryan to discuss his time in football, including his brief stint as City Manager, and Gunn's current role within the game, which sees him working with some of the best young players in the country.

THE BIG MAN

Gunny clearing his lines

had avidly followed Bryan's career at Norwich since my London-based University days back in 1986, when my mother had sent me a clipping from the sports pages of the Eastern Daily Press with the comment, 'we've signed a Scottish goalkeeper!' I wasn't worried, though, as the photo showed a smiling Gunny shaking hands with then Norwich Manager Ken Brown, a man who had an uncanny knack of making terrific signings, so I thought that maybe, just maybe, we had got ourselves a 'good 'un'. Along with thousands of other Norwich City supporters, I wasn't about to be disappointed! I opened by asking Bryan about his new role in the game, one that has meant him leaving Norwich and Norfolk, his home since 1986. Gunn was in his early twenties when he signed for Norwich from Aberdeen, and I wondered how he ended up in Norfolk rather than Glasgow Rangers?

"Yes. I had a very good relationship with Walter Smith who was the Rangers Caretaker Manager, as well as the Scotland U-21 Manager at that time, so I saw quite a lot of him as I was playing more frequently for the Scotland U-21 side than I was for Aberdeen. I knew Walter Smith liked me, and I'd also had a conversation with Fergie (now Sir Alex Ferguson) who had agreed to help get me a move to a bigger club, providing that I stayed at Aberdeen for another year, which I did. I didn't ask again, stayed for the 1985/86 season and played in quite a few games – I was also in the team for the games leading up to the 1986 Scottish Cup final – so I thought I had a good chance of playing in that."

"However, as well as I had been doing, Alex Ferguson told me shortly before the final that he was putting Jim Leighton back in the side – Jim was his first choice and he was sticking with him. He added that there was also Scotland's 1986 World Cup finals campaign to think of, which wasn't far off – Jim was the number one for the national side as well. Jim's injury, which had led to my run in the side, had been a nasty one, he'd been cleaning the blades on his lawnmower while it was still plugged in, and while he was doing so, his daughter inadvertently switched the mower on. Most people would have lost their fingers, Jim, however, had lightening reflexes and pulled his away just in time. Even so, he did lose the tip of one finger."

"So I was disappointed to be dropped, and although we won the Cup, I didn't really feel part of the achievement. I'd celebrated the cup win with the lads, but I'd fully expected to be on the pitch celebrating with them as part of the team. I did have a move to Rangers to look forward to though, so I decided to look forward, not back. With the season over I went off on holiday, paid for with my bonus money and hoping the next time I would be celebrating, it would be on the pitch with Rangers, maybe having beaten Aberdeen."

"Anyway, off I went on holiday and some drunken nights followed, but one morning, I was sat flicking through the Scottish Daily Record, as you do, and there was a big story claiming that Peter Shilton was a target for Rangers. That put me in a state of shock, followed by another drunken night. When I eventually woke up the next morning, there was another headline in the Record, this one reporting that Chris Woods had signed for Rangers from Norwich City. That spoilt my holiday to say the least. Obviously, at that time, there were no mobile phones so I had to wait – heading straight over to Pittodrie as soon as I got back."

"The boss just looked at me and said; 'Sorry, I didn't see that coming... but, Ken Brown is very interested in you, and they're looking to take you to Norwich on my recommendation.' Norwich had just been promoted and I'd seen them on TV a few times, so I was up for a move to Carrow Road. So I trained really hard during pre-season with that move in mind, then, just as the new season was about to get going, Jim Leighton got injured again meaning I was back in the Aberdeen first-team, which I feared would delay the move. However, it did give Norwich the chance to see me in action and to see first-hand what Fergie had recommended. I remember that Mel Machin came up to check me out during a League Cup game against Alloa."

"Before the game, we were having our pre-match meal, when I noticed Mel sitting next to Alex Ferguson, who introduced me to the Norwich Assistant Manager. I was thinking; 'OK Bryan, you need to play well tonight'. I then had another thought – we were playing Alloa at home, so maybe I wouldn't have that much to do! When I was out for the pre-match warm up I noticed Mel down by the tunnel watching me, so I had the best possible warm up I could – it was just like an audition. I think that visit rubber-stamped the move for me, and although I had one save to make late on in the game, I think Mel had left by then. Anyway, things moved on from there, and by October I'd signed for Norwich. I travelled down to meet Ken Brown at the airport, and that was that."

"I was very ambitious and already an U-21 international, but the move helped me to step up the pecking order for selection for the full Scotland side I think. Campbell Money was my main rival at U-21 level at the time, so the move was a big opportunity. Before I left, Fergie took me to one side and said; 'You're a top six keeper, and, with all due respect to Norwich, you can eventually achieve more.' Archie Knox, Fergie's Assistant, spoke to me as well, but he rather bizarrely said that he thought Norfolk was a place where people went to die! But that didn't stop me!"

"So Fergie had said that I was a top six keeper, and I was. In my first season at Norwich we finished fifth in Division One, then, two seasons later, we finished fourth under Dave Stringer. Then, of course, in the first season under Mike Walker, we ended up finishing third! So, a fifth, a fourth, a third… Fergie was right, but I was able to prove that and achieve it with Norwich rather than elsewhere. I remember there were rumours at one time that Tottenham were interested in me as a potential replacement for Ray Clemence, I was aware of all the press speculation at the time, but nothing came of it all and Spurs eventually signed Erik Thorstvedt while I was signed a new contract with Norwich that took me up to the 1990 World Cup finals. I was then offered another new deal with improved terms, but what was equally important was that I was able to remain at a club where I was happy and enjoying my football."

That was, I pointed out, a common factor amongst many of the Norwich players at that time who I had spoken to – they all loved living in the area and playing for Norwich.

"That's very true. As far as the money side of things was concerned, our basic wage was nothing like what the top clubs were paying at the time, which was underlined when City players moved on and told us what they were earning at their new clubs. No, our basic wages were very modest in comparison to many clubs, but our incentive scheme and bonuses were far superior to other clubs'. You have to give credit to Robert Chase for that. The more games we won, the more money we made, and, when we finished third, we got a bonus for qualifying for Europe. So, in an achieving team, there was no real reason to want to move on really. So I did end up being that top level keeper that Alex Ferguson said I would become."

Bryan had a great career at Norwich, as a player, as well as a variety of roles within the club and community, after cementing a great reputation and as an increasingly popular figure around Norfolk. It had always seemed inevitable, to me at least, that Bryan would be appointed Manager at some stage, but given what subsequently happened, and how his tenure in charge of the club had ended, had it made him want a fresh start and to move away from Norwich completely?

"Having the chance to be Norwich Manager was an unexpected opportunity. When such things arise, you often have a very short amount of time to make the decision, and as far as the Manager's job was concerned, I had only had a day to make up my mind. After the 4-0 win against Barnsley (January 17th 2009) I had the next day, the Sunday, in which to decide. I had been in Burnham Market at a friend's party that weekend, and I didn't really join in as much as I wanted to, as I was thinking about the Manager's job. We'd won against Barnsley, and won well, but I knew if it had been a 4-0 defeat, things would have been very different! Anyway, I had a quick decision to make and I knew the Board were interviewing on the Monday, with various names being linked as favourites for the job in the press, and I eventually thought; 'I'm going to have a go at this'. I immediately spoke to the Chairman and Neil Doncaster to let them know that I wanted to be considered and I was fortunate to get bolted on at the end of Monday's interview schedule."

"I'd already spoken to John Deehan and Ian Crook, who was in Australia at the time, who told me, 'I'll get on the plane now, shall I?' 'Hang on mate' I told him, 'I haven't got the job yet!' Another person very much at the forefront of my mind was Ian Butterworth, who was under contract at Hartlepool, but I wanted him as part of my coaching team, along with Dixie and Ian Crook – that was the management team that I proposed to the Board late on that Monday afternoon. It was a full-on interview, and although other candidates had come in with laptop presentations and different things, I just came in armed with my passion and knowledge of the football club – I expressed the belief that I could, along with the team I'd proposed, come in and do a good job."

"So it had all happened very quickly; from the Barnsley game, to making my decision, to contacting the others, then attending the interview – then, that same Monday night, at about 11pm, the phone rang, and that was it, I'd got the job, which was great. Of course, it changed everything. I spoke to the family about becoming Manager and about how things would change. I knew what a different job was in store for me, with lots of press involvement, more pressure, and no guarantees. But I wanted to do it, and the pressure was on from the off."

"I felt we had to change things around straight away as we'd had a lot of loan players at the club – I knew some had bad attitudes and needed to be sent back to their parent clubs. Turning things around was a massive task, and yes, there were some bad results, especially at the end of my time in the job. There are a lot of fine dividing lines in football though and, when I look back at it, the width of a post here, or with a different refereeing decision there, then things could have been different. But I was able to bring in some new players, amongst them Grant Holt. His coming to Carrow Road was a legacy of the scouting that I'd done with Peter Grant and Glenn Roeder; Holt was amongst the group of players that I'd been watching and was one that I was able to go out and sign. His arrival, of course, is a tribute to both the fans and Michael Foulger. Grant was the 'marquee' signing at the time – I'd seen him play on a number of occasions and was sure he'd be able to do a job for us and I'm genuinely delighted that it all worked out so well for him and Norwich City, he's done so well and has now proved his talent at the highest level of the game. But I had to sign a lot of players, not just one! Some of our targets were out of reach, but we still needed to get some contracted players on board, players who I thought had something to prove. I wanted to put in a bonus structure and an incentive scheme similar to the one that had worked so well for us in 1992/93. Once that was in place it encouraged some players to come here who may have been offered higher basic wages by the likes of Leeds, Brighton, Huddersfield and Charlton. The new players were also attracted by City's 25,000-plus crowds, the fantastic playing and training facilities as well as by what a great place Norwich is to live. If you get them to Norwich and show them around it's an easy job to clinch a deal, but if you're just doing business over the phone with agents, well, it's a lot more difficult and they often end up signing elsewhere I found."

How did Bryan look back at that time now after so much has changed? When he took over the Norwich side were heading for League One, but less than two years later, the club won promotion back to the Premier League. Did he have any regrets about taking the Manager's job in retrospect?

"Well, it was an experience to say the least, but an opportunity that I'm glad I took. Naturally I am disappointed with the end result, and I accept that was because of bad results. I had 21 games, of which City won six, drew five and lost ten. There were opportunities when we could have got a run going, for example, we had an excellent win at QPR, which could have really got the momentum going, but then we had a bad result by losing 2-0 at Blackpool –that's maybe one of the games that stands out for me as being a turning point. But all Managers do that when they've had a bad run or got relegated; they all claim that 'If we'd done this or just done that' then everything would have been so much different. Football Managers love hindsight!"

Was it, I suggested, more difficult managing a team that you support, or one where your heart lies?

"Well, think of all of those who have gone onto manage 'their' clubs and haven't had the best of times, there have been a few. So yes, it probably is, but at the same time, you should have an advantage – you know what's expected from the supporters on the terraces, and you put that across in the dressing-room because you're familiar with the club. I was able to tell the players what it would be like to be in a winning team at Norwich, 'you'll all be heroes'. So, it can be difficult in some ways, but not in others. Norwich City will always be special to me and is certainly one I would recommend to a young player as a great club to join."

"The whole set-up is great and the club will only improve and go forward, especially with added benefit of Premier League football. The club will always look to attract good players and to keep the momentum that has built moving forward. And good players are always going to be more interested in the prospect of joining Norwich City now. There is a great belief at the club, just as there was under Mike Walker. But I'm part of the club's history now, I've had the highs and the lows, and, ultimately, I look back, learn, and move on. And that's what I've done. I can relate both sides of the game to people, doing well at the top of the Premier League as well as being at the bottom of League One. A little bit of me will always be at Norwich. And, as I have said, I'm sure I'll be able to recommend young players to the club."

"I've been watching football at the Academy since my son Angus was nine, and I know that it produces good players and some of the current crop of Academy players will go on to have a career in professional football, I know that for sure. There will always be lads who look good when they come along at 14 or 15 years old then fall away or end up doing something else, but there will also be some special ones, and there are certainly some of those at Norwich now. There are also players who will develop, especially with the higher level of coaching they benefit from at the Academy, as soon as they're training every day you develop quickly and in different ways, knowing they have to start really delivering out on the pitch."

"I have to admit, the current batch of Academy players at Norwich reminds me of the ones we've had in the past – players like Andy Johnson, Darren Eadie, Andy Marshall, Keith O'Neill and Craig Bellamy. The most exceptional players amongst them may go onto even bigger things than Norwich can offer them, but if they do so, will generating a lot of money for the club. After all, the role of the Academy is to develop players for your club, but if that's not the case, then for other clubs, with City gaining the financial benefit from any transfer fees. And for those that don't make the grade, at least they get a good grounding in life, if they're not going to make it in professional football, there are chances to work in schemes like Football In The Community, or perhaps in a sporting environment elsewhere. The Academy's role is to develop people and help teach them discipline and to educate them about fitness and keeping healthy. It is always tragic when you have to break that news to a lad who the club has decided to let go, and I've had to do that, but you don't tell them that they aren't going to make it, or that they're rubbish, you tell them to go out there and to prove everybody wrong. That's when you'll see how much desire somebody has, how much they really want to get out there and prove you wrong."

"Another thing I found very difficult when we were struggling was the hurt I knew it caused the fans. But, ultimately, the club had the chance to take a step back, to evaluate, to rebuild, and, under Paul (Lambert) to move forward again. I really enjoyed last season (2010/11) and the club's promotion and I've been to games or have listened to games on the radio, while Angus and me have been driving home from a youth team match – we love listening to Chris Goreham and Neil Adams getting excited on the radio – we're certainly big fans!"

Talking of management again, which of the three Managers from that famous Brown-Stringer-Walker trio did Bryan most enjoy and appreciate playing under?

"Ken changed things here a lot. He brought in new players and started that fruitful Tottenham connection by signing Ian Culverhouse, Mark Bowen and Ian Crook. He also sorted out the scouting system, which had identified those quality Spurs players, so a lot changed under Ken and for the better and he re-shaped the squad by combining some really decent young players with the more experienced ones. He really started the momentum, which continued to build at the club, and which took us through the 1992/93 season. Dave worked under Ken, so he kept things going, and brought in some more quality players – people like Andy Townsend, David Phillips and John Polston. Then Mike pushed things forward a bit more. Overall, though, I do think that Ken hasn't had as much credit as he deserves in all truth. We finished fifth in my first season under him at City, and although we fell away in the season that followed and Ken left. It was a good decision to appoint Dave as his replacement, thus maintaining the continuity. The same with Mike's appointment when Dave left. But for me, I think Ken gets my vote. He was so good at relaxing the players – he also put a really good team together with Dave, Mel Machin, Ronnie Brooks and Duncan Forbes as Chief Scout. Ken had the image of being the really nice guy, which he was, but he could be very tough when needed, as could Mel Machin! Ken also brought some excellent players to the club; Dave Watson, Steve Bruce, Mike Phelan to name just three. He still comes to City to watch games and I see him on the golf course every now and then too. So, although Mike Walker was in charge of that great team and it was a fantastic time for the club between 1992 and 1994, as well as being a good Manager, he was really the final piece in the jigsaw that Ken and Dave had been putting together. Neither of them should be forgotten in that respect."

As football fans we are familiar with managers telling us that there is no such thing as an automatic pick on any club's team sheet ahead of a game, but you do get the feeling that during his time at the club, Bryan Gunn was as 'near as damn it' to being an automatic selection choice. His injury, sustained in the post-Christmas game at Nottingham Forest in 1994, is widely attributed to be the reason why Norwich, 7th in the Premier League prior to the game,

A boot-less Bryan Gunn after City's 3-3 draw at Middlesbrough

won only two of their remaining 21 League games, ending the season in 20th place and being relegated. This was, and far from it, no reflection on Andy Marshall, his successor in the Norwich side for the rest of that campaign, but a sign of the huge influence that he had at the club, on the training ground, in the dressing room, and, most of all among his fellow players, especially the back four, out on the pitch.

Norwich were relegated not because Marshall was in the side (and he was a very fine young goalkeeper) but because Gunn wasn't. It is, I think, fair to say that his injury in that game at the City Ground should go down as one of the pivotal moments in Norwich City history – who knows what the club may have achieved had the Canaries stayed up that season? But back to April 1993, a time when the Canaries were most definitely not heading for relegation.

Bryan duly took his place in the Norwich side for the 'massive title decider' against United at Carrow Road – one of eight players who started the clash at Old Trafford – and vitally, Crook was fit to return. Butterworth, Sutch and Beckford missed out, with Sutton (albeit at centre-back), Megson and Goss coming in. And, to all extents and purposes, Walker had gone for a five-man midfield, with Crook protected on each side by Goss and Megson – Phillips and Fox providing the width, with Robins ploughing a seemingly lonely furrow in attack.

With United choosing, again, to unleash their full attacking force in Sharpe, Cantona, McClair, Kanchelskis and Giggs, Mike Walker seemed to have chosen the option of stifling United's pace by giving them little room for manoeuvre against the snappy duo of Megson and Goss. The City duo would be at their fancy heels... worrying, nagging, biting and winning the ball, before allowing Crook to come alive and take possession from them.

But in all truth, United played like a team possessed and Jeremy Goss remembers the game all too well, even two decades later. He speaks of how United picked three of the quickest players in English football, pushed up, waiting to pounce and plunder. The United trio almost daring Norwich to 'come and have a go if you think you're good enough', tempting, teasing, then terrorising. That ploy wasn't in the expected script, many expected a tense game, perhaps with chances few and far between, a game where both teams circled warily around their opponent, treating them, and the occasion, with respect. However, on the night, United, who had been denied the title by Leeds United the previous season, cared little for scripts or the pundit's expectations – they were not going to lose out a second time and, in under ten frightening first-half minutes, and in front of a stunned Carrow Road crowd, Alex Ferguson's charges systematically took Norwich apart through goals from Giggs, Kanchelskis and Cantona. So swift had their breaks been that, as he admits earlier in this book, the watching Norwich City Secretary, Andrew Neville, though they were all offside. Goss, as honest a man as you will find in football, summed the goals up more accurately and very succinctly, admitting; "Three sucker punches, three goals. Game over. We couldn't match them". Was it "Game Over" for Norwich's title aspirations as well? Robins scored a second-half consolation but it made not one jot of difference to the outcome. Ouch!

Norwich had gone into the game still holding their yellow and green flag aloft at the summit of the Premier League after a fine 1-0 Carrow Road win over Aston Villa nearly a fortnight earlier – it had been one of their best performances of the season. They had followed it with a performance that was not a bad one, by any stretch of the imagination, Norwich had not really lost the game, more that United had won it, if you catch my drift. And with that defeat the Canaries' brave tilt at the title finally ended (realistically if not mathematically) following their next fixture, a 5-1 reverse at Tottenham in what probably was their worst performance of the season. Brief hope followed after an entertaining Carrow Road win over Leeds United on April 14th, Chris Sutton's hat-trick a sign of what was to come from the talented striker, and a game which, for once, had the national press purring over Walker and his team. In fact the visiting media team from BBC Radio Two, who were featuring the match with live commentary, were full of superlatives for the players, the team, and the way they played the game. Acknowledgement at last, but faint, posthumous praise, which had come only when the

Canaries' chances of winning the Premier League had all but slipped away. Maybe they felt free to express those thoughts now, the Norwich 'threat' had finally abated and everyone could relax, toast United's triumph and pat the Canaries on their feathery backs? Hadn't they done well?

Norwich had one last live TV date to prepare for that season – the small matter of trip to Ipswich – who joined Manchester United in being the only clubs to do the League double over the Canaries that season with their 3-1 win. Apart from the indignity of losing to our lesser local rivals, the result mattered because Norwich had another focus, another goal to aim for, an aspiration which Mike Walker admitted he wanted achieve to ensure City's season didn't end in real 'disappointment'. The new challenge was to qualify for Europe.

Norwich City had previously 'qualified' on three separate occasions – following the League Cup win in 1985, as well as their fifth and fourth place finishes in 1987 and 1989 – which would all, normally, have seen the club play in the following season's UEFA Cup. However, the ban on English clubs playing in Europe, which had come about as a consequence of the Heysel disaster, had put paid to those dreams, along with some other fine English club sides, notably Everton's title-winning team from 1986/87. However, the ban had finally been lifted and a peck at European glory now beckoned for a fourth time, only on this occasion, it would count. With two League games to play, players and fans had that new target – it was Europe or bust. A strange consolation prize, perhaps, but one that would be more than acceptable, even if the proposition would have been laughed all the way out of the City prior to the season's start. How times had changed, a UEFA Cup place as a consolation prize, who did Walker and Norwich think they were? A proper football club? Surely not!

SPRING IN THEIR STEPS

The Victorian Poet Laureate, Lord Tennyson, once wrote that; "In spring a young man's fancy turns to thoughts of love…" but if you're a football fan, one that's perhaps not quite as young as you once were, springtime does indeed turn your mind to a myriad of possibilities. The combination of warmer Saturdays and a fast-evaporating fixture-list often combine with dreams of winning the League or a cup, of being promoted, a fight against relegation, or even tossing the whole previous nine bloody months in the bin and buggering off on holiday early, but knowing you'll back for more next season. And sometime, as was the case in 1993, the return of the migrating swallows, and skirts short enough to distract young and (dirty) old men alike, aligned themselves with dreams of a European football adventure the following Autumn.

As earlier reminiscing has established, back in August 1992, thoughts focussed no further than top flight survival and a 2-0 half-time deficit at Highbury in their opening Premier League fixture seemed to justify fans' fears and bookies' predictions that the Canaries would be doing anything but qualifying for Europe. A new (and a relative unknown) Manager was in-situ and fans' favourite, Robert Fleck, had left the club. Not because he hadn't enjoyed his time in Norfolk, or his rapport with the City and its supporters, but because he wanted to win trophies. His departure, although predictable enough,

Chris Sutton, David Phillips and Mark Robins celebrate against Liverpool

and he was by no means the first Norwich star to leave the club when the call of big money and the chance of honours came calling, was still a major disappointment. The usual accusations would be directed at Chairman and Board that the club 'lacked ambition', and that there was more interest in 'banking the cheques than having a winning football team'. Norwich City Chairman, Robert Chase, chose to write a piece in the club programme at the time, which appealed to supporters to try to appreciate the reasons why Fleck had left, emphasising that the club was not in any position to make Fleck, or any Norwich player, a millionaire.

Chase's admission was, for many supporters, the first inkling of how the changing game, and the formation of the Premier League, initially thought by many to be no more than a 'cosmetic' re-vamp, would affect Norwich City. Suddenly players were not only playing for the glory – they were playing for big money and personal rewards as well. It had never even remotely dawned on some fans that footballers were motivated by the prospect of colossal personal wealth, indeed, in previous decades, they couldn't have been, because the money simply wasn't in the game to pay them to that degree. And, while First Division players of the 60's and 70's were hardly scratching around for every penny, they weren't earning anything like the stellar wage that the Premier League, backed by Sky's immense resources, was now able to offer clubs. The dawn of the Premier League would spawn a transfer fee and players' wage feeding frenzy, the like of which we had never seen before. Fleck himself admits earlier in this book that his head had been turned and he'd wanted to leave Norwich a year before he eventually did, but agreed to stay for one more season. It is, perhaps, fairly safe to assume that, in the last year of the 'old' First Division, the wage gap between the bigger clubs in the top league, and their less-celebrated rivals, was not hugely significant and that Norwich were not the only club that attempted some parity by including a generous bonus scheme into their players' contracts.

The gap was, however, beginning to widen and the ease by which Fleck had accepted both Chelsea's offer, and the potential increased status in the all-new Sky-driven status quo for English football, is telling. But Fleck would have known what he was doing – high viewing figures drove up advertising revenue and the games featuring the big clubs secured the big audiences. Thus the preference was to give more games to those big clubs, and more appearances meant more money – more money ensured the ability to pay the biggest wages and with it, the ability to attract the best players to their clubs. Fleck was, in other words, speculating to accumulate.

How deliciously ironic it was, therefore, when Fleck's old club, little old Norwich City, went on to have the sort of season that he would have anticipated having with his new paymasters. The penultimate fixtures of the 1992/93 season, on May 1st, saw Norwich, battered but defiant and unbowed, sitting in third place, while Chelsea, in contrast, were back in 11th having had, by their (and Fleck's) new standards of expectancy, a disappointing campaign. It was, of course, the eye of the hurricane; Chelsea's time would come, there was no doubt about that, the Premier League had been created for their benefit after all. But it was just, well, gratifying that, before it all started to get a little out of hand, Norwich could cock one last snook at the big clubs and succeed on a budget.

One player who is more qualified than most to offer an opinion on the changing influence of money in the game, is the ex-Norwich midfielder Rob Newman. Rob arrived at Norwich in 1991, after ten years and nearly 500 games for Bristol City in the lower divisions, and at a time when players at that level couldn't make a fortune from the game. Rob, like many had done, spent much of his careers at a local club, unwilling or unaware of the rewards that could be (but probably weren't) on offer elsewhere. Rob was 27 when Dave Stringer signed him, a surprise purchase for many Norwich fans at the time, but one which turned out to be a very astute piece of business, because Newman's versatility meant he was able to play in a variety of positions. He went on to make over 200 appearances for Norwich before taking on Managerial roles at Southend United (2001-2003) then Cambridge United (2005-2006), clubs where even the modest 'riches' available at Norwich would have seemed a fantasy, clubs where Rob had to make every last penny count. From one extreme to the other, then all the way back again?

THE CHARMER

Newman celebrates scoring against Sheffield Wednesday at Carrow Road

Rob now works for the world's wealthiest football club, Manchester City, where he heads up their Spanish scouting team. I managed to meet up shortly after one of his regular trips to Spain, so before we got down to the interview, we spent some time eulogising David Silva! Then, once we had calmed down having finished waxing lyrical about the magical Spaniard, our attention moved towards his own abilities as a player, and how he'd played rather a lot of games for Bristol City before Norwich came calling.

"I did, playing for Bristol City helped my career at the start back in about 1982, although it wasn't a good time for the club as they had big financial worries. They had been relegated to the old Fourth Division and, because some of the players were on big salaries for the time, the club went bankrupt. Seven of the club's highest earners were paid off and the club had to start from scratch. Obviously, as one of the younger players, and one who wasn't earning a great deal of money, it was ideal and I got a regular place in the team. But it wasn't a given for me, or any of the other younger lads, that we'd get our chance, we still had to be half-decent and an accomplished player. But clearly, those circumstances helped me as a young professional under Alan Dicks, who was my first Manager. Other Bristol City Managers during my time at the club include: Bobby Hughton, Roy Hodgson for a while, Terry Cooper, who was there for six years, followed by Joe Jordan, then when

Joe went to Hearts, Jimmy Lumsden took over. It was Jimmy who sold me to Norwich."

"Terry Cooper was the left-back in that great Leeds team of the 70's and he was unbelievable. When he came to Ashton Gate he was still playing in a left-midfield role, and never gave the ball away. If you were in trouble, or just looking for a pass, you'd give it to Terry and he'd look after it – he was a fantastic Manager too. In terms of man-management, Terry knew exactly how to treat a player, how to respond to a player, either by shouting at you, or putting an arm around your shoulder. And he did well at Bristol, getting us promoted back to the Third Division in 1984, then winning the Freight Rover Trophy in 1986 at Wembley – that was when going to Wembley meant something. Back then playing beneath the Twin Towers was reserved for the special games and occasions – the FA Cup Final, the League Cup, England internationals and the Freight Rover (now the Johnsons Paint) Trophy for the lower division clubs. I remember standing in the dressing room at Wembley thinking 'how many great players have played here... then how many great players haven't played here'? It was special. Nowadays you can finish sixth in the Second Division and end up playing at Wembley – FA Cup semi-finals are played there as too, it's just not the same. Norwich had an FA Cup semi-final while I was at Carrow Road: we played that one at Hillsborough and previously, Norwich had played one at Villa Park. And that's how it should be. I played at right-back that afternoon, but the match just passed me by. That's pretty much how it was during those early days, I was just happy to be in the team, playing regularly, and kept myself to myself. But eventually I felt more settled, more confident, more part of everything."

You said that you'd gone to Wembley for that first time and thought of all the great players who had never played there, now it's more of a case of are there any players who haven't played there?

"You look at something like the League Two play-off final, why not play it at a big ground where 40,000 fans can fill the place up and create a great atmosphere, rather than having a half-empty Wembley? Villa Park would be perfect, it's a fantastic stadium, Carrow Road would also be a great ground to choose. But the FA have got to pay for Wembley somehow I guess. Anyway, from a player's perspective, you can't beat the feeling of reaching Wembley via a semi-final though, and when Bristol City beat Hereford, the euphoria was unbelievable, the best thing ever. It is those emotions and experiences that you miss most once you stop playing and I still miss it. There's nothing like it, especially the banter in the dressing room every day. Lots of players will tell you it's what they miss the most. If you're a Manager or a Coach it's still there to a certain extent, but like I said, it's not the same."

"I miss playing, but I don't miss Management. I went to Southend under Dave Webb, firstly in charge of the reserve team, then as Assistant Manager. Then, all of a sudden, Webb had gone and, completely unexpectedly,

I became Manager. But I was never given enough time, or a decent budget, and although we finished 12th, and achieved mid-table respectability, it wasn't good enough for the Chairman and I was sacked. Maybe I'd been handed the role too early, I don't know, but I knew I had what it took to make a good go of it at Roots Hall if I had been given time, so it was extremely frustrating."

"It was a similar story when I went to Cambridge United to work as Steve Thompson's Assistant – he got sacked and, all of a sudden, the club went into administration. I became Manager, but again, had little or no money, only a youth team and about eight senior players. Because of the financial situation I was unable to sign anyone, so, with no resources and a limited playing squad, I was chucked out again. What really annoyed me at Cambridge was that after I left (in 2006) and Jimmy Quinn had taken over, he was given a budget three times the one I had to work with."

"But even with all the money in the world, unless you have got a great team spirit, with desire running through the squad, it can count for nothing – they were the two qualities that we had in abundance at Norwich back in 92/93 – along with some tremendous players. We didn't need Mike Walker or Dixie shouting at us, or showing us what we had to do... we knew we could do it, and we got on and did it. We had a squad of good players, clever and capable lads, who were aware of the situation and professional enough to deal with it. And, if someone was struggling, you helped them out, because you knew it might be you who'd be struggling in the next game – then you'd want your mates to help you out. That was the basis of the great team spirit we had."

"Looking back at that opening game at Arsenal, though, two down at half-time, we were shell shocked, as it should have been six. I sat there during the break thinking, 'right, damage limitation', there was no way anyone would have thought we'd turn it around and win 4-2. But we played well, and the confidence grew. By the end, if we'd stayed out on the pitch, we would have kept on scoring goals, we were that confident. Look at the Arsenal team, which included Jensen, Smith, Campbell, Merson, Limpar, with Ian Wright on the bench, they were not a bad team to beat! It felt like we'd won the League by the end of the game, so it was a great trip home, followed by a great night out in Norwich. It was an especially good day all round for Gossy, who met his future wife that night. And it all kicked on from there. Looking back, we must have been a nice team for the neutrals to watch, as there weren't too many 0-0 draws (just three in 42 League games) that season."

With Rob having had a long playing career, as well as experiencing management and coaching roles at both the very bottom and the bottom of the Football League pyramid, I wondered what he thought had progressed the most in the game since he'd started out at Bristol City?

"That has to be improved diets and the science of eating properly. It was just coming into the game when I joined Norwich, although I'd been aware of it at Bristol City as Joe Jordan had played in Italy and had brought back ideas about healthy diet with him, meaning we were eating pasta, chicken and fish as our pre-match meal long before anyone else. Although, in saying that, there was a market stall near where we trained, so we'd also nip over if we had the munchies and buy a burger! But Joe found out and put a stop to it – he also took pasties off the menu at the training ground! In that aspect, Joe and the club were ten years ahead of everyone else – my pre-match meal then was chicken, beans and brown toast."

During his time in the game players Rob had been called upon to play in more than one position, but once he'd tucked in to his pre-match chicken and beans, what role did he prefer to play in?

"It was right midfield. I'd played as a defender too, and could play in attack, but Norwich bought me as an attacking central-midfielder. If a player can play in more than one position, then he's a good player for a team like Norwich to have. And I could just about play anywhere, but right-midfield is the one I enjoyed, even though defence was arguably my best position. I think it was hard on Gossy when I signed because he'd been there a long time, getting small pay rises, and not as many games as he should have. Then someone like me, who plays in his position, comes in on a big transfer fee and what have you. But he didn't have a problem with me; it would have been with the management. I have to admit that he came close to leaving the club on a couple of occasions, it was hard for him, as it was for me, because he was my best mate at the club. We used to go out together, me, him and Mark Walton, and we all got on very well. Unlike me, Gossy could get up and down the pitch and run all day... but I could pass the ball!"

"Ian Crook and I used to see who could hit the best ball, the longest ball. We loved it. Then, when Mike played the back three system, with Ian Culverhouse as a Sweeper, I loved that too. I'd get the ball from Gunny, then ping a 60 or 70-yard ball out to Darren Eadie – Chippy might be doing the same to Foxy. I always used to say to them; 'look, if I hit a ball up to you and it goes over your head and directly out of play, that's my fault, I'll hold my hands up and apologise. However, if it goes over your head and then bounces just ahead of you and then goes out, that's your fault.' When we all went out onto the pitch, everybody knew what was going to happen and who was capable of doing what and when. For example, if you gave it to Chippy, you knew he'd do something with it, he'd find someone, or some space. I'm sure he and Taff (Mark Bowen) had a mental telepathy thing going on, time and time again you'd see Taff playing the ball into Chippy, who'd do a reverse pass over the opposing right-back's head and find Taff again. Teams would expect it, they'd have been told about it, but they still couldn't cope. You watch footage of those games, you'll see them do that time and time again, but we were a passing side, all of us were comfortable in possession, and all of us could pass the ball well. When I joined Norwich I was 'introduced' to training routines designed to make your passing improve for the first time. David Williams was a fantastic coach who had us trying intricate short, sharp passing drills, and I have to admit that for the first three months or so, I couldn't do them!"

I wondered, at that point, if they didn't practice passing in training at Bristol City?

"Well, it wasn't that they didn't do them there, it was more a case of the gulf between the top level, where we were at Norwich, and those below. I've since taken similar drills on and use them in training myself, players love them, it makes them think. Training has to be interesting and you need to know not only how to pass the ball and where, but what to do after you've passed it. It's about knowing what to do, your awareness and speed of thought – if you can master those aspects, you'll go a long way in the game."

This was interesting. It sounded as if Rob was saying that one of the main differences between the players who make it, and those that don't, is their 'footballing IQ'. I applied it to myself, a midfielder who had graced the heights of the North West Norfolk League, and a fundamental difference between someone like Rob, whose played at the highest level is that you can have ability (and I think I had some), but if you don't have the footballing intelligence, that speed of thought, then you're never going to be a professional footballer.

"It's an important distinction. Now, if we're out playing, and I get the ball, even as the ball is coming towards me, I'm thinking either, 'right, I'm passing this onto Gossy, to Darren Eadie or Neil Adams...' Then when I got the ball, I'd execute the pass immediately, with one touch and without having to look. I was then ready for what came next, just knowing. But with you, it would be a case of here comes the ball, okay, hope I can control this, one, two touches, right, got it, look up, where is everyone, whose in space, whose being marked, what options do I have? I know. They know. You wouldn't. Sorry, but you're too slow. And yes, that is one of the big differences between the varying levels of the game, speed of thought as well as capability."

I suggested to Rob that the familiar old phrase that football was a 'simple game' was now just outdated nonsense in that case.

"It is and it isn't. Great players make the game look simple. Look at Gossy, he was a great player. He'd get the ball, move it on, hit a great ball, to feet (take a look of the footage of Norwich's 4-2 win at Arsenal on that opening day of the 1992/93 season, for Norwich's third goal, Gossy plays an exquisite, inch-perfect through ball for Ruel Fox to run onto in the Arsenal penalty area, which he scored from) and move on, ready for what he had to do next. He was a great runner, an energetic ball-winning midfielder. But he could hit a great pass. That, as I said earlier, was the thing about that side: good players, intelligent players, all of whom knew how to play the game. You combine that with the team spirit we had and you can begin to understand why Norwich did so well that season. It's silly isn't it, depending on the player and team, a 40-yard pass is either a 'long punt up the park' or a 'superb, defence-splitting pass'? It's one or the other, depending on the player and the level. We played through Chippy because he could produce those passes – he really could put a ball on a sixpence. He was unlucky at Tottenham in having Glenn Hoddle in front of him. But would he have made it at Tottenham even if Glenn hadn't been there? He came to Norwich, a team with no superstars, just a bunch of lads that got on well and wanted to play good football. It was, perhaps, what he needed, the right club and the right environment? There were no cliques at Norwich, none at all. The best way to illustrate how it was back then is to see us all when we get together now. Although reunions only come now and again, but whenever we are together, everything clicks back into place, just as it did when we were playing. Everyone gets on, there's lots of chat and banter straight away. And another thing, if a player from that team needed someone's help or support, it would never be a problem – I absolutely know that we'd help each other out, and that it would only take one phone call. That team spirit will last forever."

Despite the magnificent team spirit and camaraderie, did Rob ever play alongside someone he disliked?

"No, not really. I wasn't too happy about Jon Newsome coming here and taking my place (Newsome joined Norwich from Leeds in 1994, the club's first £1,000,000 signing) but it wasn't personal. He was, perhaps, a little quicker than me – but I was a better passer of the ball. But he cost a lot of money, so he was always going to play. One thing about Jon, when he made a mistake, it was never down to him, it was always down to someone else somewhere along the line. When I made a mistake, I knew it was my mistake. Maybe he came in just a little bit too late to be part of the great team spirit that we originally built-up there, a time when a lot of the first-team players that I'd played alongside were in and out of the side. Others (Ian Culverhouse, Ian Butterworth, Ruel Fox, David Phillips and Chris Sutton) had all gone, whilst some weren't getting as many games, or were in the reserves or on the bench. You didn't ask for a run out in the reserves at that time, you were told. So it had changed by the time Jon came along. There were a lot of young players coming through as well, who hadn't learned the ropes as we had – there wasn't so much cleaning of boots by that stage. In my day, woe betide you if you didn't knock on the dressing room door and, in my case, I did chores and had looked up to Gerry Sweeney for two years… you didn't mess with him. The game was changing, as was the club."

Did you ever get the chance of a move from Norwich?

"No, and I wouldn't have been interested if one had been offered to me. To be fair, I was as settled at Bristol City and I didn't ask for a move from Ashton Gate. But the club accepted the bid from Norwich, then told me about an opportunity for me to play at a higher level. So I took it. Bristol and

Norwich City are similar sorts of clubs and I was very happy at both. I had a good career, made a good living, had a good lifestyle, with some fantastic memories. I did okay and I don't envy today's generation. I've got a great job now, the scouting network at Manchester City is second-to-none and we're secure as the roles are ring-fenced. We also have total autonomy to get on with the job and a great network and I have built up a fantastic database about all the players in Spain. I do the rounds and put the work in – people know that I'm loyal and that I work hard. Manchester City want to be the very best at everything that it does, and although it has a way to go yet in some aspects, it will end up being the very best, I have no doubt about that."

It seems that Rob has got the dream job, one to call his own and one he can develop in the way he chooses. But I wondered if, for example, a nice little Assistant Manager's role came up, at a Championship club – would he be interested?

"No, I wouldn't want to know, unless they were a really huge (laughs) club. Like I said, I've got a great job, within a great set-up at Manchester City. I love it, why would I ever want to go anywhere else?"

And who could argue with that? After such a distinguished career I think he deserves his role at the City of Manchester Stadium for many years to come. He came across as a real student of the game, someone who loves football and appreciated a career doing something he loves.

Rob was in the Norwich side for their last home game of the 1992/93 season against Liverpool. The Anfield Reds, like Manchester United (see previous chapter) were a side that Norwich had a more than respectable record against. Yet, despite some of those Anfield wins (2-0 in 1983 and 1-0 in 1988), there had also been a fair few poundings for Norwich on Merseyside, including an ignominious 6-2 plucking in 1986, and, of course, the 4-1 reverse back in October 1992. With the UEFA Cup in mind therefore, revenge, of sorts, over Liverpool was not just desirable, but, with Blackburn Rovers breathing down our necks, it was essential.

With Bryan Gunn deservedly picking up the club's Player of the Year award before the game (typical of the club's season perhaps, in that, despite being top of the table for long periods, the winner of the trophy was the goalkeeper!) there was a cautiously celebratory air at Carrow Road that afternoon. Although victory would not secure European qualification for the next campaign, it would certainly mean that the long trip to Middlesbrough for the final match would at least have some significance that wasn't, for once, connected with the prospect of Norwich relegation. Indeed, it was our opponents who were doomed to relegation on Teesside that following Saturday. But there was that small matter of Liverpool FC to contend with first.

Norwich duly won the game 1-0, with the decisive goal coming courtesy of a Dave Phillips penalty – the result of one of David "Calamity" James' early masterpieces. A Norwich corner resulted in John Polston challenging James for the ball, which was won, by James. Then, as the players prepared for play

Efan Ekoku congratulates Andy Johnson after scoring the third at 'Boro

to continue, James proceeded to kick Polston on the shin, in full view of the referee. Red card and pandemonium at Carrow Road ensued but Phillips, playing in his last home game for the club (local legend has it he was sold to Nottingham Forest to help pay for the club's under-soil heating) dispatched the penalty with consummate ease and Norwich held on for the win. To add insult to injury, Liverpool would ultimately finish 13 points beneath City in the table that season. And so to Middlesbrough.

By that stage Norwich's end of season fate had been confirmed – City travelled to Ayresome Park needing a point to finish third, however, that would still not guarantee their place in the following seasons UEFA Cup, unless Arsenal went onto beat Sheffield Wednesday in the following weekend's FA Cup final. To come this far, as they had so many times previously in their history, then have to rely on another club getting a certain result so that Norwich got what they deserved was unfortunate, so the bonus for Arsenal was that they 'inherited' thousands of temporary fans from Norfolk prior to that match following Norwich's thrilling 3-3 draw at Ayresome Park. For the City fans who witnessed the draw, the match proved to be a sign of things to come too, with Efan Ekoku, signed from Bournemouth, getting two of the Norwich goals, with youth team product, Andy Johnson, getting the other. Johnson's goal, on 68 minutes, had provoked wild celebrations amongst the City fans, and rightly so. A little over twenty minutes to go, 3-2 up, 'Boro already relegated; surely it was game, set and match? Not as far as John Hendrie was concerned unfortunately, who countered Johnson's strike just five minutes later as Middlesbrough dominated the remainder of the game, determined, perhaps, to snatch away our European spot in exchange for City snubbing out their Premier League status? Had 'Boro scored again of course, and they had chances to, then Norwich would have finished fourth, below Blackburn on goal difference, with no hope of Europe. A season that had promised so much would have "merely" equalled their best ever top-flight finish – thankfully City's Player of the Season kept hearts and minds together and the point was won as the curtain fell upon the inaugural Premier League season.

Norwich's UEFA Cup place, cruelly denied previously on three occasions through no fault of the club or its supporters was finally, and deservedly, confirmed with Arsenal's FA Cup final replay over Sheffield Wednesday with ex-Norwich centre-half, Andy Linighan, scoring the goal which helped take the Cup back to Highbury and had the City players checking that their passports were up-to-date ahead of some high profile jet-setting exploits the following season. I doubt Andy was aware of it at the time, but I hope someone told him how significant that his goal also was for the Canaries – cheers Old Boy!

Manchester United were therefore crowned as Champions, their first title success since 1967. Alex Ferguson's Red Devils have won the Premier League a further 12 times since 1993, and in doing so, have virtually made the trophy their own personal property. Indeed, such has been the ever-expanding gap between those 'haves' and 'have nots' since the 1992/93 season, despite the fact that 45 different clubs have enjoyed Premier League membership in that time, only four of have won it. Few of us will need reminding that, up until the end of the 2010/11 season, only Manchester United, Arsenal, Chelsea and Blackburn Rovers have replicated the feat. Aston Villa finished in second place, with Blackburn Rovers a point behind Norwich in fourth.

For Norwich of course, the question was: what now? Mike Walker had already signalled his intentions of strengthening the squad – the signing of Ekoku and the elevation of Andy Johnson to the first team had been the precursor to another exciting youth team introduction, that of Darren Eadie. Undoubtedly, the success that had been enjoyed by everyone connected with Norwich City Football club had raised the club's profile suitably, and maybe, just maybe, players would now choose to join Norwich because they wanted to win trophies or acknowledge they could in fact achieve their ambitions at Carrow Road.

The previous summer had seen Norwich's star player leave Carrow Road for 'bigger and better things'. Would the next one see players joining Norwich for similar reasons – a summer of intent, rather than one of discontent? Only time would tell.

LOOKING BACK...

Whenever the inaugural season of Premier League football in England is looked back upon and recollections or reflections are shared by those who 'were there', in whatever capacity, what will be the over-riding memory of the majority of people? Will it be of a certain player?

Maybe Teddy Sheringham's name will crop up – he was the leading League goalscorer that season with 22 in total and, more to the point, he scored the first-ever goal in a live Sky fixture during Nottingham Forest's 1-0 win over Liverpool. Not long after that he upped and left for Tottenham, the long-time North London rivals of Arsenal, who possessed the nation's top scorer in all competitions, Ian Wright with 31. His total that included ten, yes TEN, in the FA Cup that season.

Norwich's leading league goalscorer, Mark Robins with 16 strikes (15 league and one in the League Cup), is omitted from the 'official' list of the Premier League top scorers for that season, even though his ex-Manchester United team-mate Mark Hughes' are included with an identical tally, both in total and make up.

Or what about the big transfers? Money was rife and clubs weren't afraid to wave their wads, witness Darren Anderton, Portsmouth to Tottenham's physio's table, £2,000,000? Mark Pembridge maybe (now residing in the "Where Are They Now?" file), he cost Derby £1,250,000 when he signed from Luton. Paul Stewart anyone? Liverpool signed him from Tottenham for

£2,300,000 in July 1992, and duly rewarded his new employers with one goal in 24 league appearances, which works out at, let's see, £2,300,000 per goal. Nice one Paul! That single goal, incidentally, came in his club's second game of the season, a 2-1 win over Sheffield United.

At £800,000, Mark Robins was Norwich's biggest cash outlay in a summer of big spending by the Premier League clubs that saw over £20 million was spent in total. Amongst all of that excess however, came one of the bargains of the summer, Norwich's acquisition of Gary Megson from Manchester City on a free transfer. Is everything flooding back to you now?

What about the big games and the shock results? The afore mentioned Liverpool lost 5-1 to Coventry City on December 19th, while reigning Champions, Leeds United, failed to win a single away League game all season. Their eventual successors, Manchester United, failed to win in their first three League games of the season, losing to Sheffield United (for whom Brian Deane scored the first goal in the Premier League) before drawing to Everton and Ipswich, thus spending an ignominious week or so in 20th place!

Shock results? By the reaction of the media, every Norwich win was seen as a shock, and every defeat, as a sign that the Canaries were, finally, about to "topple from their lofty perch". Among the Canaries' best results were the 3-2 win at Aston Villa and 1-0 Anfield success against Liverpool. Typically, the latter was reported as a sign of Liverpool's continuing impotency under Graeme Souness, rather than a sign of Norwich's quality.

The abiding memory of the season probably relates to Manchester United as well. By April it seemed that the whole nation was urging them to win the title and the collective hysteria clearly got to the referee who, with the score at 1-0 to Sheffield Wednesday in the Old Trafford clash on April 10th, awarded the Red Devils as much injury time as they needed to score the goals they required to retain the League leadership. Ironic therefore, that it was an ex-Norwich player, Steve Bruce, who popped up to score the brace required, the second of which was recorded as crossing the line early on the Sunday morning. Brian Kidd ran onto the pitch to celebrate and a nation rejoiced...

For me, though, the abiding memory of that season is the build-up, execution and aftermath of Norwich's third game, the televised match against Nottingham Forest. Watching that game and that third goal go in said a lot, not least that City were a side that needed to be taken seriously and a squad of players that were not going to tumble down with the Autumn leaves. Watch it again if you get the chance... City have the ball on the half-way line, three quick passes, a swift execution and a quality finish are accompanied by the excited voices and reactions of Ian Darke and Andy Gray speaking to the watching nation. City were a side who had no intention of making a brief visit to the top spot, they were in it for the long haul.

We can all look back and pick out the Norwich 'high spots' from that season; whether it be the opening day win at Arsenal, one of six games that

Norwich went onto win despite falling behind, Chelsea (home and away), Wimbledon (home), Crystal Palace (home) and Leeds United (home). The highest ever League placing (which may possibly never be beaten, although we can all keep the faith!), one that would now have secured a place in the following season's Champions League, with no need to pre-qualify for the group stages! The joy of UEFA Cup qualification, a consolation prize according to some, plus two Manager of the Month awards for Mike Walker, deservedly won not just because of the results on the pitch, but for the attractive, passing game that he perfected in his time at Carrow Road. He had transformed players who were relatively unknown outside of Norfolk, or even Norwich at the start of the season, into household names. Ian Crook for example – why he never got an England call-up will forever rankle with me; also Jerry Goss, the previously perpetual reserve, who formed such an inspirational midfield partnership with Crook, he had the heart of a lion, ran all day and passed the ball with laser-like precision. Mark Robins, rescued from his bit-part role at Old Trafford, blossomed and scored 15 League goals in the process including those two at Arsenal and an exquisite hat-trick at Oldham. And I could go on and on and on!

As this book is all about great Norwich City memories, I decided to catch up with some Norwich fans (and one legendary football commentator) and ask them about their 1992/93 Norwich City recollections too.

Name: Charlie Wyett.
Age: 40
Occupation: Sports writer for The Sun newspaper
"My first Norwich match was on March 7 1979, at home to Wolves. It was a 0-0 draw, and I remember sitting in the South Stand, watching the partially-built River End slowly taking shape to my left. Apart from the fact that Justin Fashanu and Martin Peters were playing for Norwich, and Paul Bradshaw and George Berry for Wolves, I remember little else about the game, although I do recall the theme tune for the 1978 World Cup TV coverage was played before kick-off. My first away match was not until much later as it was almost impossible getting to away matches as a youngster living in the north-west of the county and my first game was on April 20 1987 with Norwich drawing 1-1 at Nottingham Forest. Because my mate was a Forest fan, I ended up watching the game from the Trent End. The home fans used to sing 'You'll never beat Des Walker' although I'm pretty sure Robert Rosario did exactly that to score the opening goal."

"I started working in journalism in 1990 on local papers in Cambridgeshire. As a result, most of my trips to Norwich during the early Nineties, when my non-League clubs were not playing, were as a supporter rather than a journalist. It would be a lie to say I travelled down to Highbury on August 15 1992 with much hope. Norwich had not finished the previous season well,

Dave Stringer had left the club and we knew relatively little about Mike Walker. The fact that Norwich were relegation favourites was hardly a surprise, and at half-time at Highbury, I was convinced the bookies were right. The second-half of that game, with Norwich scoring four times, counts among my favourite moments as a supporter of this club. It was also the first, and probably last, time I have watched a match with a massive mural erected at the other side of the ground. What happened over the course of that season was unbelievable. It is also incredible to think that despite finishing third, Norwich were not guaranteed a European place and had a goal from Canaries old boy, Andy Linighan, to thank for the qualification. These days, third place would have seen Norwich in an automatic Champions League place and a guaranteed £25million."

"However, while Norwich were not expected to do well during the campaign, I still feel the fans took some of the success for granted, because during some previous seasons, particularly 1988/89, City had started challenging for the top spots. The UEFA Cup run was fantastic. There was such a belief within the club and the team felt they could win every game. I missed the home game against Arnhem as I had to cover an Eastern Counties League match, but I made the trip for the return leg, on an official coach from Norwich. When we finally arrived in Arnhem, I remember being taken to a compound and the club's coach steward warning us that the Dutch club's fans had a bit of a bad reputation. He then told us that the police in Arnhem were quite strict and hilariously, in a broad Norfolk accent, claimed: "The dogs over here don't know the meaning of 'let go'". Sadly, I missed both Bayern matches due to work, although it was a special night for my uncle Paul who had lived in Munich since 1975 and hated the club, choosing to support rivals Munich 1860 instead. On the day of the game, he went to the main railway station in Munich to buy an English paper and heard one Norwich fan asking the newsagent for an Eastern Daily Press."

"The trip to Milan was also memorable, although it was a shame the match was so badly supported. Mind you, considering we could not sell out our match against Arnhem, you can hardly criticise Inter for failing to do the same. Had Norwich won that match against Inter, I really believe we could have got into the last four at least, but sadly, that did not happen. The Norwich side was badly hit by suspensions for the match in the San Siro though. After that narrow defeat, I remember Mike Walker's 'release the purse strings' speech, and while Robert Chase was criticised for failing to do so, you sometimes have to look at the financial situation from his perspective. The club was losing money and was nowhere near as well supported as it is now. For example, at the start of the 2011/2012 season, I went to the Carling Cup game against Milton Keynes Dons, and while 13,000 seemed like a small crowd, you have to remember we used to get those kind of attendance figures in both the 1980s and 1990s. So the money just wasn't there.

Most clubs gather fans when they enjoy success, but it seems that Norwich's fanbase has grown beyond recognition during our most difficult decade."

"If I had to pick a few stand-out players from that squad, you would have to start with Bryan Gunn. While I remember Kevin Keelan, I still rate Gunn as the better keeper. Jerry Goss is the player that most non-Norwich fans remember from those days, and rightly so, but while Chris Sutton and Mark Robins played massive parts during those two years, I still feel the full-back pairing of Mark Bowen and Ian Culverhouse should be praised, because they didn't always get the credit they deserved. I think the game itself has certainly changed since those days, both for the better and worse. Since 1996, I have been a football writer for The Sun and even within the last three years, the profession has changed beyond recognition, and the relationship between players and journalists is totally different. But more worrying, is that the relationship between players and fans is equally as bad, due to the amount of money they earn – players genuinely live in a different world. I'd even go as far as to say that some stars at the top clubs think they even breathe different air to the rest of us."

"Some people say that Norwich can never finish third in the Premier League ever again, and although that may be the case, I have no doubt that this club could one day return to Europe and enjoy an even better run than last time. You only have to look at Fulham under Roy Hodgson when they reached the Europa League final. As for the future of the Premier League, it will change but I am not sure whether a Euro League will ever happen – most Manchester United fans would still rather play Liverpool, Manchester City, Leeds or Arsenal every week rather than Feyenoord, Dortmund, Marseille or Partizan Belgrade. But I do believe that the controversial '39th game' will, eventually, come to this country. TV is king these days and it will have even more of an influence in the coming years, particularly as we are approaching a time when the Premier League receives more from overseas TV rights than Sky Sports. Mind you, it could be worse... Fancy Norwich v Manchester United in New York?"

Name: Paul King.
Age: 48
Occupation: Teacher/NVQ Assessor. Club Canary steward since 1995
"Although 20 years is a relatively short period of time, within football, it could be classed as a lifetime – therefore it is interesting to look back and compare the Norwich of 1992/93 and the current set-up. It's easy to forget, for those of us who were about in 1992, that Carrow Road and the surrounding area was shabby by comparison. The re-development of Riverside had yet to start and the area itself was less than desirable. Walking down Carrow Road in 1992 the first thing you saw ahead of you was the big green gates, which let you out of the old South Stand after games, and a black fence surrounding

the old Barclay stand. Beyond that you could see the grassy mound that you had to climb to take your position on the terraces. On the right-hand side of Carrow Road were the derelict, unsightly railway sheds, and on the corner of Carrow Road and Kerrison Road, was the now much-missed fish and chip shop. Walking around past the Main Stand you had the old Boulton and Paul factory opposite and the old car park behind The River End. Behind the old South Stand were small business units and, quite often, if it had been raining, you could be walking in several inches of mud and water because of the state of the road surface. Things couldn't be more different now; the whole area has been redeveloped with a new road layout, shops and flats, which give it an entirely different feel – one to make you proud. Walk down Carrow Road to a game today and the first thing you will see is the smart Holiday Inn next to the Barclay Stand with its welcome sign on top. No more walking in puddles round the back of the Jarrold Stand, which makes it a far more pleasurable and inviting area to visit."

"Inside the ground 20 years ago, however, was a slightly different story. There was still standing in the Barclay and River End although both Barclay and South Stand were looking past their best. The Barclay finally came down after a 3-1 home defeat to Arsenal on April 8th 1992 – the honour of scoring the final goal in front of the old stand went to Ian Butterworth in front of barely 13,000 spectators. At the start of the 92/93 season Carrow Road started to be transformed – the bottom tier of the new Barclay was open for the first game against Chelsea, with the top tier ready for the local derby with Ipswich Town during Christmas week. Initially the top tier was for visiting supporters, but that arrangement only lasted for next four games (interestingly both Coventry and Spurs twice) before it was returned to home supporters. In the River End you had to reserve seats for the big games, but otherwise you could sit where you liked until the 94/95 season. And, possibly for the first time in its history, the ground was now four separate stands – the infills didn't start until the following season. Today the ground is possibly one of the best in the country – Carrow Road has state of the art facilities and, apart from the Hotel corner, is a virtual bowl, which gives a marvellous atmosphere, especially at night matches."

"From a personal point of view, while the ground is far removed from the 90's, I do think it has lost that special atmosphere it had on night games when standing was allowed. Who can forget Ipswich (Milk Cup), Southampton (FA Cup) and Manchester United (League Cup), amongst many others, for that unique atmosphere that possibly only Norwich and Norfolk could generate? Ground facilities are seen as all-important now, and a vital part of the match experience, but back in 1992, there were few pre-match facilities around!"

"There was no Riverside development, and if you wanted a pre-match drink, it was either The Kingsway or Ferry Boat on King Street. Away supporters tended to use The Clarence Harbour on Carrow Road and there was the fish and chip shop on the corner of Kerrison Road, but very little else. Within the ground it was the usual standard kiosks serving hot drinks and food, although there was a small lounge in the corner of the South Stand where you could sit down and have something to eat. Nowadays, it's totally different. All three pubs mentioned are long-gone, but in their place there are many establishments on the Riverside, of which The Queen of Iceni is the most popular. Within the ground there are several members only restaurants including; The Gunn Club and Darren Huckerby's Lounge in The Jarrold Stand – in both of these you can have a meal, watch Sky games on the large screens and (certainly in the Gunn Club) watch interviews with players past and present. Also, within the stands, you now get a wide range of drinks, food and confectionary. A far cry from the days of the old River End when you had to queue at one kiosk for a Bovril. As far as we fans were concerned, back in the 1992/93 season, Carrow Road was far from being sold out. Despite the overall capacity being lower than it is today (21,500 approx), the first home game of the season, against Chelsea, saw a crowd of just over 15,000 – followed by 14,000 for the visit of Everton the following Saturday. In fact the game that cemented our place at the top of the League, against Southampton, saw an attendance of only 12,452. With the exception of the games against the so-called bigger teams, crowds rarely crept over 16,000. Even the following season, our first ever UEFA cup game against Vitesse Arnhem couldn't sell out, and only 16,818 witnessed history being made. And in 1998, only 9,818 attended the 3-3 draw against Birmingham City."

"During the 1992/93 season the Norwich City provided air travel for the Monday night game at Oldham which we won 3-2, and later on in the season, 10,000 took up the free travel to Wimbledon. Unfortunately, while the supporters turned up, the team didn't, City losing 3-0. It is widely considered that the upturn in attendances coincided with run to the play-off final in Cardiff in 2002. Since then, Carrow Road has rarely been less than full, and has earned a reputation for being one of the most vociferous grounds in the country. We also have one of the largest season ticket renewals, currently standing at around 22,000. Nowadays 26,000 is the norm, even in the Championship, and we even averaged 25,000 in League One. Our away support is phenomenal and puts a lot of clubs to shame, especially when you consider the distances we have to travel just to get on a dual carriageway or motorway. Such is the demand for away tickets that a few years ago the Away Season Ticket was introduced, guaranteeing match tickets to all games, a scheme that is currently capped at 700 supporters.

With regard to the team, it is easy to forget that Norwich nearly didn't make it into the inaugural Premier League. Following a 4-3 home win against Everton on 21st March 1992, City didn't pick up another point until the last home game of the season, when Robert Fleck's equaliser against Wimbledon ensured survival. It also proved to be the last game in charge for Dave Stringer who resigned later that week. Initially Mike Walker had only brought in Gary Megson from Manchester City, then, with four days "til the start of the season, Robert Fleck left for Chelsea, prompting the purchase of Mark Robins from Manchester United. Optimism was not high at the start it has to be said, but with the team spirit within the club, soon improved!"

"Apart from bogey sides like Manchester City and Wimbledon (both beaten at home in the 1992/93 season!), I always though Norwich could beat anybody at Carrow Road in the Premier League, which was a much more level playing field than it is today. The players were all in it together, playing as a single unit, and that showed in the results. In fact (as far as I know) Norwich are still the only team to be 2-0 down at half-time, away from home, and win twice (Arsenal, Chelsea) since the start of the Premier League! We had Culverhouse and Bowen defending and bombing down the flanks, Crooky and Megson in midfield, and Sutton and Robins providing the goals. Prior to 1992/93 Dave Stringer had been in charge for just under five years producing, what some pundits called, football that could only be bettered by Liverpool at that time. Mike Walker and John Deehan, who inherited Stringers team, they got them playing in a style that was lovely to watch, but, not only that, produced a team that was very hard to beat. In fact if City hadn't blown up in April, we could well have been Premier League Champions. Overall, though, the player that stood out for me was Dave Phillips. He had special qualities and could provide the perfect pass, was a good tackler and, of course, scored some crucial goals that season... Arsenal away, Villa away, not forgetting that sideways volley against Crystal Palace. Phillips would easily win a spot in my all time City XI, a player who would have contributed greatly to our UEFA Cup run if had still been at the club."

Name: Peter Rogers
Occupation: Norwich City Programme Editor-"On The Ball City"
"Like most City fans, the 1992/93 and 1993/94 seasons are two campaigns I always look back upon with particularly fond memories. As a member of matchday staff in the Canary Store at the time, and a regular away traveller, I decided in the summer of 1992 that during the forthcoming campaign I would look to attend every game home and away. For the past three or four seasons I had always managed around two-thirds of the away games and had always been impressed by these 'super fans' whenever they were revealed as attending the 500th, 750th or 1,000th consecutive City match – but little did I know that I really could not have picked a better season to 'watch the lot'. Although there were some tricky ones to get to along the way – time off work at short notice for a midweek League Cup game away at Carlisle was not an easy one to negotiate with my then employers, but it was well worth the effort. They didn't need to know my family bereavement was only a goldfish did they?"

"Some of the football played by Mike Walker's team during that season really was a pleasure to witness and, I guess, on a par with some of the memorable displays produced by a Martin Peters-inspired City side in the late 70s – an era I often hear recalled fondly by players and fans alike from that period. The season produced so many memorable games and moments that it is almost impossible to record a favourite game, although the opening day victory at Highbury set the tone for the season, and securing that third place finish with the 3-3 against Middlesbrough at Ayresome Park was another fantastic occasion. The fact that we then had to rely on Arsenal winning the FA Cup to get us into Europe, a result that was not settled until the final minute of extra-time in a replay, just goes to show that Norwich City never do much the easy way!"

"Despite the pride I took from attending every game in 1992/93 (and it took some real effort to find the enthusiasm to return to Ewood Park for a League Cup game with Blackburn three weeks after our 7-1 mauling at the hands of Rovers). I knew I would not be able to repeat the feat again in 1993/94, therefore watching City in Europe the following season was always going to be my priority, and even if our European dream was to end up being a single game on foreign soil, I wanted to be there. I knew overseas travel would not come cheap, and if I had to forfeit the old trip to Hillsborough or White Hart Lane, then so be it. In the end I managed to watch all of City's six games in that memorable UEFA Cup campaign and am so glad that I did. It could be a while before the opportunity arrives again."

"My favourite City player at the time was Robert Fleck. As an impressionable teenager watching Flecky in his prime, I always felt something exciting could happen with him around. With pace and a superb eye for goal, he was arguably our most influential player at the time. The City fans loved him and the away fans loathed him – Fleck knew it and thrived on it. You always felt with him in the side that City had a chance whoever the opponents. It is ironic that his departure was then followed by one of the most successful periods in the Club's history, but I can't help but wonder 'what might have been' if Fleck was also available to Mike Walker during that 1992/93 campaign?"

"I started attending matches a decade earlier when, after several weeks of harassing my dad into taking me to watch Norwich City, I attended my first game at Carrow Road on Monday, April 4, 1983. A 0-0 draw with Ipswich Town. Despite a lack of goals I was instantly hooked – not just on the football but the crowd and size of it all. As a nine-year-old I was fascinated by the atmosphere and colourful language from the stands as much as the action on the pitch. Suffice to say I was keen to get down to Carrow Road again as soon as possible. My dad worked most Saturday's, so regular trips were not possible, but we did also attend the final home game of the 1982/83 season against FA Cup finalist Brighton and Hove Albion. That match was to serve as my first Norwich victory with Mick Channon taking the mantle of being the first player I saw score a Norwich City goal. I managed to see a good number of home games in 1983/84, including the opening home game against champions Liverpool, as well as the thrilling 3-3 draw with Manchester United, but by that stage I was able to attend games with either my dad or a friend and his father, meaning visits to Carrow Road were becoming more of a regular occurrence."

"My first away match was the Milk Cup Final, with my first League away game coming the following season – a 2-1 win at Crystal Palace during the Club's 1985/86 Second Division championship-winning campaign. Peter Mendham scored Norwich's opening goal and had an excellent match; the win also broke a then club record, Norwich's tenth successive unbeaten away game. But my big break in watching the Canaries on a regular basis came in 1987 when, via a family friend, I was asked to become a senior ball boy at Carrow Road. The deal was that I would be able to act as a ball boy for all of City's first-team fixtures providing I also carried out the duties for all reserve games and Norfolk Senior Cup ties played at Carrow Road – I jumped at the chance. I had a seat on the touchline, access to players for autographs and the ability to save pocket money and paper round money for away games. The end of my ball boy days coincided with me leaving school, although I then took on a role working matchdays in the Canary Store – a position I held until I joined the Club's full-time staff as Programme Editor in October 2000."

Name: John Motson
Occupation: Legendary Match of the Day commentator

Finally, and with the title of this book in mind, I sought out the BBC's John Motson to ask him about his thoughts on the changing face of football and his memories of commentating on Canary games between 1992-94.

John has been covering football matches (as well as a myriad of other sports) for BBC Radio and Television for twice as long as the Premier League has been in existence. He first came to the wider footballing nation's attention in February 1972, commentating on the FA Cup Third Round replay between Hereford United and Newcastle United, having joined the BBC as a sports presenter on Radio 2 four years earlier. Motty (he even refers to himself as such on his voicemail message!) is therefore steeped in the recent history of English League and Cup football, and, although the number of matches he has covered in that time must run to well over a thousand, his recollections of the Canaries' feats in the 1992/93 Premier League campaign, as well as the UEFA Cup run the following season, return as easily as if they were yesterday.

With football now changed out of all recognition to how it was two decades ago, I asked Motty if he thought that one of the so-called 'lesser' clubs would ever have the sort of season that Norwich had enjoyed again or finish in what is now a qualifying position for the Champions League?

"You have to remember that the financial imbalance between clubs was much smaller at that time. We had previously seen Southampton finish second in 1984, while Ipswich, under Bobby Robson, finished the season in that position twice. So it wasn't unheard of for a smaller team to have a good season and finish in a high position."

Was there any specific reason, I wondered, why the rise and rise of Norwich that campaign was regarded as more of a shock than those seasons that, as you have said, Southampton and Ipswich enjoyed, or when Watford finished as Division One runners up in 1983?

"Well, what was special about Norwich that their achievement came at a time when it was becoming harder to compete with the bigger clubs – the financial imbalance was just beginning to kick in, so the gap between the leading clubs and the smaller ones was becoming wider. The pivotal moment, maybe, the event that meant that the game was on a course of change, was the implementation of the Taylor Report."

"That led to the big changes in English football – grounds had to become all-seater, there was more prominent and improved stewarding and more families were encouraged to come to matches. The game was marketed as being an attractive prospect to more people, the audience became wider and the overall appeal became more popular. Sponsorship and commercial opportunities were there for the clubs to make the best of, and it was a lot easier for the bigger clubs to make money. In contrast, of course, it was harder for the smaller ones to compete financially. Many clubs have struggled to catch up and sometimes suffered as a result. Leeds United are perhaps the best example of what can happen if you don't get it right."

Of the Norwich games that Motty attended (and I think he probably would have been able to list all of them!), which stood out in his memory now?

"I remember the game at Leeds that I commentated on, with Norwich winning 4-0, especially Jeremy Goss's volley. And, when Norwich played in Munich in the UEFA Cup, I especially remember watching them training before the game. Norwich were so relaxed and natural, there seemed to be no nerves at all. Jeremy Goss and Mark Bowen got the goals. I commentated on the return-leg at Carrow Road as well."

"As far as players are concerned, it would have to be Jeremy Goss. He scored some crucial goals. The changes that have happened in the game, plus those that are, I am sure, yet to come, make the achievements of Norwich that season seem all the more unlikely ever to be repeated."

"Will we see a club of Norwich's size and stature feature so strongly and claim a top three place in the Premier League again? I don't think so. It was a one-off. Norwich's achievements came right at the cusp of those big changes in the game. But what they did was absolutely fantastic. I don't think there is any possibility now that a club of that size will have that sort of season again."

Motty's final comment is one that many will share – an inevitable and somewhat sad consequence of the rise and rise of football in England in the last 20 years. The launch of the Premier League certainly provided the catalyst for the game's massive development and expansion, but at what cost to the game as a whole?

The Premier League is now one of the biggest commercial successes in sport: the value of the overseas TV rights to the Premier League in terms of income, a contract that expired in 2010, was £625 million. In 2001, it was 'just' £178 million. The broadcaster *Now TV* recently paid the Premier League £100 million for the coverage rights in Hong Kong alone! Games are broadcast to over 600 million homes in over 200 countries across the globe, and, as 'long ago' as November 2007, an estimated 1 billion people watched the Premier League game between Arsenal and Manchester United, which equates to nearly a fifth of the entire population of the planet.

To maximise their increasing wealth, the top clubs regularly play friendly matches around the world in an effort to raise awareness of their brand and to increase support. Supporters, after all, are now far more than just those who turn up at the game every week, they are anyone who can be sold a club shirt, regardless of whether they live in Manchester, Maanshan or Melbourne. Plans are even being considered for a '39th game', a match to be added to the regular Premier League season that would bring a competitive fixture to outposts all around the globe – yet more TV and digital contracts to be signed, yet more money to be made.

For clubs such as Manchester United, Manchester City, Arsenal, Chelsea and Liverpool, who are already posturing, ahead of the day they will be able to negotiate their own TV deals the future looks to be an increasingly wealthy one. For these clubs, their financial forecasts must be beyond even the excesses of a football agent's imagination, but I wonder how much Sky will have to pay to outbid their new competitors, the clubs themselves?

For a clubs like Norwich City, success is now regarded as actually reaching the Premier League, then hopefully staying there. It is sad to concur with Motty's assertion that no club of Norwich's size and resources will ever finish as high as third in the Premier League ever again, but what is sadder, is the fact that to finish 17th, and therefore hang on for 'one more year', when the club's ambition will be to simply repeat the same achievement, comes at the expense of any peripheral glory in the FA or League Cup, competitions that are now regarded by most 'lesser' clubs as distractions to their Premier League survival.

A top three finish should always be regarded as an achievement, but we now witness wild celebrations for narrowly avoiding relegation and near deification for Manager and players (as happened with Wolverhampton Wanderers at the end of the 2010/11 season) for doing so – isn't that celebrating failure? Admittedly, I'm sure that football supporters would rather raise their glasses to success but, at a time when success is subject to the size of your club's spending power, should we just make the most of whatever scraps are left at the foot of the table for the rest of us?

And remember Mike Walker and Norwich City for their magnificent achievements during that legendary season. The last of a kind.

Thanks and Acknowledgements

This book would not have been possible had it not been for the support, help and input of a great deal of people. I would therefore like to offer grateful and heartfelt thanks to the following.

Norwich City FC, in particular, Peter Rogers and Will Hoy.

The Management and staff of the Holiday Inn at Carrow Road.

The players of Norwich City – Ian Butterworth, Darren Eadie, Robert Fleck, Jeremy Goss, Bryan Gunn, Rob Newman, John Polston and Mark Walton.

Chris Goreham of BBC Radio Norfolk and all on The Scrimmage.

Those true gentlemen of the Press, Mick Dennis and Charlie Wyett.

Ed Balls MP and his Westminster team.

Kevin Baldwin, Paul McVeigh, John Motson, Andrew Neville, Peter Walsh and the Eastern Daily Press, John Eastwood and Mike Davage, co-authors of Canary Citizens, Rob Hadgraft, author of Norwich City – The Modern Era, original and new editions, also Rick Waghorn, author of 12 Canary Greats.

Sarah Povey, Gordon and Janet Lake, Michael and Emmie West, Dr Russell Saunders, Nigel Nudds, Hugh Townsend and Paul King.

And to David Lane of Legends Publishing for his infinite tolerance, patience and support!

Dedications...
spirit of '92/93
role-call

The following list of people took advantage of our advanced purchase Dedication scheme so that their names would be included in the book, or were included as requested by a friend or family member who bought *Fantasy Football* **for them.**

Dorothy 'Dottie' Hart
James Green
Keith Bray
Royston Symonds
Mike Hilton
Brian Knight
Matthew Goreham
Stephen Varley
Swindon Canary
Russell Saunders
Matthew K Gouldby
Matthew Baker
David Nunn
Nathan Armes
Tim Allman
Robert Jolly
Ben Dunton
Edmund Clarke
Terry Treacy
Iain Hilton
Michael Hilton
Alan Stannard

John Todd
Alan Martin
Peter Johnson
Kirstin Holsey
David Edwards
Elliot Huntley
Neil Burrage
John Ward
S Tyrrell
Roger Billings
David Youngman
Craig Elliott
Janet Lake
Richard Andrew Brady
Margaret Gibson
Ray Hammond
David 'Spud' Thornhill
Eric Witham
Gary Stone
Harriet Husbands
Jim Baxter
John Easton

"Let all tonight then drink with me
To the football game we love,
And wish it may successful be
And in one grand united toast
Join player, game and song
And fondly pledge your pride and toast
Success to the City club..."